In Gotham's Shadow

IN GOTHAM'S SHADOW

GLOBALIZATION AND COMMUNITY CHANGE IN CENTRAL NEW YORK

ALEXANDER R. THOMAS

STATE UNIVERSITY OF NEW YORK PRESS

Published by
State University of New York Press, Albany

For information, address State University of New York Press,
90 State Street, Suite 700, Albany, NY 12207

Production by Kelli Williams
Marketing by Anne M. Valentine

Library of Congress Cataloging-in-Publication Data

Thomas, Alexander R., 1969–
    In Gotham's shadow : globalization and community change in central
New York / Alexander R. Thomas.
        p. cm.
Includes bibliographical references and index.
    ISBN 0-7914-5595-5 (hard : alk. paper) — ISBN 0-7914-5596-3 (pbk. :
alk. paper)
    1. Cities and towns—New York (State) 2. Urban renewal—New York
(State)—Utica. 3. New York (State)—Economic conditions. 4. New York
(State)—Social conditions. 5. New York (State)—Rural conditions. I. Title.
HT123.5.N7 T47 2002
307.76'09747—dc21   2002002465

10 9 8 7 6 5 4 3 2 1

*In memory of my father,
Alexander A. Thomas,
whose encouragement and support
helped make this book a reality.*

Contents

Illustrations

Newspapers and Their Abbreviations

BG ... *Boston Globe,* Boston, Massachusetts

BS ... *Baltimore Sun,* Baltimore, Maryland

DP ... *Daily Press,* Utica, New York

DS ... *Daily Star,* Oneonta, New York

FJ ... *Freeman's Journal,* Cooperstown, New York

NYT ... *New York Times,* New York, New York

OD ... *Observer-Dispatch,* Utica, New York

JA ... *New York Journal American,* New York, New York

Preface

In Gotham's Shadow is the result of my own homecoming. I spent six years as a graduate student in Boston, Massachusetts, and during that time my own perception of the world changed. I came to think of major cities as those with fully developed subways and city centers that could be conceptually divided up with names such as "the financial district," the "Back Bay," and "the Fens." My childhood home in upstate New York was two hundred miles and a world away. Boston represented opportunities that beckoned me to stay, but I returned home in 1998. Home had changed.

I was to write my doctoral dissertation on Cooperstown and Hartwick while teaching part time at Utica College. Cooperstown was struggling with its increasing popularity as a tourist destination, whereas my hometown of Hartwick eight miles away had changed hardly at all. Utica was reeling from what appeared a string of misfortunes. Yet, in the media and on my trips to Boston and New York, people cheered the booming economy. I would drive to friends and family in the New York City area and for meetings in Boston and be reminded of how unequal the boom really was: new office parks, stores, shopping centers, homes, everything. And none of it where I lived. A friend in Cooperstown commented that it seemed as though there was something exciting being built everywhere but here. And on my trips to New York and Boston, it seemed like that to me as well. But strangely, as I wrote my dissertation, I found very little research about the inequities between my various homes. Sitting on ragged couches in upper east side coffee bars or in smoky clubs by Fenway Park, conversations rarely if ever turned to the hinterlands surrounding the great cities but abounded with the exotic tales of foreign countries or distant cities much like our east coast megalopolis. When "upstate" came up, the economic

xiii

misfortunes were often considered to be the defining feature of the area, but ultimately not the concern of New Yorkers. What was missing was any sense of the region or the state as a cohesive unit: New York is a center of the world economy, and it need not look to its immediate hinterland for survival. For New Yorkers, the world is the hinterland.

The story of central New York tells of the conditions found in late Capitalism. It points to the dynamic found between urban and rural areas in the construction of an economy, and what happens as that dynamic grows. This book discusses the relationship between urban and rural areas in central New York State, in the shadow of the great metropolis that is New York City.

Will Holton invested much work in earlier versions of this book, playing the role of editor and critic. Jan DeAmicis has similarly played a vital role throughout the writing of this book, having endured countless readings of the material. Similarly, Jack Levin and Gordana Rabrenovic were both very influential with their opinions and ideas for improvement. Bob Smith provided insightful comments on later drafts of this book, and Dan Larkin challenged me to improve the final drafts into the current form. Leo Lincourt and Carrie Kane have been persistent in their support and ideas.

Several institutions proved priceless in their services: Kinney Memorial Library, Fort Stanwix National Monument, The National Baseball Hall of Fame and Museum, The New York State Historical Association, The New York State Library, Syracuse University Libraries, The Town of Hartwick Historical Society, Utica College of Syracuse University, The Village Library of Cooperstown, and the Oneida County Historical Society. Special thanks must go to the State University of New York College at Oneonta library, whose staff are among the most helpful and insightful people I know.

A special thank you is necessary for the folks at SUNY Press. Ron Helfrich and Kelli Williams have been very patient and very helpful. The anonymous reviewers provided insightful comments to the manuscript, and in doing so challenged me to improve this version of *In Gotham's Shadow*.

Barbara Thomas and the late Alexander Thomas have always been supportive both emotionally and financially, and without their encouragement of their only son this work could not have been imagined, much less accomplished.

Polly Smith-Thomas, my wife and my best friend, has been a constant source of love, insight, friendship, criticism, and hope. Always in the right proportion, at the right moment, in the right way. Robert and Todd have been patient in their waiting for "the end of the book."

I also thank the many people in the communities who spent their time answering questions and sharing their thoughts. Without them, there would be no *In Gotham's Shadow*.

Portions of this book have been adapted from the article, *Untowning Hartwick: Restructuring a Rural Town*, originally published in 1999 by the Electronic Journal of Sociology (http://www.sociology.org). Reprinted with permission of the publisher.

Chapter 1

One Summer Day

It was a warm Saturday afternoon in the summer of 2001. The state office building loomed over the concrete plaza below, across the street from the Radisson Hotel in the heart of Utica, New York. A block away, the stately steeple of Grace Church stood illuminated by the afternoon sun and cast its shadow on the fifteen-story Adirondack Bank building. And yet, for all the warmth of a Saturday afternoon, the downtown streets were empty. In a metropolitan area of nearly three hundred thousand people, I stood alone on Genesee Street.

To leave Utica and her suburbs is to pass landmarks of American industrial history: the makers of the Thompson Sub-Machine gun, the Remington typewriter, General Electric radios, and Duofold underwear. The highway runs on the original route of the Erie Canal, that great westward highway through the Appalachian Mountains to the Great Lakes, alongside the former New York Central tracks and, at one point, under the first commercial telegraph line on earth. A hundred years earlier the region had been one of the great textile centers of the world, but today Utica is a city of broken windows. More than forty thousand people have left the metropolitan area since 1970, following in the footsteps of the firms who left before.

Forty-five minutes to the south of Utica is Cooperstown, a village of about two thousand people at the source of the Susquehanna River. The village parking lot is overflowing and Main Street is packed with visitors from distant cities. They gawk at the storefronts and fondle authentic country goods made in Chicago and Hong Kong, experiencing the idyllic small town setting before returning to split level homes in the suburbs of their choice. Home to the National Baseball Hall of Fame, Cooperstown is perhaps best known for its role in the baseball creation myth as the home of Abner Doubleday. At the south end of the asphalt parking lot, a Depression-era stadium commemorates the hallowed ground where that first baseball game supposedly took place.

Follow a thin ribbon of oil-and-stone for six miles west of Cooperstown into Hartwick, a rural village of six hundred residents. The highway, once called Main Street before being renamed for 911 service, is devoid of activity. Parking lots inhabit the space once held by commercial buildings and crabgrass has found a home in the sidewalks. And yet, Hartwick does not stand out as an unusual community. The village is quite ordinary in this region of New York State, and shares with Cooperstown and Utica a common predicament: the global economy seems disinterested in their fates. Despite the disparity in their sizes and histories, all three communities are faced with the challenge of surviving a global economy that seems to have forgotten them. They are too far from the coast, from major transportation routes, from other major cities, from centers of power, from the trends and fashions and tastes that seem to so excite investors. And yet, less than four hours away by car, is that great hub of the global economy: New York.

A Nice Place to Raise a Family

Here, in the shadow of arguably the greatest city on earth, one may be surprised to find that there is no Citibank or Chase Manhattan branch, no Macy's or Tower Records. Not even a Barnes & Noble. The issue is not distance, because all of the above have outlets in places far more distant than Utica, New York. They are looking for something more: a healthy market with a cosmopolitan culture that promises growth. And central New York no longer has the desired growth rate or potential for high profits, so their fellow New Yorkers look elsewhere for places to invest. Utica and her surroundings are not "in."

All three communities are pleasant enough; more than one resident of each community lauded the merit of each place for raising children. Crime rates are lower than the national average; the Utica-Rome metropolitan area yearly ranks among the safest in the country (FBI 2001). Central New York is home to numerous colleges of every kind, an array of sports teams and an impressive list of historical sites and attractions. It is nearly impossible to wander more than an hour's drive from a metropolitan center, and some of the nation's greatest cities (New York, Philadelphia, and Boston) are within four hours' driving and two of Canada's (Toronto and Montreal) are within six.

The landscape is quite striking. The Mohawk River cuts through an eroded plateau and, with the Hudson River, cuts a path from the Atlantic Ocean, through the Appalachians, and to the Great Lakes.

The headwaters of the Susquehanna and Delaware Rivers also begin their journeys to the Atlantic in the hills to the south. Numerous creeks have carved their own valleys as they flow into one of the three rivers. Plains run beside each meandering body of water and then give way to high hills wooded with maple and oak trees. It is the very landscape immortalized by James Fenimore Cooper in his many novels and Currier and Ives in their serene prints.

A Currier and Ives print was produced of Utica, showing the stately steeple of Grace Church with children skating on the river in the foreground. The reality of the scene was never truly the major point of the work; Utica at the time was an industrial city and the view from the Mohawk River would have been of the historic Triangle neighborhood that stood between the river and the church several blocks away. Thanks to urban renewal programs in the middle part of the twentieth century, a visitor stands a better chance of seeing the church from the painting's vantage point today than a hundred years ago, but the river itself was moved a quarter mile to the north in 1916. Still, Utica as a city was what Mary Ryan (1981) termed the "cradle of the middle class" due to its influence in setting the tone for middle-class values and expectations. For the most part, Utica is still typical of many older American metropolitan areas today. The city has lost population,[1] residents and stores have moved to the suburbs, and although more than half of the metropolitan areas in the United States are smaller than the Utica-Rome metropolitan area, almost half are larger (USBC 2000).[2]

Similarly, Cooperstown is set in a beautiful area of New York State, but at the headwaters of the Susquehanna River rather than in the Mohawk River valley. Whereas the Mohawk Valley turned into a major transportation (and immigration) corridor, the Susquehanna Valley did not and thus Cooperstown has experienced considerably more stability in terms of its population and local culture than has Utica. Home to James Fenimore Cooper and the county seat of Otsego County, the village has a long tradition of elite patronage and thus features some of the most beautiful architecture in the region. Located at the southern tip of Otsego Lake, the architecture has often accentuated the natural beauty of the region and been ennobled by it. The village is quaint; reminiscent of a Currier and Ives print.

On an evening in Hartwick, the howls of outdoor dogs and occasional whirr of distant automobiles traveling the tiny roads contrast with the secluded silence the village has to offer. Planes fly overhead to distant cities, their occupants blissfully unaware that there even is a Hartwick. Highways connect major cities, as do the bus lines that serve them like the trains that ran before; the village has only a small state road and a similar county road to connect its residents to the outside world. Hartwick is off the radar and its people feel most comfortable at such a distance. The village is the essence of a Currier and Ives print; the reality that Cooperstown seeks to emulate, and that was portrayed in the print of Utica.

There is a conservative tilt to the local culture in all three communities. Cooperstown and Hartwick, like Otsego County of which they are part, rarely vote anything but Republican. Yet, the Green Party has begun to make inroads as newer and younger residents sense the threats to the life they have grown to revere. In Utica, the Democratic political machine took power from an older and more resilient Republican machine during the 1920s. Set in predominantly Republican Oneida County, the fall of the machine brought the city ill repute during the 1950s and eventually regained the entire metropolitan area for the Republicans. But conservatism goes well beyond politics.

Many newer residents to Cooperstown and Hartwick have described the local social structure as cliquish, finding it difficult to make friends. The various factions of social life even formed the basis for a steamy romance novel entitled *The Sex Cure* (Dorian 1962). A thinly disguised work of fiction, the novel chronicled the affairs of the local elite and brazenly confronted the exclusivity of the local culture. Some have even referred to the area as being "cold," as some residents report that it can take years before finally feeling welcomed into their new homes. Native and newcomer, however, find the community to be a comforting and desirable alternative to life in metropolitan America, and it is for this that many come to the area.

Many residents are confused by the emphasis on "diversity," living as they do in an area where it is common for townships to be more than 97 percent white. Diversity is found in cities, such as Utica, where it is not always perceived as an asset. Uticans, in contrast, take a more pragmatic approach to racial and ethnic diversity, as they have had to do in the past. Utica, like most American cities, has witnessed wave after wave of immigrants from around the world. Every major wave of immigration has found its way to the city, including a new wave of Bosnian and Vietnamese immigrants during the 1990s. Although Utica has at times handled such conditions no better than other cities, it has handled them no worse.

A Victim of the World

The changes that have taken place in central New York are a reflection of the changes in the global economy that have taken place since World War II. The United States, through a series of international treaties, took upon itself a central role in the overall functioning of the global economy (Wallerstein 1979). The system was organized around core countries, such as the United States and those in Europe, which were central in the formation of capital for investment, intellectual innovation, and in other economic functions found in modern industrial nations. Relationships were forged with developing nations, so-called peripheral nations in reference to their economic, political, and military positions in the global economy, which instead stressed their utility in terms of raw materials and as a source of inexpensive labor (Wallerstein 1979). In many cases, nations of the periphery were former colonies of European empires, but in others they functioned as satellites of the core countries (Frank 1967). As these relationships became the dominant feature of the global economy, they would have an impact on the regions that had once provided these functions within core countries, especially the United States. In central New York, a region that had developed an economy based on agricultural production and manufacturing, the increased willingness on the part of once-local firms to locate in other states and nations signaled a dramatic shift in the way ordinary residents experienced their communities.

The economies of local communities throughout New York State were changed dramatically. As in other older industrial regions in the United States, cities lost manufacturing employment as factories moved to the suburbs, to other states, and to developing nations (Harrison and Bluestone 1988). Central New York, in comparison to other economic regions, offered unionized workforces accustomed to good pay, and in many cases companies left for "right-to-work" states and nonunionized countries where wages were lower (Markusen 1987; Storper and Walker 1989). In Utica during the 1950s, civic and business leaders praised the good relations between labor and management, only to see those relations disintegrate as companies left the area in the following decades. In many cases, the corporate concentration of factory owners, and, later, service industries as well, led to the eventual closing of facilities. During World War I, Utica was home to two of the largest textile firms in the world, but by 1950 both had been taken over by out-of-town firms and their factories eventually moved to southern states. Some products still bear the "Utica" name, a corporate testimony to tradition and a local reminder of the pain of deindustrialization. As many cities benefited from an increase in services, Utica witnessed some of its banks and other service industries grow from the takeover of institutions headquartered in smaller towns, but by 1990 several of Utica's premier businesses were themselves taken over by companies headquartered in rival cities. Once an urban beacon for rural residents throughout the region, the city's proximity to Syracuse (forty-five miles) and other cities became a liability for

Utica, as such proximity has done to such other medium-sized metropolitan areas as Pittsfield, Massachusetts (Nash 1989), and Schenectady, New York (Rabrenovic 1996).

Rural areas have suffered these same trends of economic restructuring found in urban areas (Mattson 1997), although there is considerable variation even among them (Ames and Ellsworth 1997; Fitchen 1992). During the 1950s and 1960s, many residents of rural communities moved into the suburbs of metropolitan areas as well, and the fate of rural America was uncertain (Johnson 1989). But by the 1970s and 1980s, many Americans began moving back to small town America, and the media began to speak of a new rural renaissance. But such enthusiasm was short-lived, as the 1980s dealt many rural communities a devastating blow:

Growing international competition in goods-producing industries hit rural areas hard in the early 1980s. Manufacturing industries—the chief source of rural jobs in the 1960s and 1970s—laid off workers, closed up shop, or moved overseas. Mining and timber companies introduced changes in management and technology that resulted in dramatic productivity gains, and these in turn prompted substantial reductions in their labor forces. Farm-dependent communities suffered as farmers' debt increased and dropped. (Duncan and Sweet 1992: xxii)

But even when times were good, population and economic growth was not distributed equally: in general, the less "rural" an area, the better it fared (Thomas 1998). Communities near interstate highways experienced more growth than those without access due to their ability to attract businesses and people interested in an easy escape from country life (Lichter and Fuguitt 1980). Those fortunate enough to be in close proximity to major cities fared best, as they enjoyed arguably the best of both worlds (Aronoff 1997). Similarly, larger rural towns also experienced more growth than their smaller neighbors (Brown et al. 1996); in very small villages, so much of the economic base was lost that they ceased to function as independent communities, acting instead as economic satellites of larger villages nearby (Thomas 1999).

In the face of such restructuring, rural communities have employed a variety of strategies for coping with social change. Communities near metropolitan areas have been found to try to attract urban corporations by marketing both their rural character and urban proximity (Aronoff 1997). Others have responded by attempting to attract urban tourists, often with varying degrees of success (Matsuoka and Benson 1996). Such strategies are often the result of political and economic elites acting in a manner similar to urban growth machines (Bourke and Luloff 1995; Humphrey and Wilkinson 1993).

The Drive for Profit

Profit has to some degree been a motivation for private business for generations. It has not only inspired great invention, but also devised attempts to mitigate the negative potentialities of profit-seeking behavior. In this, the Community Investment Act, which requires banks to reinvest funds in the communities in which they do business, and the medieval prohibitions against usury (interest) share in their ultimate goal. In the past, the limits of transportation and communications technologies placed an additional restraint upon the workings of capitalism. Today, as seen in central New York, the limits have been transgressed.

It has long been understood that larger economies, or bigger markets, can translate into higher profits for the firms that do business there. Due to economies of scale, a company manufacturing a given object in a large community can make a higher profit than one in a smaller community making the same item. Both firms will need the same machinery, the same generated power, and ultimately the same labor. But the firm in the larger community can sell more goods and/ or command higher prices as the larger market translates into a higher demand. Companies in larger markets thus have an advantage over those in smaller markets and can grow larger. In time, a smaller firm will be in most cases either bought by a larger company or forced out of business. Such economic dynamics are not neutral for individual communities, but rather indicate a major advantage for larger cities and towns.

It is not surprising that central New York has witnessed similar dynamics. Utica's prowess in textiles was built not only on the strength of the city's own companies but by their ability to buy smaller mills throughout upstate New York. In time, Utica owners closed their smaller mills in the vicinity of Cooperstown.

Similar dynamics exist in agriculture. Cities are ultimately limited by their abilities to feed their populations. Whereas in smaller communities agricultural production can take place near or even in the town, the sheer number of inhabitants and the land area they develop for non-agricultural purposes forces city leaders to look to the surrounding countryside. Expansion of the city's influence in the country is necessary if the city hopes to grow, as Marx (1985 [1848]) discussed:

The bourgeoisie has subjected the country to the rule of the towns. It has created enormous cities, has greatly increased the urban population as compared to the rural, and has thus rescued a considerable part of the population from the idiocy of rural life. (84)

As did most American cities, Utica grew rapidly during the nineteenth century, and necessarily looked to its hinterland for food, water, and raw materials.

Expansion of the urban sphere of influence has another function: its ability to control the "fixed costs" of keeping the urban labor force alive. By importing food from a large number of producers, the competition between them forces prices down and ultimately lowers the costs of labor for urban industries. Whereas Marx (1990 [1867]) suggested that the wages of labor could only be lowered to the point where workers are kept minimally alive, the suppression of agricultural producers can further depress this point by forcing them to accept lower prices for food. In effect, the surplus labor of the farmer is also transferred to the owners of capital. In central New York, there was a gradual creation of a middle-class lifestyle that assumed and depended upon the interlocking network of urban elites that provided not only manufactured goods but also foodstuffs processed by urban companies (see Ryan 1981). As in manufacturing, however, larger firms, often based in larger cities, are capable of outcompeting smaller firms, and so it is not surprising that such firms as Chicago-based Kraft General Foods now own several once-local food companies.

Such changes in the scale of business firms thus also affect the communities in which production takes place, and the whole process can be called upscaling. Upscaling involves an emphasis on larger economies of scale for investment, and thus gives bigger cities an infrastructure capable of outcompeting smaller metropolitan areas, which typically receive such investments last if at all. There are also cultural ramifications, as the minimum market size required to support modern institutions (e.g., shopping malls, media outlets, dance clubs) becomes increasingly larger. As such institutions are accepted as "necessary" in everyday life, smaller communities come to be seen as cultural backwaters, as only the largest are capable of competing among the diminishing number of cities that can support such institutions. Whereas Utica in the 1950s was considered to be a major city within New York State, by the 1990s the city was the butt of jokes on such television shows as *The Simpsons* and *Jenny*. In *Jenny* in particular, Utica was presented as a "small town" that by nature was boring and ill-bred (see chapter 9) despite being larger than half of the metropolitan areas in the United States (USBC 2000). That Utica could be considered a small town by the cultural standards now dominant in the United States signals a sea change in the way Americans perceive urban and rural life.

Advances in transportation and communications technologies have aggravated such dynamics, and today both rural and urban communities face increasing challenges brought about by the automobile (Kay

1998; Kunstler 1994; Wachs and Crawford 1992). In metropolitan areas, suburbanization has created a decentralized agglomeration of housing, business, and industrial functions spread over great distances (Kunstler 1994; Garreau 1992). Rural areas experienced similar changes: villages larger than others in their respective regions were better able to maintain a diversity of economic goods and services available to residents (Frisbie and Poston 1978; Pinkerton et al. 1995). Not surprisingly, the relative economic health also helped such communities maintain population growth despite dramatic restructuring of their retail and administrative functions (Ballard and Fuguitt 1985; Thomas 1998). In addition, since the 1960s settlement patterns have changed from that of contiguous settlement in villages to one of deconcentrated settlement patterns throughout the hinterland (Ballard and Fuguitt 1984). In other words, rural areas have experienced increased economic centralization at the same time they have experienced residential deconcentration.

The Community Question

It might be argued that attributing such weight to structural considerations in seeking to understand community change comes dangerously close to a deterministic argument. While community cannot be understood without economics, it must also be understood in terms of the interaction of its members.

The location of a community and the ultimate growth of said community is dependent upon numerous factors, including the geography, economic system, and culture. Utica, for instance, grew to a metropolitan area of more than three hundred thousand residents because of its location on the Mohawk River, and easy transportation helped the city to industrialize. In contrast, Hartwick's location was amenable to farming and settlement but not transportation, which hindered its industrial growth and relegated the village to an agricultural economy for most of its history. While Utica accepted wave after wave of immigrants that ultimately shaped the culture of the city, Hartwick's population peaked in 1820 and thus experienced relatively little immigration and the cultural change it brings. It is not surprising that the difference between urban and rural found in the region is more than demographic: Utica, like other urban centers, has been shaped by different cultural forces, which even today influence the city's response to new events.

It is tempting to consider community as a place, or a class, or even a municipality. As these days of Internet chat rooms and virtual communities remind us, a community is composed of people. Specifically, a community is composed of a number of individuals in regular inter-action with one another who through such interaction generate a self-referential culture. Community is thus generated on a continual basis and is thus subject to rapid changes in composition of ideas (although such rapid changes may not occur) (Collins 1975). Individuals who share the culture understand the proper interpretation of the various values, beliefs, and ideas and thus reproduce these cultural traits at a later time with other individuals. Social interaction is, however, struc-tured by the space in which people live and communicate.

As the study of Internet communities is relatively new, it is under-standable that sociologists have long recognized the concept of settle-ment space as central to the identity of a community. Settlement space can be understood as

the built environment in which people live. Settlement space is both con-structed and organized. It is built by people who have followed some mean-ingful plan for the purposes of containing economic, political, and cultural activities. Within it people organize their daily actions according to the mean-ingful aspects of the constructed space. (Gottdeiner 1994, 16)

Conflicts arise over the development of settlement space, giving rise to such fixtures of the urban social landscape as political machines (Allswang 1977), community organizations (Rabrenovic 1996), and social movements (Castells 1977). Individuals seldom experience settle-ment space as coterminous with the space they experience on a daily basis, and the space experienced regularly by an individual may be understood as viable space. Viable space differs from that of settle-ment space in that it recognizes that community residents often inter-act more regularly within particular neighborhoods and not in others, and that this has an effect on how people perceive and experience community:

Most individuals experience their communities as limited to the space most easily accessible to them. This space is experienced at regular and frequent intervals, and is familiar and comfortable. In contrast, space experienced in-frequently or not at all comes to be perceived as outside the realm of everyday life. (Thomas 1998, 20)

Space thus provides the environment in which interaction may occur, and is influential in encouraging or discouraging social interaction. It is the relationship between settlement space and viable space that determines the level of urbanism in a community.

Gans (1962) demonstrated the difference between settlement and viable space in his classic study of the West End of Boston. Residents of the neighborhood selectively perceived their environment; buildings often frequented were part of the cognitive map of the neighborhood, whereas less important structures or buildings in a state of decay were often ignored or treated as "filler" in the urban streetscape. Similarly, residents of the neighborhood perceived the community as their own "urban village" that, although contiguously urbanized with the remainder of the metropolitan area, was uniquely their own. Despite being residents of a large city, everyday life was experienced as a small community. That is, although the settlement space was quite large, the viable space was relatively small and nonthreatening. Residents of Utica's inner city discuss their neighborhoods in a similar fashion.

In contrast, the viable space in a rural small town is often larger than the total settlement space of the village. In the United States, it is common to find that small towns are composed of a dense settlement space (village)—much as in cities—surrounded by agricultural land. The result is that the settlement space of rural towns often is smaller than the area within which one may reasonably be expected to travel. That is, the viable space is larger than the settlement space. This is the general pattern still found today in both Cooperstown and Hartwick.

A community contains any number of attractor points: physical settings in the settlement space that attract community members on a regular basis for social interaction. Attractor points may attract the vast majority of community members, as in the case of the neighborhood business district, or perhaps a smaller but important class of residents. For instance, a neighborhood school functions to attract members of the community affiliated with the school system; namely, students, parents, and staff. For this particular population, the school functions as an attractor point. Because of the number of people who interact at attractor points, economies of scale are high. This has a reciprocal effect, as it is the high economies of scale that attract individuals for purposes of interaction. People are attracted by the economies of scale in the area and, via the act of being present (or not present), change them. The attractor points are thus subject to rapid changes in location and strength, and should be considered dynamic.

Interaction in urban and rural communities takes place within a system of attractor points and social networks that are structured by their relationship to space. Urban community systems are marked by a viable space that is smaller than the settlement space, but easy access to attractor points in other settled areas creates a constant outflow of community members to other attractor points in nearby communities or of a more regional variety. For instance, Utica historically had tight-knit ethnic enclaves with their own neighborhood business districts, but with an overall outflow of residents who worked in adjoining neighborhoods or traveled to the central business district for various activities. In contrast, rural community systems have typically been more self-contained. With a settlement space smaller than the viable space, such attractor points as the business district and the local school often bring in community members who live outside of the settlement space. Whereas urban community systems, structured as they were by contiguous urbanization, have historically looked outside of the viable space with a sense of opportunity and possible expansionism, rural community systems have looked within the viable space for a sense of self-sufficiency and uniqueness (Fitchen 1991).

Not surprisingly, much of the restructuring of the concept of "community" has taken place as former attractor points, such as schools, factories, shopping districts, and the like, have been restructured. The demise of the Hartwick business district deprived residents of not only places to shop, but places in which to interact with other members of the community.

Community and Economic Change

Much of the change in both rural and urban communities is thus due to the expansion of the viable space of communities and the resultant changes in economies of scale. In Utica, for instance, the automobile made it possible for businesses to relocate to non-downtown neighborhoods with a reasonable expectation that shoppers could drive to their stores. Although this is a trend that some might assume began with the postwar suburban housing boom and new paradigms for suburban-style strip malls, this shift to non-downtown business districts began with the car as early as 1909 (see chapter 10). Increased economic activity of residents outside of their neighborhoods created opportunities for interaction all over the metropolitan area, but also limited the amount of interaction in the immediate neighborhood. This occurred at the same time as the deindustrialization of the region and the increased concentration of local businesses into larger and, increasingly, non-local firms. Many of these changes were, as discussed, the result of the globalization of local economy, and thus seemingly beyond the control of the local community.

Such expansion of viable space forces attractor points to compete for influence within the overall system. In metropolitan Utica, the expansion of viable space forced the central business district to compete against suburban shopping centers, and over time a strip in the town of New Hartford became the dominant attractor of retail shoppers. Similarly, the expansion of viable space in the area of Cooperstown and Hartwick forced Hartwick merchants to compete against those in

Cooperstown, with devastating results for Hartwick. This of course is both a result and cause of upscaling in the region, as Cooperstown merchants were also faced during the 1980s with competition from larger communities.

Perhaps the single biggest difference between urban and rural communities, after population, is the presence of institutions that are necessary for the overall functioning of the society but not necessarily for the survival of the community. Colleges, for instance, provide education and income for community members, but rarely grow food. Most cities have educational institutions, hospitals, industrial and commercial firms, among others. In rural communities, the presence of one or another of these institutions in the viable space is often quite unique when compared to surrounding communities, and thus they may be referred to as unique institutions. As such institutions are necessary for contemporary society, urban areas typically have a full array of unique institutions as part of their infrastructure. This grants urban community members access to such services without leaving their own viable space; in many cases, urban residents have a choice of service providers. Rural communities, in contrast, may have few or even none of these institutions, and residents are thus forced to choose between access to such institutions and staying near to home. While Utica has several colleges, neither Cooperstown nor Hartwick have colleges within their own settlement spaces. While Utica and Cooperstown have school districts, Hartwick youngsters are bused to Cooperstown. While Utica provides a choice of three hospitals, Cooperstown has one hospital and Hartwick has none.

A unique institution may be understood as an institution in a community that serves to enhance the community's integration with the larger society. The unique institutions in Cooperstown, such as Bassett Hospital and the Otsego County offices, function as conduits between Cooperstown and the largely urban power structure with which it must negotiate and seek investment. They also make Cooperstown an important attractor for residents of other local communities who seek such services, as these are typically not available in their own communities. It should be noted that unique institutions might also be understood as forms of internal colonization. By enforcing regulations created by and in the interests of urban elites (e.g., loan guidelines), they typically serve the interests of the larger urban society as opposed to local interests. It was the presence of unique institutions and their associated resources in Cooperstown that ultimately enabled the village to survive and dominate other local communities during the 1960s and 1970s. Indeed, Cooperstown's unique institutions have proven so effective for the village that the 1990s brought clear challenges to institutions in Utica (see chapter 11).

Differing Adaptations

Given such variation in their size and character, one might argue that to compare Utica, Cooperstown, and Hartwick is similar to comparing apples and oranges. But much is to be learned about fruit by comparing apples and oranges, just as much is to be learned about the world economy by examining the relative positions of Utica, Cooperstown, and Hartwick. The adaptations to globalization found in each community tell of the relative advantages given larger cities in the competition for capital investment. None of these communities are "global cities," and it is not surprising that they have adapted to globalization so differently. They have experienced economic and social trends together as a region, but each has adapted to them based on its own particular demographic and historical circumstances.

Chapter 2

An American Story

For thousands of years, central New York was home to the Mohawk, Oneida, and Onondaga tribes. Part of the larger Iroquoian cultural group, they had first arrived in the Great Lakes region about 4000 B.C.E. (Tuck 1977). During the late sixteenth century five Iroquoian tribes, the Cayuga, Mohawk, Oneida, Onondaga, and Seneca, formed the Iroquois Confederacy in order to bring peace to the territory and defend against attack from other Iroquoian and Algonquian tribes.[1] The existence of the confederacy made the Iroquois a powerful force in the Great Lakes, and throughout the late seventeenth and early eighteenth centuries, the confederacy traded furs with the Dutch, British, and French for such items as firearms and rum. The existence of the confederacy and other native populations were also construed as an impediment to the expansion of the colonies into the interior of the continent, including central New York. It is not surprising that policies at the time were aimed at dislocating the Iroquois from their ancestral homelands.

The threat of European encroachment on Iroquois lands was a tense issue for decades before the American Revolution, even being commented upon in the 1768 Treaty of Fort Stanwix, which placed the western boundary of New York at the Unadilla River in Otsego County. The treaty stated that its purpose was to

prevent those Intrusions and Encroachments of which we had so Long and Loudly Complained and to put a stop to the many fraudulent advantages which had so often taken us in Land affairs. (National Archives 1998a)

When the American Revolution began in 1775, border raids on the part of Iroquois still loyal to Great Britain served as an excuse for the colonial military to attack the confederacy. In May 1779, General George

Washington ordered that "parties should be detached to lay waste all settlements around . . . that the country may not be merely *overrun* but *destroyed*" (U.S. Library of Congress 31 May 1779; emphasis in original). Later that year, American forces under James Clinton destroyed Iroquois villages in the Onondaga territory, and then turned their attention to the Susquehanna Valley (Fischer 1997; Graymont 1990). They built a dam at the future site of Cooperstown and then broke it, flooding the Iroquois fields downstream. They later met with another army led by General Sullivan, working his way up the Susquehanna from Pennsylvania. The army targeted not only warriors but also the native population as a whole, destroying "the villages of the Indians, slaughtering their livestock, and burning their fields" (Ellis et al. 1957: 116; see also Mulligan 1972). Peace could be obtained only after "you (Generals Clinton and Sullivan) have very thoroughly completed the destruction of their settlements . . . but you will not by any means, listen to any overture of peace before the total ruin of their settlements is effected" (USLOC 31 May 1779). In a campaign that foreshadowed Sherman's march to the sea, two objectives were accomplished: the border raids occurred less frequently, and the Iroquois population was by and large suppressed in central New York.

The dispossession of the Iroquois made the settlement of central New York by the Americans possible. Those natives who survived faced few options: to migrate west or to face poverty in the new communities springing up through upstate New York. The French traveler Alexis de Tocqueville summarized their plight:

The Americans of the United States do not let their dogs hunt the Indians as do the Spaniards in Mexico, but at bottom it is the same pitiless feeling which here, as everywhere else, animates the European race. This world here belongs to us, they tell themselves every day: the Indian race is destined for final destruction which one cannot prevent and which it is not desirable to delay. Heaven has not made them to become civilized; it is necessary that they die. Besides I do not want to get mixed up in it. I will not do anything against them: I will limit myself to providing everything that will hasten their ruin. In time I will have their lands and will be innocent of their death.

To this day, Iroquois names animate the geography of New York, in places such as Oneonta and Oneida, in rivers such as the Mohawk and the Susquehanna, in lakes such as Canadarago and Otsego. And every year, the General Clinton Regatta celebrates the campaign of 1779 as hundreds of canoeists race from Cooperstown down the Susquehanna.

The Western District

The first European explorers of the Mohawk River traveled west from the Hudson through a narrow valley that, ninety miles upstream, broadens into the ancient great lakes floodplain. Near the site of this widening was a site the Iroquois called "Unundadages," a fording spot at the bend along one of the river's many meanders. The Iroquois had utilized this spot as a crossing point for several trails, including the westward Seneca Trail. In 1786, the future city of Utica consisted of "three rude huts, all occupied by boatmen" (Clarke 1952: 15). In 1791, Moses Bagg built a hotel just south of the ford at what would later be known as Bagg's Square. When in 1797 the state of New York authorized thirteen thousand dollars for the construction of the Genesee Highway along the route of the Seneca Trail, the position of Utica as a gateway town for westward expansion was established. A year later, a meeting at Bagg's Hotel drew the name "Utica" from a hat containing thirteen proposed names for the new settlement.

Utica's position at the start of the Genesee Highway, and later the upgraded Seneca Turnpike along the same route, helped the community to flourish. Surrounded by the marshy Mohawk floodplain, the village had little to offer farmers but much to offer merchants and craftsmen. The result was that Utica grew as a dense commercial city almost from the beginning. Its transformation from a marshy ford to a commercial gateway town was summarized by DeWitt Clinton in 1810:

Utica is a flourishing village on the south side of the Mohawk; it arrogates to itself being the capital of the Western District. Twenty-two years ago there was but one house; there are now three hundred, a Presbyterian Church, an Episcopal, a Welsh Presbyterian and a Welsh Baptist; a Bank, being a branch of the Manhattan Company; a Post Office, the office of the Clerk of the County, and the Clerk of the Supreme Court. (Quoted in Ellis 1979: 110)

In time, Utica would become the seat of the federal courts for the Northern District of New York and a major power center in state politics.

The great expanse south of the Mohawk River was also developed after the revolution as settlers looked to the hills near the rapidly filling valley. It is commonly held that hearty pioneers staking claims on untitled and untamed property settled the American frontier, but the reality is one of aggressive marketing of territory by land speculators. Throughout northern and western New York, speculators of either aristocratic origin or aspiration would divide the Iroquoian homeland despite the promises of the past (Ellis et al. 1957: 90; Taylor 1995).

William Cooper was a poor Quaker from Burlington, New Jersey, who longed to be a part of the polite society he knew in Philadelphia (Taylor 1995). After the Revolution, Cooper was able to gain control of the Croghan Patent, whose loyalist owners were in exile and out of the newly formed United States.[2] Shortly thereafter, Cooper began to settle his patent and plan his great city: Cooperstown. In 1786, several farms

were established at the site. By 1787, more settlers arrived, "princi-
pally from Connecticut, and most of the land on the patent was taken
up" (Cooper et al. 1976: 10). He envisioned Cooperstown to one day
be a great city, writing in 1810 that the site on the Susquehanna would
prove as important as the mouth of the Buffalo River (Buffalo) and
boasted of the village's superior construction to Utica (Cooper 1936
[1810]). And with the frontier wide open, such hopeful expectations
seemed within reach. In fact, Cooper's dreams of profit and a great
city named after himself were rather tame in comparison to those of
one of his neighbors.

John Christopher Hartwick was a German minister attracted to the
colonies to preach to Lutheran settlers. He originally arrived to minister to the Palatine German settlers who had settled the central
Mohawk Valley during the eighteenth century, but he rather quickly
tired of the decidedly American characteristics he found in them. He
believed the settlers were losing their piety in the openness of the
frontier and tried tirelessly to correct the situation. His efforts led him
to travel extensively throughout the northeastern United States, and
he was decisive in establishing the Lutheran Church in this country
(Arndt 1937). But his enthusiasm was perceived by many of his pa-
rishioners to be rather extreme, and he was considered to be something of a nuisance. As result, he found himself a teacher in an ill-fated
search for a following.

Hartwick blamed his pattern of rejection on the sparse settlements
and democratic ideology of the American colonies (Taylor 1995). This
was likely a factor, but much of the fault was with Hartwick himself.
By most accounts, he was a slovenly and irritating man, stubbornly
devout and considered misogynistic even by the standards of the late
eighteenth century.[3] Birdsall (1925: 29) related the following incident:

On one occasion when disturbed in preaching by a dog, he exclaimed with
much earnestness that dogs and children had better be kept at home, and it
would not be much matter, he added, if the women were kept there too!

As a congregation seemed to be out of reach in the sparsely settled
Mohawk Valley, Hartwick resolved to build his own community of the
pious somewhere else. In 1761, he received a patent for the land that
approximates the present Town of Hartwick.[4] On this land, he dreamed
of recreating a medieval German village, densely settled and hierar-
chically organized around him. It was to be called "New Jerusalem,"
but it is unclear if there were any settlers on the patent prior to
the Revolution.[5]

Cooper and Hartwick represented a conflict of feudalistic conservatism and bourgeois liberalism. Cooper was, above all, a businessman

who viewed landholdings as a source of wealth and income. He sold land to settlers even while many aristocrats clung to the semifeudal land lease system, and in doing so helped to undermine the system (Butterfield, 29 Apr. 1955: 10). He sought to develop a thriving commercial city that would attract new settlers and raise property values in his village. The main impetus of his work would be familiar to any modern capitalist: to earn a profit.

In stark contrast, there was Hartwick, obsessed as he was with a city based on piety, hierarchy, and feudalistic social arrangements. As his goals were different, his approach to settlement was vastly different from that of Cooper. His lease required potential settlers to acknowledge Hartwick as their "pastor, teacher, and spirtual counselor" and "to attend regularly, decently, attentively, and devoutly, Divine service, and instruction performed and given" by Hartwick. (Arndt 1937: 295). These stipulations were unpopular among the settlers in central New York: Hartwick and New Jerusalem represented a return to a medieval past that few were willing to make.

Low Bridge Ahead

Utica was a gateway city; the last gasp of home before the wilds of the Seneca Turnpike, the Great Lakes, and the Ohio Country. Transportation was slow, however, relying as it did on stagecoach and riverboats that required portage at several rapids along the Mohawk. As a result, Cooperstown did enjoy its share of traffic along the southern branch of the Western Turnpike built through the village and some water traffic from Otsego Lake. In 1825, the necessary infrastructure for urban success changed with the completion of the Erie Canal, and with it the nature of the competition between Cooperstown and Utica. Built through Utica, the canal provided the only American water route from New York on the Atlantic to Buffalo on the Great Lakes.

The effect of the Erie Canal on New York State was tremendous. Prior to the completion of the canal, New York City faced stiff competition from such other seaports as Philadelphia and Boston. The Erie Canal gave New York an inexpensive route to the Great Lakes and the interior; even today, one can boat from New York to Chicago via the canal if they desire. The canal brought about the dominance of the Port of New York and filtered millions of dollars through the upstate New York countryside. It allowed farmers and manufacturers throughout the state a worldwide market, spawned several new cities and grew others. Various feeder canals brought not only more water to the Erie, but industry and residents to other regions in the state such as the Finger Lakes and the Champlain Valley (Larkin 1998). Within a few decades New York was the most populous state in the nation and the Erie Canal corridor was known as the "Urban Streak" due to the number of cities along its shores.

Contemporary descriptions of the city testify to Utica's prosperity. Duke Bernhard of Saxe-Weinar Eisenbach in 1830 called the city the "most flourishing town in New York," despite a rather negative impression of the country as a whole. Alexis de Toqueville wrote of Utica in 1832:

Charming town of 10,000 inhabitants. Very pretty shops. Founded since the War of Independence. In the middle of a pretty plain.

But even in the midst of such prosperity, the rate of growth slowed during the 1830s as cities to the west, especially Syracuse, Rochester, and Buffalo, began to give Utica stiff competition. Utica had lost its status as a gateway city, as the "canal boats which passed through Utica by the hundreds enriched the western counties of the state, but added little to the prosperity of Utica" (Clarke 1952: 36).

The physical layout of the city changed as a result of the canal. Prior to 1825, development in the city was in relation to the Mohawk River. Bagg's Square sat at the fording spot in the river, although it now had a bridge to the other side. The oldest streets were built close to the river, and the city as a whole grew primarily along the shore. After 1825, development shifted to the south along the canal. East and west of the original settlement, the land along the river went largely undeveloped as the entire city began to shift south and along the east-west corridor created by the canal. It was quite understandable. The river flooded yearly and was bound by swamps. When the canal went through the city to south of the river, the superior property along its banks was more easily developed. The river was all but abandoned, and in the early twentieth century was moved entirely to make room for expanded rail yards. Even today, Utica barely acknowledges the river's presence. The entire metropolitan area straddles either side of the basin in which the river meanders—an undeveloped swath that is interrupted only at the oldest part of the city. William Cullen Bryant's *Picturesque America* commented:

It is clear that the impetus of the city is not derived from the river, but from the Erie Canal, for the streets are all built in the proximity of the latter, and the former is outside the town altogether. (Quoted in Wyld 1962: 46)

As Utica faced a future of growth, Cooperstown and the nearby village of Hartwick found themselves relegated to the outside of the burgeoning economy spawned by the canal. Cooperstown had been named the seat of government for Otsego County, but by 1830 the county's population had nearly peaked. Between 1830 and 1960, the population hovered between forty-six and fifty-one thousand, growing most significantly during the 1960s due to the expansion of the county's two colleges in Oneonta. Since 1970, the population has remained relatively stable at around sixty thousand residents. In comparison, the Township of Utica's population had grown to 8,323 in 1830 (Shupe et al. 1987). In the town of Otsego, the township to which Cooperstown belonged, the population was only 4,363, twice the population ever to be attained by the township of Hartwick (Shupe et al. 1987). As Utica grew over the next century, the town of Otsego would never reach five thousand residents. By 1900, Utica contained more residents than all of Otsego County and was growing suburbs. Not surprisingly, by 1840 Utica no longer competed with Cooperstown, but rather with the cities to the west.

Consolidating Utica

It was during the 1840s that Utica shed its skin of the frontier days, becoming an established site of civilization. The city became the kind of environment from which the pioneers had escaped rather than what they sought in the frontier. Over the coming decades, Utica's business elite helped to shape the entire nation, as discussed by Walsh (1982):

(They) developed means of transportation; constructed the telegraph system of the state; established newspapers; organized the Associated Press; opened California with the Overland Mail; created the American Express Company; supplied the country with textiles, clothing, knitgoods, and shoes; and were in the vanguard of the social movements for temperance and the abolition of slavery. (iii)

Some companies, such as Western Union and American Express, were founded in the city (under different names) and later moved their headquarters to other cities. The city was home to the first association of journalists in the nation (Schwarzlose 1980). For F. W. Woolworth, his failed five and dime on Bleeker Street provided a bitter lessen, and when he later tried again in York, Pennsylvania, he insisted that his store would not be on a side street. Years later, Woolworth would build what was then the tallest six story building in the world in the heart of downtown Utica for the triumphant return of his five and dime. Throughout the second half of the nineteenth century, Utica and the surrounding region would develop and reflect the middle-class culture that so predominates American life today (Ryan 1981). It was through the prosperity of its middle class that the city was able to do this; it was the relative decline of the early 1840s that made it possible.

In 1845, the business community was alarmed to learn that the New York State Census showed a small decline in population for the city. The city had never lost population before, and so many other cities were growing quickly. With about twelve thousand residents, Utica had gained more than four thousand residents since 1830, but remained ranked as the twenty-ninth largest city in the United States (USBC 2000). Forced to face the reality that the frontier had passed through and beyond Utica, city leaders debated about how to save the city from being nothing more than a reasonably large market town. It was decided to send a delegation of three Utica businessmen on a fact-finding mission concerning the use of steam power in manufacturing. After a tour of New England factories, they enthusiastically suggested the development of an industrial base, and set into motion the financial mechanism to make it happen.

Oneida County, of which Utica is part, already had a small manufacturing sector, primarily along the fast-moving streams that rushed to the Mohawk. Utica had lagged behind its future suburbs due to its lack of good sources of water power, but due to steam power Utica mills would define the region's character and shape its future.

By 1850, the Globe Woolen Mills, the Utica Steam Cotton Mills, and the Utica Steam Woolen Mills had been established. The implication of their founding is self-evident: Utica was to be an industrial city. But the hidden significance lies in their immediate incorporation. City elites formed a commission, chose a course of action, and implemented a plan in short order. In less than five years, the direction of the city's history was thoroughly altered. Most authors suggest that the process went smoothly, being supported by both city leaders and ordinary citizens (Crisafulli 1960; Ellis and Preston 1982; Walsh 1982). Just as important, the business community acted in the interests of the overall community. While it seems likely that there were dissenters at the time, the establishment of the mills was a product of the community and of collective action on the part of city leaders. They were founded, funded, and operated by local elites. While there was, of course, a sense of self-interest, that sense of self-interest was identified with the well-being of the community and did not rely solely on the health of a single company or individual.

The opening and growth of the mills coincided with the influx of successive waves of foreign-born immigrants between the 1840s and the 1920s (Noble 1999). Early on, it was the English, Scottish, and Welsh. Germans came as well, establishing Lutheran and Catholic churches in the midst of the Anglican and Calvinist sects. For the early 1800s, many of the residents were rooted in New England Yankee customs and traditions. When the potato blight hit Ireland in the 1840s, thousands of Irish found their way to Utica's west side by the Erie and Chenango Canals during the following decades. Later came the Polish and Italians, and small populations of Jews and African Americans fluctuated throughout the nineteenth century.[6] Ellis and Preston (1982) summed up nicely:

If one adds the children of foreign born in this country, one finds that upward of two out of three residents had close foreign ties. In this city of immigrants one would hear Irish brogues near the locks, the lilt of Welsh voices in song, and the guttural tones of Germans in shops and stores. (59)

Marginalizing Otsego

Without a transportation infrastructure competitive with the canals and railroads to the north, there were fewer opportunities for commerce in northern Otsego County in comparison to Utica and other canal towns. This was especially evident in regard to manufacturing. In Cooperstown and Hartwick, industrialization was minor and firms had fewer transportation options. Small mills built in Toddsville, Phoenix Mills, and other hamlets were outcompeted or bought by urban companies. Utica benefited from the ability of its textile firms to buy smaller companies located in Otsego County and other rural communities in central New York (Bohls 1991). Factories in Utica also had the advantage of full time workers who were typically brought in specifically to work (of necessity) in the mills (Pula and Dziedzic 1991). The mills in central Otsego County frequently hired those who sought to supplement their incomes, and were much smaller in productive capacity.[7] A basic pattern of upscaling was found in the early textile industry in central New York State as smaller companies located in rural towns were bought by larger companies headquartered in major cities, transferring not only administrative (white collar) employment to the cities but in time closing the rural factories themselves. By 1920, Utica was home to two of the largest textile firms in the world (Przybycien and Romanelli 1977).

Like the larger cities, villages tended to be densely populated urban centers surrounded by rural hinterland and often developed around specific forms of production. Toddsville, Index, and Phoenix Mills, for instance, grew up around the small textile mills in those communities. Hartwick developed around several small grist and lumber mills and attracted a large enough population to develop a commercial district as well. Cooperstown had mills, the county seat, and a commercial district. There was trade among these different villages, but due to the distances involved contact was rather irregular. Each community was economically integrated with the others, but social life tended to be centered in the home villages: villages were centers of regular social interaction between residents and this created a tight knit social structure.[8]

Between 1830 and 1870, the area was actually quite isolated from the outside world. Members of the area elite, such as James Fenimore Cooper, were often integrated into social circles outside of the area. For members of the lower and middle classes, however, the typical day revolved around the farm or the place of work in the village. The stability of the population actually is indicative of significant emigration during this period. As much of the farmland had been taken up, the first son was typically the child who inherited the family farm. This forced the other children to look elsewhere for their economic well-being, and this search typically took them westward for land or into the cities for work. As a result, there were relatively few opportunities for immigrants in the area and so few arrived. The dominant New England culture that arrived with the first settlers remained dominant in Otsego County even as it was increasingly challenged in Utica and other cities in the face of immigration from around the world.

The area remained relatively isolated until the 1870s, when the Cooperstown and Susquehanna Valley Railroad, a consortium of private interests and town governments, was built to connect with the lines of the Albany and Susquehanna (later the Delaware and Hudson) (Birdsall 1925; Grills 1969). Although plans were made to extend the line to Canajoharie in the north and deeper into the Catskills to the south, such plans never materialized. Cooperstown was made more accessible, but was still a spur off the main line.

Between 1897 and 1905, an interurban railway known simply as "the trolley" was constructed from Oneonta to Hartwick, Cooperstown, and Mohawk on the Mohawk River. Besieged by financial problems almost from the beginning, it ran sporadically until the 1940s when the tracks were recycled for the effort to fight World War II (Garrison 1992; Nestle 1959).

The effect of both rail systems was to bring in new populations and break the cultural isolation of the area. While there had been migrant farm workers for quite some time, it was the rail workers who became permanent residents. By 1905, about two hundred interurban workers, many of whom were Italian Catholics, lived in shanties near Hartwick village. They brought with them the concerns of the largely urban labor movement, including some that were not particularly welcomed in the area. In 1901, after working without pay, rail workers rioted in Hartwick village and in 1903 they blocked the rails in Mohawk.

Quiltwork Neighborhoods

As Utica grew, its many neighborhoods developed individual identities. As early as the 1820s, Utica's elite built homes at distance from the lower classes, and such segregation has continued throughout the city's history. As new forms of transportation allowed the elite to move farther from the city center, they did.[9] They moved first to Rutger Street, today adjoining the central business district but then on the outskirts of town, a neighborhood within walking distance of Bagg's Square but on a hill overlooking the town as it was then. When the trolley arrived, many moved farther from the city center, and the area surrounding Rutger Street developed for the working class in neighborhoods marked by double- and triple-decker apartment houses.

The new ethnic groups that settled in the city en masse added a new dimension of segregation. Increasingly, German and Irish immigrants moved to the west side, the Welsh to Corn Hill. Later, Poles moved into west Utica as well, and Italians moved into the east side (Pula 1994). Change was constant. For instance, the Jewish Community had originally been concentrated in the "Jewish Quarter" northeast of downtown, later in an area called "the triangle" northwest of downtown, then in Corn Hill and central Utica, and is today rather dispersed throughout the metropolitan area (Kohn 1959; 1994). The African American neighborhood population likewise moved from an area near downtown, to the Triangle, to Corn Hill (DeAmicis 1994). Even today, people of Latin American, African American, Vietnamese, and Bosnian descent increasingly populate neighborhoods once considered to be "Italian." This dynamic had been established by 1850.

Utica grew slowly compared to many other cities. In 1830 and 1840, Utica was the twenty-ninth largest city in the United States. In 1840, the city was larger than Detroit, Cleveland, and Chicago. One hundred years later, Utica was ranked ninety-second and was best compared to Charlotte, North Carolina, Peoria, Illinois, and Little Rock, Arkansas. In 1950, Utica had fallen off the list of the one hundred largest cities in the country (Gibson 1998).

By the end of the nineteenth century, Utica was an industrial city dominated by textile mills and populated by immigrants from throughout the world. Despite falling behind the larger cities to the west, Utica was the major economic and cultural center of the Mohawk Valley region. Home to the Utica Knit, Utica blankets, Oneita Clothing, Duofold underwear, and many other textile companies, metropolitan Utica was dominated by textile interests. Although there were many other companies, such as Utica Cutlery, Utica Boilers, and Remington Corporation, textiles remained the most important industry into the 1940s. Utica continued to grow and prosper, but other

Figure 2.1. Populations of Major Upstate Cities, 1790–1990

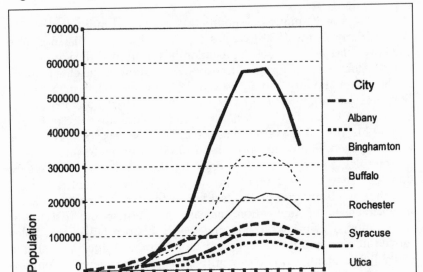

Source: Shupe et al. 1987

cities did so more rapidly. Utica was prosperous and stable, and in its contentment the city grew complacent and fell behind the other great cities. As Kohn (1959) described:

Utica offered less in opportunity in comparison with neighboring cities. Syracuse had become a center of the salt and chemical industry and grew rapidly. Rochester . . . became a great industrial city and a center of the clothing industry. Buffalo outstripped most of the cities of New York State because of its rail and water-borne industries. Utica with its textile mills, worked mostly by unskilled, foreign labor at low wages and controlled by old-settled families, showed no encouragement to new industries employing skilled labor. Thus, Utica was permitted only a slow economic growth. (21)

Through World War II, life in the city was comfortable. Not necessarily financially—many workers, like their counterparts elsewhere, made very little—but socially. The economy and the population grew, and generations grew up and stayed in the area. There were certainly ups and downs, periods of growth and recession, times of great change and seeming stagnation, but nothing foresaw the changes that would come after World War II.

To the south, Cooperstown and Hartwick had experienced a very different period. As Utica grew, they remained stable. As Utica industrialized, Cooperstown and Hartwick lost industry. As Utica looked to other cities as neighbors and kindred spirits, Cooperstown and Hartwick looked to each other.

Cooper's Town

Although the initial goal of building a great inland city was not fulfilled, Cooperstown did acquire the infrastructure for its later development. Cooperstown thrived not only as the county seat and market town but attracted the tutelage of the upper class as well. It was the reputation and infrastructure of early tourism in the village that led to the subsequent development of a modern tourist economy.

The early popularity of James Fenimore Cooper, who is regarded by some as America's first novelist, brought visitors from distant locales as early as the 1840s. Such tales as *The Last of the Mohicans* showcase upstate New York as a rugged frontier. Vivid descriptions of the landscape give the stories a certain romantic quality. The son of William Cooper, James spent much of his life in Cooperstown and Albany. Relations between the aristocratic Cooper and his Yankee neighbors in Cooperstown were apparently quite ornery at times (Birdsall 1925), and the villagers were presented as hooligans in such stories as *The Pioneers*. But Cooper also brought the village a notoriety not conferred upon most rural villages, and the tourism industry began with his death and burial on the grounds of the Episcopalian Church. When pilgrims to his grave eventually arrived, local merchants were quite happy to have the extra income.

By 1900, several resort hotels had been established for the visitors, and some built large estates on the shores of Otsego Lake. Throughout this period, tourism was centered on private homes and in resorts. While there was certainly a large economic impact, the visitors generally had little contact with area residents. The resorts catered to every need, so there was little reason to leave. Often, visitors would stay for weeks on end, enjoying the hospitality of the resort and the particularly appealing scenery of the countryside. The resorts were a social scene connected to but not integrated with the local community. The impact on the local community was rather minimal, as many visitors felt little need to go downtown. Not only was the architecture fairly Spartan in comparison to upper-class areas in most major cities, but the stores were aimed primarily toward the local population. Cooperstown was, away from the hotels, an upstate New York market town, and visitors did not travel a full day or more to see just another market town. They went for the countryside, the lake, and the social scene.

Following World War I, members of the upper class began to take shorter vacations closer to home. Communities on Long Island's South Fork, collectively known as "the Hamptons," had begun as early as 1900 to impact the elite social scene in Cooperstown. They were closer to New York, more easily accessible, and had an ocean. The resorts of central New York were conceivably in trouble and the resort owners needed to find a way to stem the decline.

Cooperstown's initial advantage over similar villages nearby was the upper-class presence. Faced with massive investments in a tourism infrastructure, a failure to stem the decline could translate into massive losses for the local elite. One solution was to persuade the New York State Historical Association to make Cooperstown its home in 1939 (NYSHA 1997). The association would manage two history museums. The Farmer's Museum was devoted to the preservation and exhibition of agriculture techniques and tools, and included a recreation of a rural hamlet (the Village Crossroads). Across the street is the Fenimore House Art Museum, which boasts one of the largest American Folk Art collections in the world. But the jewel would be the National Baseball Hall of Fame and Museum, also dedicated in 1939.

Viva Baseball

The fifteenth edition of Encyclopedia Britannica (1976: 729) states:

In the early days of modern U.S. baseball, no one who wrote of it seemed to doubt that it was an evolution from an English children's game known then and thereafter as rounders. A simple change in the rules, according to these authorities, transformed it into a man's game.... The rules of the pioneer Knickerbocker Baseball Club of New York, drawn up in 1845, constitute the earliest known documentary record of (modern baseball rules).

By the late nineteenth century, baseball was already celebrated as "America's game." Professional leagues were organized much as they are today, and modern rules had by and large been institutionalized. What was lacking was evidence that baseball was in fact an American game. And if the game had, in fact, evolved from rounders, then an American genesis of the game needed to be created. Springwood (1996) would refer to this as "the Immaculate Conception of baseball" (30).

The co-founder of the National League, Albert Spaulding, had for some years been involved in a dispute with the editor of his *Spaulding's Official Base Ball Guide*, Henry Chadwick. Whereas the British-born

Chadwick was certain of the game's British origins, the American Spaulding was equally certain that the game was wholly American. Chadwick would later describe "the whole matter (as) a joke between Albert and myself" (quoted in Levine 1985: 115). Spaulding transformed the private joke into a nationalistic showdown with his 1905 formation of the Mills Commission. Named after its chair, Abraham Mills, the commission was to investigate the game's origins.

With the formation of the committee, considerably more than history was at stake. Composed of business leaders, former baseball players (American), and two federal senators, the committee from the outset was unlikely to find a non-American origin. As Springwood noted (1996: 31–32):

In truth, very little actual work was performed by the committee. As a prominent group of figureheads it served mainly to suggest a stronger sense of authority. Most of the official analysis was done by Mills. Spaulding largely controlled the flow of historical materials that came his way, and indeed, he seemed to draw on every possible shred of testimony, however tenuous, that might support an indigenous theory of baseball's origin.

By 1907, the search for American origins seemed hopelessly elusive. In that year, however, Spaulding received an intriguing letter from a seventy-three-year-old man named Abner Graves. Graves claimed that Abner Doubleday, who would become a well-known Civil War officer, had gone "diligently among the boys in the town (Cooperstown), and in several schools, explaining the plan, and inducing them to play Base Ball in lieu of other games" (Birdsall 1925: 254). Such a story was exactly what Spaulding had wanted. Despite a fifteen-year age difference between Graves and Doubleday, which would have made Graves a five-year-old playing baseball with a twenty-year-old Doubleday, Spaulding supported the story of a perfect stranger (Vlasich 1990).

There was good evidence that the first organized game had occurred in Hoboken, New Jersey, in 1842 (Frommer 1988), but the story of an 1839 game in bucolic Cooperstown contrasted well with the industrialized Hoboken. The Doubleday myth also played to the nationalistic impulse that brought the committee together in the first place. In addition, it allowed fans to pinpoint the time and place for the game's beginning—thus avoiding the cognitive ambiguities of a slow cultural evolution (Gould 1989). The game was American, not British; it formed out of an earlier time of innocence, not the smoky streets of slum filled cities—the game was born of an American hero in the home of America's first novelist.

As Abner Doubleday was a West Point cadet in 1839, it would seem unlikely that he traveled to Cooperstown to play "his" new game (Vlasich 1990). Had such a game occurred, it is perhaps more likely that Doubleday had taught the local boys, accustomed to playing a New England-based variation of the game (Town Ball), a New York City variant of the game that he learned at West Point. More likely, however, is that the story was a concoction. In his history of Cooperstown, Birdsall (1925) was particularly skeptical that the event had even occurred (254–55). Moreover, "a significant shadow of doubt has been cast on Graves's credibility, and apparently no record exists of any attempt to cross examine his claims" (Springwood 1996, 33).

The findings of the Mills Commission were published in 1908, and met with little celebration in Cooperstown. Birdsall (1925) makes brief mention of interest immediately after the finding, but it was not until 1917 that the Doubleday Memorial fund was formed (Springwood 1996). With the Chamber of Commerce, this group raised money to purchase the pasture of Elihu Phinney and turn it into a village baseball field. In 1934, local fund raising and New Deal program money resulted in the construction of the grandstand, and Doubleday field "was re-dedicated as the 'birthplace of Baseball' " (Springwood 1996: 37). The organizers of the event promoted the patriotic virtues of the myth by stating:

It is hoped that the flag of the United States will be generally displayed in the village and that all will plan to have a share in making this an event long to be remembered in Cooperstown and in the annals of base ball throughout the country. (FJ, 25 July 1934)

Throughout the early twentieth century, the local elite had worked to solidify Cooperstown as a major resort center. Facing the downturn in tourism regionally, many backed an idea to expand the baseball legacy: a Hall of Fame (Kulik 1989). The primary financial backer was not an ardent baseball fan, but rather the owner of several tourism-related institutions. A museum would bring tourists into downtown to help the ailing Depression-era economy (Vlasich 1990). With the additional support from Major League Baseball, the first Hall of Fame election inducted Ty Cobb, Walter Johnson, Christy Mathewson, Babe Ruth, and Honus Wagner in 1936 (Springwood 1996). The newly built Hall of Fame and Museum was dedicated June 12th, 1939, one hundred years after the supposed invention of the game two blocks away.

The Hall of Fame not only signified a new era for baseball, but for tourism as well. The period of resort tourism was over, and a new period would begin.

New Jerusalem

John Christopher Hartwick never did build his great holy city. After being named as leasing agent over the Hartwick Patent, William Cooper systematically ignored Hartwick's wishes and utilized his own system for settling Hartwick by selling off the territory (Arndt 1937; Butterfield 1969). Facing the reality that New Jerusalem would never be built, Hartwick willed a Lutheran Seminary to be built with what remained of his estate. It took nearly fifteen years, but the Hartwick Seminary was finally built in the fields four miles south of Cooperstown and six miles east of Hartwick village in 1812. The settlement that grew around it never rivaled either of the villages, and in the 1920s the Board of Trustees closed the seminary and used the proceeds to build a liberal arts college in Oneonta a short time later. Hartwick College today dates its birth from the 1797 death of John Christopher Hartwick; it is not only the remnants of New Jerusalem, but testimony to its founder's ultimate failure. The site today is a mobile home park.

In the central portion of the township, Hartwick village grew at a crossroads in the Otego Creek Valley. Like many agricultural towns in central New York, the village thrived during the middle and late nineteenth century by growing hops. The village developed a central business district that served village residents and nearby farmers, as well as such community institutions as a school system, three Calvinist churches, and a local newspaper. By the turn of the twentieth century, however, most hops production moved to Washington State and, like many nearby agricultural communities, Hartwick suffered a decline—the result of a "blue mold" that infected the local hops. The arrival of the interurban trolley in Hartwick saved the village from an economic calamity: the trolley established its main car yard, power plant, and offices in Hartwick. By the Great Depression, however, the trolley too was in a state of decline. In short, by World War II the village had a history of economic decline and revival. As in Utica and Cooperstown, there was no reason to believe that an economic downturn could be permanent. The new science of economics showed that such patterns were normal, even desirable. Economic changes were signs of progress for the nation as a whole rather than omens of impending decline. And in the name of progress, omens came.

Chapter 3

Loom to Boom

A period of history rarely begins when it says it does. The events of the 1950s were the direct result of the fact that "by 1919, two-thirds of Utica's gainfully employed were working in clothing and textile factories" (Bean 1994: 216). The fall of the industry was thus from a lofty height:

At the time of the first world war the city of Utica was one of the richest per capita in the U.S. [But] after the war the tide turned sharply . . . the trek of the textile mills out of Utica to the south began. By 1924 there were only six (of 22 in 1910) working mills left in Utica, and some $15 million of capital was tied up in idle industrial properties. (Sheehan, Dec. 1949: 170).

In 1910, Utica was home to two of the largest textile producers in the world. The Utica Knitting Company proudly wore the name of its home city, and the Utica and Mohawk Cotton Mills produced world famous "Utica Sheets" (Przybycien and Romanelli 1977). By 1960, neither firm had any operations in the city. The textile industry as a whole had begun its exodus from its stronghold in the northeast to the anti-union and anti-tax havens of the deep South, a trek it would continue as it moved out of the United States entirely later in the century. It is thus no surprise that in 1922, Utica Gas & Electric Company planned a massive expansion in service for the metropolitan area, but by 1928 had scaled back their plans (UGEC 1923; Williams 11 Nov. 1957). Although Utica had failed to keep pace with its neighbors to the west, the city was still accustomed to growth. For instance, in 1900, Syracuse had grown to nearly twice the size of Utica (108,374 vs. 56,383).[1] Over the next two decades, Syracuse would add over seventy thousand residents, whereas Utica would gain only forty thousand.

33

But even while lagging behind, Utica was accustomed to adding twenty thousand residents per decade, and at that rate the city should have contained almost 115 thousand people by 1930. It grew to only 101,740.[2] Something was amiss.

The Chamber of Commerce recognized the omens in the numbers. In the 1840s, city leaders responded to the threat of impending decline by sending a delegation to Massachusetts to study the possibility of reviving the city with textiles. In 1928, the Chamber of Commerce responded to the threat of impending decline by

seeking something to replace textiles. They concluded that Utica's salvation lay in the diversification of industry and that the change would be a tough job that would take a lot of doing. (Williams 11 Nov. 1957: 7)

Members of the chamber had the vision to see that Utica needed change once again. The group needed a way of making it happen.

Their first attempt involved hiring an executive director to bring about the desired changes with the notion that

the "right man" could push the proper buttons and obtain immediate results, industrially or otherwise. It didn't work that way in Utica. The $10,000 executive hired in June of 1928 was fired the next March. And the assistant who was supposed to be his good right hand wasn't much better, either. (Williams 11 Nov. 1957: 8)

The necessary coalition became apparent with the coming of the Great Depression. As the local Democrats brought votes to Franklin Roosevelt, the New Deal helped to keep the city afloat.

Seeking Respect

It was during the 1880s that Utica politics were given over to the immigrant populations who struggled for respect and livelihood in the city's mills. In the east side neighborhoods home to Irish and Italian immigrants, a coalition with politicians from the less populated west side solidified the influence of the city's working class through the first political machine. Thriving on a system of patronage fueled by public funds and illicit profits, the machine acted as much as an inefficient means of social justice as a political entity.[3] The machine controlled both political parties throughout the 1880s and early 1890s until rival Irish politicians wrestled the Democratic Party from machine control and ran a reform ticket, leaving the machine to the Republicans (Bean 1994).

In the 1920s, however, a rival machine came to power based upon a resurgence of immigrant anxiety caused by both national and local events. Locally, the first phase of Utica's deindustrialization hit the Italian and Polish immigrants hardest. As textile mills closed, the increasingly assimilated Irish politicians found that they could rely less upon their own neighbors than upon the disenfranchised workers (Ehrenhalt 1992). This allowed the Democratic machine to gain power with the help of some good guesswork.

In 1928, the Irish Catholic Al Smith ran unsuccessfully for president of the United States. Like many Catholic voters, east Utica Italians were unnerved by the anti-Catholic tone the campaign had taken (Ehrenhalt 1992). This was, in part, the reason they voted at levels 200 percent above previous presidential elections (Bean 1994). But Al Smith had left the governorship of New York to pursue his presidential bid, and Franklin Delano Roosevelt sought to take his place. When Roosevelt arrived in Utica in 1928 after a string of uninspiring campaign stops in the western cities, the leaders of Utica's Democratic machine, Charles Donnelly and Rufus Elefante, met him at the city's Hotel Hamilton and escorted him to a rally in the heart of Utica's "Little Italy." Rufus Elefante commented in 1986 that Roosevelt was, "so highly elated and he was so pleased after all the other meetings were flops. He took a liking to me and Charlie Donnelly" (OD, 28 Sept. 1986: 8A). After Roosevelt was elected, the two would "go and visit the governor and ask for political favors, which we got" (OD, 28 Sept. 1986: 8A).[4]

After Roosevelt was elected president, the local Democratic machine was able to utilize federal patronage to hold power continuously for nearly thirty years. In addition to the five thousand Works Progress Administration (WPA) jobs, the machine also benefited from the fact that William Bray, another Utica Democrat, was lieutenant governor during the administration of Herbert Lehman from 1933 to 1938 (Witt 1963). The machine was organized in much the same way as political machines in other cities, with a tight core of leaders at the top of the organization who controlled policy, a middle level of precinct and block captains responsible for maintaining the loyalty of those who lived in their neighborhoods, and the general membership who more often than not would vote with their machines (Allswang 1977; Ehrenhalt 1992).

The machine provided a centralized organization for conducting city business and requesting patronage. Stuart Witt (1963) related the following example:

Dean Cope of Syracuse University, formerly an assistant dean at Utica College, tells a story which illustrates the organization of the party at the highest level. When Cope first came to Utica College in the mid-'fifties, he was told by some of his colleagues that he was a fool if he were a democrat in this city. To illustrate their point, they took him to Marino's (Restaurant) for lunch. While the group was having lunch, one of Cope's knowledgeable colleagues pointed out the various booths in the restaurant: one for contracts, one for welfare, another for jobs, etc. As the group was leaving the restaurant, one of Rufus Elefante's lieutenants stopped them at the door and asked them what they wanted to see Rufie about. After they responded that they did not particularly want to talk with Elefante and had come merely for lunch, the lieutenant said in disbelief, "Oh, come now; everybody who comes in here wants to see Rufie." Then he realized that they were from Utica College, which was currently conducting a million-dollar fund-raising drive, and gave the men his unsolicited assurance that they would get their money. (9–10)

The episode demonstrates the resolve on the part of some local elites to vote against what they perceived as corruption. But for others, it represented the efficiency of machine rule, and some local businessmen perceived this to be a benefit. A 1949 *Fortune Magazine* article highlighted the benefits for local businesses (Sheehan 1949). The new relationship between the business community and the political machine was related in the following description of a walk from industrialist Richard Balch's tackle factory to Marino's as

leading across Genesee (Street) and down shabby Catherine Street, and along the way Dick will give his easy greeting to at least a dozen people, many of them in rough working clothes. At the restaurant he will pause to ask what's new of proprietor Frank Marino, who usually works the bar himself at noon, and then sit down to lunch with one of the frequenters—Charlie Donnelly, the postmaster; Joe Davoli, educational director of the Textile Worker's Union; or maybe the Great Dictator, Rufus Elefante himself. (The Truth is Dick dabbles a bit in politics, and democratic party politics, at that.) "What do your uptown friends think of your consorting with the boys at Marino's?" you ask Dick. He gives you a grin. "I think they think it's romantic," he says. (129; commentary in original)

Richard Balch would serve as chairman of the State Democratic Committee from 1952 to 1955. Such efficiency was what the Chamber of Commerce needed in order to fulfill its goal of rebuilding the area economy *sans* textiles after World War II. It is what they sought in the ten thousand dollar executive, and what they ultimately found in the political machine.

A Marriage of Convenience

It is difficult to say exactly when the business establishment of Utica recognized the utility of working with the machine. Certainly, as the nation suffered through the Great Depression, the ability of Elefante and Donnelly to ask for favors in Washington and Albany demonstrated that the machine was not merely a local phenomenon. The WPA employed nearly five thousand people in Utica alone for such jobs as building new sidewalks and demolishing dilapidated buildings. In addition, the federal government backed loans that allowed Utica to buy its then-private water company. In hindsight, the government was controlled by a political machine, but at the time it was simply the way politics was conducted. Simply stated, the machine worked for Utica.

By the end of World War II, both the political machine and the business elite had recognized the utility of "efficient government," as one business leader of the time called it. For business, the machine offered a means of accomplishing needed tasks quickly. By the middle of the 1950s, the Democrats controlled the city council and the mayoralty, and peacefully coexisted with the Republicans who controlled the county. The two parties were reluctant to run strong candidates against the other party in what was deemed "their territory" (Witt 1963).[5] The machine was also heavily involved with organized labor leader Rocco DePerno, a Republican who nonetheless supported the political machine. Ehrenhalt (1992) described the alliance as a "virtually seamless political web":

Dues from Teamster members paid for a considerable amount of the generosity the machine was able to bestow on its friends. All in all, the machine probably took in far more money than it needed to spend in election campaigns. When the Democrats controlled City Hall (virtually the entire 1950s), city employees were required to kick back to the party 4 percent of their salaries each election year. In off years they only had to pay 2 percent. But those kickbacks alone, allies of the machine agree, were sufficient to pay the campaign expenses. Union money and all other sources of machine income were more or less available for Elefante to dole out as he saw fit. (109; author's commentary)

Such connections with organized labor not only helped the machine in terms of finances and votes, but local industry benefited as well.

The 1949 *Fortune Magazine* article favorably documented the success of Utica's budding urban growth machine. Discussing first the scene at the Fort Schuyler Club, a private fraternity of Utica's business elite, the magazine stressed that many of the decisions affecting business in the city were made over lunch at "the Club." Among the membership was Vincent Carrou, the Democratic mayor during the Depression, Richard Balch, State Democratic Chairman from 1952 to 1955, and other powerful figures.[6] The magazine praised the city for what it described as a new

spirit in town, a kind of wave of good feeling that has swept groups that were once dangerously dissident in Utica somewhat closer together—the haves and have-nots, the native and the foreign-born, and especially management and labor. And Utica is a community that particularly needs such harmony and understanding.

The arrangement between the business elite and the political machine would aid business immeasurably.

The ability of representatives of the business elite to talk directly with the power brokers of the local unions and city government helped them accomplish city policy objectives and control labor. For instance, *Fortune* related that Richard Balch's firm, Horrock-Ibbotson, had not suffered a single strike as of 1949. Indeed, the unions were frequently able to convert factories into "union shops" due to such relationships with business leaders in the community (Sheehan 1949).

With the mechanism in place by which Utica could act quickly, the city leadership turned its attention to reviving its declining textile-based economy.

Greener Pastures

As World War II came to a close, the nation as a whole welcomed the returning soldiers with a steep recession and countless labor struggles. Throughout 1945 and 1946, the Utica *Observer-Dispatch* published news of strikes in every corner of the country, occasionally citing the good fortune that kept such events safely far from home. In Utica, the city and its leadership turned their attention to such issues as housing the returning soldiers and transforming its industrial base. Into the 1950s, Utica would have to struggle to hold its population and maintain employment while both people and jobs seemed determined to leave the city behind.

At the close of World War II, the Utica metropolitan area constituted about 2 percent of those who lived in New York State but employed 10 percent of the New Yorkers who worked in textile mills.[7] Even with the restructuring the industry experienced during the 1920s, "it was still the leading industry as late as 1947" (Crisafulli 1960: 179). More than twelve thousand workers were employed in the region's textile industry, representing 23.5 percent of the metropolitan area's total non-agricultural employment.[8] Most of the workers were employed in the city, although a number of major facilities operated in such suburbs as New York Mills, Ilion, Mohawk, Herkimer, and others.

After the war the textile industry was again in a state of change. The advent of air conditioning allowed mills to operate in the South all year long despite the heat produced by the heavy machinery. Over the preceding decades, companies headquartered in other cities had bought several of the mills and they did not have the concern for the community that was expected from those headquartered in Utica. More importantly, however, was the fact that the mills had not been able to compete effectively against southern competition since before World War I. Southern labor was less expensive, and despite the rhetoric of willingness to work with labor unions, the southern states of choice had passed "right to work" laws that severely curtailed the ability to unionize. Many of the Utica mills chose to abandon the city after a series of contentious strikes (Bean 1991; Pula and Dziedzic 1991).[9] But unionization was not solely responsible for the flight of the mills, and it is likely that the other factors would have led to the exodus of the industry anyway. As Crisafulli had pointed out in 1960, "the decline of the local economy actually has been in process since World War I when the textile industry passed its peak of development" (178). Therefore, the dislocations to come were merely a continuation of past trends (see Figure 3.1).

The metropolitan area lost 8,800 textile jobs alone. Hardest hit were the textile mill workers, who plummeted from 9,700 jobs in 1947 to 1,700 jobs in 1957. As a total share of manufacturing jobs, the textile industry dropped from almost 24 percent in 1947 to just over 7 percent ten years later. As a result, Utica had one of the highest unemploy-

Figure 3.1. Textile Industry Employment, 1947–1982

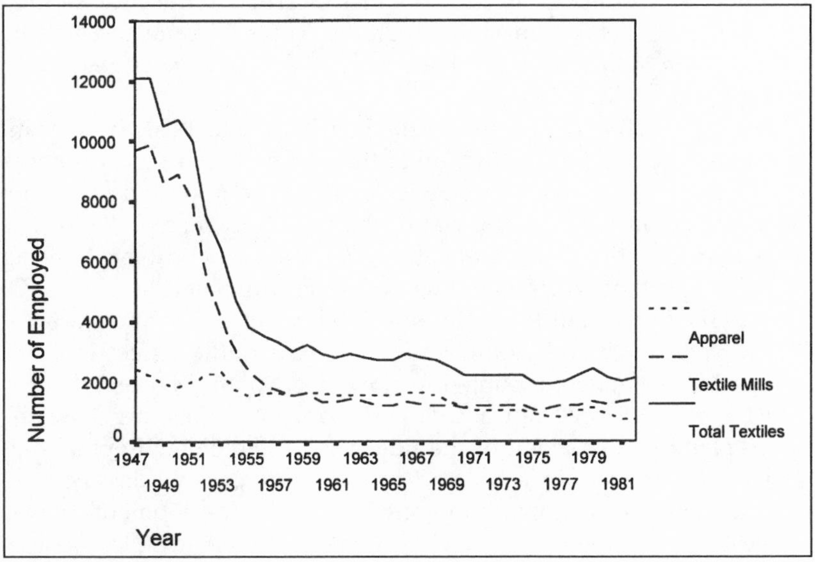

Source: USBLS 1984

ment rates in New York State for years after the layoffs and would not have an unemployment rate below the state average until the 1990s.[10] Local leaders at the time recognized the need to reinvigorate the economy. It was for this task that the alliance between the business elite, labor, and the political machine was crucial.

As in other cities, Utica's political and business elites found a coalition that agreed on the basics of what would be necessary. The Elefante political machine of the 1930s that so ably brought patronage to the city would become a classic urban growth machine after World War II. Urban growth machines are political mechanisms whereby a consensus of opinion among various business, labor, and political elites guides the design and implementation of economic development policies (Logan and Molotch 1987). In Utica, this took the form of common social networks (as discussed earlier) in which those involved came to see the future prospects of the city in similar ways.

City leaders believed that good labor relations were important to attracting new industry, and subsequent research has proven them correct (Markusen 1987; Storper and Walker 1989). The cooperation of labor leaders with the machine aided in this effort, but by far the two major players in the growth machine were the established political machine and the business elite. The political machine benefited from a continued ability to distribute patronage to its membership as ties with the business community expanded its abilities to do so. And as the *Observer-Dispatch* showed in a series of articles critical of the machine in 1958, such key machine figures as Rufus Elefante had become businessmen in their own right and benefited from city contracts (OD, 6 May 1958; 16 May 1958).

The approach adopted during the late 1940s and 1950s was meant to expand the basic infrastructure of the city, both in a physical and a social sense.[11] City planning policies stressed the importance of slum clearance because, as one official of the time commented, "Utica has more than the normal share of substandard, old and obsolete housing facilities, much of which is in blighted or in slum condition" (OD, 30 Dec. 1957; 2A). In addition, the development of a system of arterial highways through and around the city, to ease traffic congestion, and the need for increased parking downtown were both persistent themes. The *Observer-Dispatch* ran a series of stories documenting how the major planning document of the time, the Bartholomew Report, suggested altering the street system to create more parking, less congestion, and new downtown shopping areas.[12] Redevelopment, it was suggested, would improve the city's finances by replacing low assessment buildings with high paying buildings.

The discussion of physical investments in the city began even before the end of World War II. The Sunday edition of the *Observer-Dispatch* ran numerous stories and op-ed pages about the need for a new civic center (usually including some combination of city hall, memorial auditorium, state and/or federal office building, etc.), highways, new commercial areas downtown, and a variety of other pet projects. Most often it was the city's most prominent citizens that were given the opportunity to share their views, but it is notable that such a discourse was given the freedom to take place.

The growth machine also supported efforts to transform the labor force from one of relatively uneducated and unskilled textile workers into one of educated engineers and other such skilled laborers.[13] To this end, the machine lobbied extensively for the establishment of Utica College of Syracuse University, Mohawk Valley Community College (then Mohawk Valley Technical Institute), and the State University of New York Institute of Technology (SUNY Tech). In addition to these three colleges all being built, the machine also discussed the possibility of moving Ithaca College to Utica (OD, 21 Oct. 1946) only four months after the announcement that Syracuse University would build a Utica campus (13 Jun. 1946). The machine also lobbied the state to build the main campus of the State University of New York (SUNY) in Utica, only to witness the decision to build four research universities in other parts of the state instead. Newspaper reports of the time suggest that the Utica machine believed that Utica deserved the SUNY campus due to its being the largest city in New York without a major university.[14]

The result of the transformation of the growth machine was that although Utica lost jobs in textiles and other outmoded industrial sectors, the metropolitan area gained jobs in other areas. As Crisafulli (1960) commented:

It is a picture of a general decline and rebirth which supports our remarks that the textile industry has been only one aspect of industrial change.

In actuality the area recovered well under the circumstances, and numerous historians have branded this period of Utica's history as the "loom to boom" era. In 1946, General Electric announced that it would boost its local workforce to nine hundred, and in the ensuing years the workforce would climb even higher (OD, 6 Jan. 1946). In 1948, Chicago Pneumatic announced that it would build a factory that would employ two thousand, and Remington Rand announced that it would build the world's first commercial computer (Univac) in Utica. Despite the dislocations of the textile industry, Utica's industrial base appeared to be in the process of rebounding. Some local leaders realized that the future of the city was to be in white-collar service jobs such as insurance and finance and in high technology fields such as aerospace and computers, and worked to bring in more of such jobs.

The speed with which the machine worked would be envied today. For instance, when local leaders decided that there was a need for a new commercial airport in August 1945, the necessary voting had been completed in November of that same year (OD, 15 Nov. 1945) and by January nine airlines had been lined up to serve the community (OD, 3 Jan. 1946). By the middle of the 1950s, it appeared that the Mohawk Valley, once a driving force of the textile industry, was to be America's first Silicon Valley.

The fact that the unemployment rate was among the highest in the state appeared to be a temporary phenomenon, as it seemed to reflect the turnover of employers as the economy modernized. Crisafulli (1960) showed that eight of the twelve companies lost during this period produced textile goods, whereas five of the eight companies gained during this same time period produced goods in the electronics and aerospace industries (293–94). Two of those companies, Kelsey-Hayes Company and General Electric, opened multiple facilities in the metropolitan area (four and two, respectively)

The American Dream

Every Sunday throughout the 1950s, the *Observer-Dispatch* proudly showed pictures of new neighborhoods, both inside and outside the city limits. In most cases, the captions would express a sentiment that the city was growing, that the housing stock and thus the lifestyles of metropolitan area residents was improving, and that this was a period of imminent progress. There was some variation, of course. When the newspaper highlighted new neighborhoods in the suburbs, the caption was often a rather condescending comment about how the once-small town was growing. At other times, the photo was not of a new neighborhood but rather an older neighborhood that was being modernized—the trees lining the streets cut down, the pavement widened and more parking for all. The fact that in other sections of the newspaper the story was that neighborhood residents often disapproved of the "modernization" on aesthetic grounds was normally not acknowledged in the Sunday living section. In any case, the fact that the city was undergoing a massive expansion of residential areas while the population only grew by 1,013 during the 1940s did not seem to bother local residents, the newspaper, or city leaders. The expansion of residential areas was perceived as not a threat to the general sense of balance in the city economy and social structure but as a modernization of the city infrastructure and an expansion of the metropolitan area's geographic boundaries. The population of the metropolitan area did grow from 263,163 in 1940 to 330,771 in 1960 at a time when the city's population was stable at about 101,000 people (Shupe et al. 1987). Whereas prior to 1950 the Utica metropolitan area was a collection of cities and villages that were closely spaced but not necessarily contiguously urbanized, the expansion of residential areas and increasing suburbanization promised to make the area one contiguously settled urban mass within a few decades.

This was exactly the case among Utica's neighbors, as the Albany-Troy metropolitan area became the Albany-Schenectady-Troy metropolitan area within a few decades on the basis of increased suburbanization. Indeed, given continued growth in both the Utica and Syracuse metropolitan areas, it was reasonable to assume that in time the two metropolitan areas would also be contiguously urbanized. The urbanized areas included a string of communities of moderate size (five to twenty thousand) and the cities of Syracuse, Utica, and Rome. Indeed, this area between Syracuse and Utica remains among the most urbanized regions of the state despite the fact that economic and demographic change precluded all of the communities from growing together in a solidly urbanized setting. Such expansion of the geographical boundaries was defined as "growth," despite the fact that it was primarily a redistribution of residents and businesses, and thus defined as positive. Simply stated, such a prospect was exciting as it could be considered the difference between a major metropolitan region and a mere collection of discontinuous cities.

Much effort was placed in restructuring the physical environment of the metropolitan area as a whole. In most cases, when city leaders and planners talked of "modernization" during the 1940s and 1950s, they meant restructuring the metropolitan area to make room for the automobile. The public and private discussions led, with the help of the state and federal governments, to Utica being selected as one of only a few cities to begin an urban renewal pilot program. In time, the strategies for urban renewal that were developed in Utica were replicated in cities of similar size (100,000 to 300,000) across the United States. As discussed, the needs for arterial highways throughout the city led to numerous plans for everything from a system of boulevards to a comprehensive expressway system. In 1954, the New York State Thruway opened.

In each case, however, the 1950s welcomed such changes as indicators of progress. And Utica, a city of more than one hundred thousand people, enjoyed the status of being a major city within New York State politics. Prior to World War II, the population of the Utica metropolitan area was 263,163, making it only slightly smaller than metropolitan Syracuse's population of 295,108 (USBC 1947). It would be decades before the impact of progress would be clearly understood.

Chapter 4

On the Road

At the end of World War II, neither Cooperstown nor Hartwick had grown into the great cities envisioned by their creators. Hartwick village never surpassed one thousand residents. Cooperstown peaked at 2,909 people in 1930 and has lost population in every census since 1950. Cooper's (1936) boasts of a city rivaling Buffalo proved pathetically optimistic; Hartwick's dense Lutheran citadel was rather a sparsely settled, predominantly Calvinist town. Still, both villages thrived in ways unforeseen by these men.

A Unique Experience

A unique institution may be understood as a community institution that functions to integrate the community with the larger urban culture and economy. It does not merely integrate the community with its neighbors. It integrates the community with the mainstream urban society as a whole. Further, it is typically uncommon in rural communities (unlike the post office) and thus necessitates that local residents travel for its services. Hospitals, large manufacturing facilities, museums, colleges, etc., are examples of unique institutions. Such institutions are most often associated with urban areas, and their presence in a rural community serves to ensure the continued attention of the urban elite to the community. The relationship between the urban elite and the community with unique institutions is often dialectical: the urban elite is often attracted to the community because of the existence of a unique institution and then becomes responsible for continued maintenance of the institution. Cooperstown is heavily endowed with such institutions.

Cooperstown was (and still is) the seat of government for Otsego County, home to the New York State Historical Association (NYSHA), and the mythological birthplace of baseball so immortalized in the Baseball Hall of Fame. Home to 2,727 residents in 1950, the village had a thriving business district along Main Street and the patronage of several elite families. The most prominent of these was the Clark family, of Singer Sewing Machine fame, who helped to bring the village unique institutions it would likely not have had without them (such as NYSHA, Bassett Hospital, and the Baseball Hall of Fame, among others). In addition to the presence of unique institutions, Cooperstown was by far the largest community in the northern half of Otsego County, and was thus the largest market as well. This combination of unique institutions and the sheer size of the potential market, when compared to other nearby villages, made Cooperstown an attractive place for investment from outside companies. But having the largest potential market in the area is a predominantly local phenomenon; its unique institutions are what gave Cooperstown a reputation for elegance and refinement.

During the nineteenth and early twentieth centuries, Cooperstown had experienced the first of its three periods of tourism: the resort period (see chapter 2). It was at the end of this period that the infrastructure was put in place for the next major period: the supplemental period. The supplemental period was built upon the reputation of the resort period but relied upon the new infrastructure of museums. It was this infrastructure and the changing reputation of the supplemental period that would later lead Cooperstown to its third period of tourism: the dominant tourism period of the late 1980s and 1990s.

Even though the resort period faded out of existence during the Great Depression, the supplemental period had to wait for the end of World War II. Supplemental tourism differs from resort tourism in that visitors stay for shorter periods of time and are most likely of working and middle socioeconomic status. In both periods, tourism functioned to supplement the local economy—the production and distribution of goods and services remained the dominant sector of the economy. In Cooperstown, this was primarily manifest in agriculture and retail sales.

It was during the 1950s that tourism became a major industry in Cooperstown, increasing substantially during the next two decades. Attendance at the Baseball Hall of Fame surged from 22,066 to an average of nearly 127,000 per year during the 1950s. Growth was steady through the 1960s until leveling off during the mid-1970s. The museums of the New York State Historical Association also experienced growth. Annual attendance at Fenimore House doubled during the 1950s, and at the Farmer's Museum it increased by 120 percent.

Given such dramatic growth in the tourism industry, it might have been expected that the village would be dramatically restructured. It was not.

Rather than reinventing itself during this time, Cooperstown instead developed two distinct cultural identities. Historic Cooperstown was the center for tourism. It revolved around the refined tastes of the village elite and sought to attract a predominantly middle- and upper-middle-class clientele. A small art scene developed, and its practitioners extolled rural virtues through a variety of mediums. The museums all conformed to historical themes, and new motels were built on Otsego Lake to house the visitors. The movement of visitors from one attraction to the next also meant that tourism was more intrusive than the resorts had been. Throughout this period, however, the community-oriented economy continued to thrive.

Local Cooperstown was related but different. Community-oriented businesses supplied the village and its hinterland with a variety of goods and services. Most of the products one would want to buy were available in town, and most residents traveled elsewhere only sporadically. Although these two identities supported one another, they remained separate because of the strength of the community-oriented economy. Indeed, during the 1950s the community-oriented economy of Cooperstown was so strong that it tended to attract shoppers from the smaller communities that surrounded the village, including Hartwick.

The More Mundane

In contrast to Cooperstown, the village of Hartwick was more typical of the rural small towns of central New York.[1] As agriculture had been the dominant form of production in the region, the overall pattern in the area was one of small commercial villages every seven to ten miles that served the respective village populations and the hinterland until approximately the halfway mark to the next nearest village. Such distinct spheres of influence also meant that the relatively few local residents tended to shop in the same businesses, that children attended relatively small school districts centered in the villages, and that the more devout attended services in the village churches. In short, they were the centers of social interaction that was patterned by numerous structured (schools, churches) and unstructured (shops) institutions. Hartwick was one of many communities that fit this pattern.

In 1950, Hartwick was the commercial hub of the northern Otego Creek Valley and had a sphere of influence that extended approximately four to five miles in any direction. In each direction, there were similar villages (Laurens, Milford, Schuyler Lake, and Morris), but only Cooperstown was substantially larger than Hartwick and its neighbors. Along Main Street, the central business district sported twenty-two commercial storefronts and additional commercial structures spread out throughout the remainder of the village.[2] Some specialty goods, such as new automobiles, were not available for purchase in the village although others, such as appliances, hardware, and groceries, were available. As in other communities, a local print shop published a small weekly newspaper. Most transactions of everyday life could be conducted in the village, and along with such everyday transactions came the opportunity to interact with neighbors, friends, and business owners. The entire economy presupposed that local residents would work, shop, and pray in the village—a fair assumption when travel to other villages was uncomfortable, costly, or time-consuming. It became a more tenuous assumption when modern transportation technology made other villages more easily accessible.

The automobile had already begun to make an impact on the village prior to 1950. There were seven different establishments in and around Hartwick that sold gasoline, for instance. Some residents had already begun to drive to Cooperstown and Oneonta for items bought less regularly, such as clothing and furniture. In the 1950 Hartwick High School Yearbook, *The Hub,* twenty-two Hartwick area businesses and organizations bought advertisements, as did seventeen in Oneonta and twenty-five in Cooperstown. Most of the out of town advertisements were for businesses with no equivalent in Hartwick: automobiles, farm implements, and clothing. Other advertisements were for restaurants and other destinations for road trips out of town. The car made travel easy, but there was still a home to which to return.

See the U.S.A.

It was during the 1950s that the automobile became the dominant form of transportation.[3] As early as the 1920s, federal programs had improved and paved local highways. The 1930s in particular had witnessed the improvement (straightening, paving, etc.) of highways throughout the country under the auspices of the Works Progress Administration; Otsego County received its share of resources. Hartwick in particular benefited from the expansion of government services during the New Deal: the village received new sidewalks, paved highways extended to all corners of the county and state, and Hartwick was chosen as the home of the Otsego Rural Electrification Cooperative (REA). During the 1950s there was a great expansion of such efforts, the most obvious program being the Interstate Highway System. Due to federal funding for such initiatives, many in Otsego

County were able to, among other things, buy cars and take advantage of the newly paved highways.

Soon after World War II, the state also addressed the need for improved highways by building the New York State Thruway. The Thruway was to be a toll-supported highway specifically built for intercity travel, and in time the fact that the majority of the communities along its route did not have exits would impact much of upstate New York. The Thruway bypassed Otsego County entirely, but arrived in Utica in 1954. When the original length from the New York City suburb of Yonkers to Buffalo was complete in 1956, only forty-four exits served the 423 miles in between. Utica, the largest city of the sixth largest metropolitan area in the state only had one exit; most rural communities had only the hulking lanes pass disrespectfully through their environs without an exit. Distances of twenty miles without an exit were common, and the eastern suburbs of Utica, which stretch for a distance of nearly fifteen miles down the Mohawk Valley, still have only one exit (in Herkimer).[4] The Thruway would be an intercity road, and this would allow travelers the luxury of moving through Utica and noticing little more than the wetlands through which the highway passes. As one trucker from New England commented, "To tell you the truth, you don't really notice Utica when you drive through. It might as well be Weedsport" (a small community through which the thruway passes).[5]

Utica also lost its most valued historic friend. With the 1959 opening of the Saint Lawrence Seaway in Canada, traffic on the Erie Canal dropped dramatically. (The Erie Canal had been improved as part of the Barge Canal in 1903.) Prior to its opening, state and federal officials claimed that the Seaway would have little impact on the fortunes of the Erie Canal and the cities along its banks. But it did. Although traffic on the Erie Canal had peaked in the mid-1950s, the canal stood nearly idle twenty-five years later. Larkin (1998) summed it up nicely:

The sad situation becomes much more vivid when commodities are viewed from a "last year shipped" perspective: The Barge Canal last carried flour in 1950, brick in 1954, iron ore in 1955, and oats in 1959; coal has not been seen on the canal since 1962, lumber since 1963, wheat since 1968, paper since 1972, and sugar since 1976. During the two years prior to 1991, no freight at all was handled at 49 of the canal's 66 terminals, and only 5 of its 53 warehouses were used for their intended purpose. In June 1995, when this author spent three delightful days on the canal steaming from Syracuse to Buffalo, the only other commercial traffic seen were two or three dinner boats. (87).

By the 1990s the canal had become almost the exclusive domain of pleasure boaters, and tourism officials predicted a renaissance. In water freight transportation, however, the Saint Lawrence Seaway has resulted in Utica having a status similar to that of Cooperstown and Hartwick in regard to highway transportation.

As much as the Thruway served to make Utica a way station off the main line of traffic, it solidified the status of Cooperstown and Hartwick as lying off the beaten track. At its closest point, the Thruway passes twenty-five miles north of the two villages, separated from them by narrow, two-lane, curvy, and hilly roads. Although it was easier for people to get to the area, only those who specifically wanted to make the trip would visit. Gone were the days of travelers discovering the area while on their way somewhere else.

The new technologies of the automobile and refrigeration also made it possible to transport milk and other agricultural products over great distances in a relatively short period of time. As dairy cooperatives and other interests recognized this benefit of new technology, it would affect the viability of agriculture itself over the next fifty years.

From Farm to ?

The restructuring of production that took place in Utica during the early 1950s had a parallel in Cooperstown and Hartwick, but without the drama of the events in Utica. Whereas in Utica factory closings typically left hundreds or thousands unemployed, the restructuring of production was much slower in Cooperstown and Hartwick. When factory closings in Utica during the 1920s indicated the economic fortunes on the horizon, the sheer drama of the events and the timing of the Great Depression and World War II gave the city time to plan a strategy. As the restructuring of agriculture began in Otsego County after World War II, the relatively slow time frame made it difficult to notice. In addition, the economic units being affected were individual families and not entire corporations. Simply stated, it was easier to perceive a crisis when a company of thousands restructured; the slow demise of agriculture appeared to many to simply be "family troubles—you'd never think it was any bigger than that."

In 1945, there were 3,914 farms in Otsego County.[6] Farms accounted for 79.3 percent of the land in the county; with 78,187 head of cattle, the 1940 human population was outnumbered by more than thirty-two thousand. One local resident shared:

You'd go up and down all these roads, and all'd you see was farms. Mostly dairy; but they'd grow corn as feed and sell some to the locals for real cheap.

Another resident said:

You see all these empty fields. Well, the land don't grow that way—should be trees. All these fields used to be farms; corn, cows, shit like that. An' now they're all out of business . . . Well, most of 'em anyway.

Throughout the 1950s and 1960s, the number of farms in the county fell, from 3,914 in 1945 to 1,427 in 1969—a loss of 2,487 in twenty-four years, or an average of more than one hundred per year. Some of this drop was due to a concentration of operations onto larger farms owned by fewer operators. During the same period, the average farm in the county grew from 131 acres to 228 acres. Mostly, though, farmers ceased to operate farms. While 79.3 percent of the land was devoted to farming in 1945, by 1969 only 50.2 percent of the land was so utilized. Agriculture has been declining ever since. The 1987 Census of Agriculture showed that, for the first time on record, people outnumbered cattle, due by and large to the decline in dairy farms. In 1997, there were 865 farms left (USBC 1997a). In 1950, at least three of the retail businesses in Hartwick and several more in Cooperstown were aimed exclusively at farmers.

With the ability to transport milk greater distances with large tanker trucks, the milk processing industry itself was transformed. Hartwick had a small milk-processing center (creamery) until 1962, when increased competition made it apparent that such a small facility was no longer efficient. The plant closed, and five people lost their jobs. A tragedy for those involved, such a small event could not garner the attention that the closing of a textile mill could. In time, Otsego County lost most of its dairy processing industry as it became centralized in the cities of Binghamton and Oneida, both more than seventy miles away. Such trends continued into the 1990s, as some local farmers began sending their milk as far away as Massachusetts and Vermont for processing. As one merchant explained:

(I know this farmer) who sends his milk to Vermont. Anyway, he's right up the road here. And the store gets the milk that he makes, but it has to go all the way to Vermont and then back before we drink any of it.

Larger trucks and a shift of dairy processing out of the local area nibbled away at the employment base throughout the decades—one trucker here, a farm hand there. Rarely would more than five jobs be lost at once as a consequence of the same economic event; the impact of the decline would not be apparent until the late 1970s when Hartwick's economy, rather belatedly, collapsed. And when it did, the deep roots of the crisis were easily overlooked.

Go, Huskies, . . . Gone!

The new advantages in transportation also allowed the transportation of students over greater distances. With the increased importance of the high school diploma during the 1950s and the postwar baby boomers starting school, school districts throughout New York State found more students in the classroom. In addition, state requirements were being increased, putting fiscal pressure on local school districts. By the middle of the 1950s, the New York State Board of Regents was actively encouraging the consolidation of school districts in both urban and rural areas. As in other forms of upscaling, school consolidation ultimately would benefit larger communities over small.

In September 1956, the senior class of Hartwick High School started the school year unaware that they would be the institution's last graduates. Members of Hartwick's school board contemplated a consolidation with Cooperstown throughout the winter and spring of 1957. The consolidation would be beneficial for both school districts. Cooperstown desired to build a new High School—consolidation would spread the costs of such a building program around a larger tax base. Hartwick could transfer its elementary students to the former high school, which was newer than the former elementary school. On April 17, 1957, the Cooperstown *Freeman's Journal* reported that the two school boards agreed to send Hartwick High School students to Cooperstown High School and begin discussions of consolidation.[7] In less than four months, a decision that would dramatically alter both communities had been discussed and decided.

The loss of the school would have a greater impact, however. As in other communities, the local school was an institution that residents could call their own. It provided a centralized point on which to focus community pride, and this was immediately apparent in regard to varsity sports. Hartwick High School had had a streak of good fortune in a number of sports since the end of World War II, and "few schools captured the public fancy as (had) Hartwick and her teams" (Parce 1957). In a column in the Oneonta *Daily Star* describing a Hartwick man who could "name the heroes, goats, records, pitches, and situations over the past few years with the quickness of an IBM machine," the rhetorical question was raised as to what the man would do in the absence of Hartwick High School (Parce 1957):[8]

Next Year? Jim hasn't looked that far ahead, but we'll put a bob on the line that he'll know the facts and figures on the Cooperstown Redskins forwards and backwards. . . . Thus, educational progress has ended a sports era.

An end of an era indeed.

The decision had been made purely on economic terms in order to provide more services from a stagnant tax base—the grim side effect of population stability. A broadened curriculum and improved facilities were promised and by and large received. On July 1, 1958, the

Cooperstown Central School District, containing the village and portions of the towns of Otsego, Hartwick, and Middlefield was formed. New York State recommended further consolidation with the Milford Central School District, eight miles south of Cooperstown, but this did not ultimately happen. Throughout the 1960s school consolidation plans were continuously discussed, the most ambitious being a 1964 plan to merge Cooperstown with school districts in Cherry Valley, Edmeston, Milford, Richfield Springs, Springfield, Van Hornesville, and Westville. Had it occurred, the new school district would have stretched forty miles from end to end.

Similarities

As in Utica, the restructuring of production began to play a major role in the health of the economies of both Cooperstown and Hartwick. The time between 1945 and 1957 was not a revolutionary period, but rather a period when the dynamics of history were altered in such a way as to make the future possible. Utica lost the remnants of its textile industry, but remained predominantly a manufacturing city. Agriculture started to decline throughout the region, but not enough to be called a crisis. The structure of tourism changed in Cooperstown, but continued to be relatively unobtrusive in the everyday lives of local residents. Hartwick residents began to drive elsewhere, but the village appeared to thrive anyway; even the merging of its schools ensured that Hartwick would still have an elementary school. Change had begun, but it had done so slowly.

Chapter 5

Sin City

The urban growth machine of the 1950s in Utica was a coalition between the political machine and the business elite. By 1957, Utica appeared to be on the way to a full recovery from the economic dislocations of the previous ten years. The metropolitan area was home to the first commercial computer in the world, new colleges, and several large manufacturing facilities to take the place of the mills fleeing to the south. The city administration practiced a progressive urban policy that stressed the need for improved education, infrastructure, and quality of life (see Clavel and Kleniewski 1990). But underlying the lubricating mechanism of the emerging urban growth machine was a parallel organization silently coexisting with the city's more noble endeavors. As a result, a series of events toward the end of the year jeopardized the power of the political machine, and the coalition between business and the machine fell apart within two years. The impact would be devastating.

Wide-Open Town

Alcohol has been called America's drug of choice, and so it is not that the roots of Utica's so-called "sin city" scandals are rooted ultimately in Prohibition. However, with the prohibition of alcohol mandated by the Eighteenth Amengment in 1919 an old market for the drug was energized with a dynamism never before seen in the United States (Inciardi 1992; Levine and Reinarman 1992). As the legitimate business enterprises dealing in alcoholic beverages were forced to shift their focus to drinks such as root beer and sarsaparilla, those willing to risk

55

prison to supply an overeager market would enjoy profits only dreamed of by the former suppliers. Like many other cities, Utica spawned its own class of bootleggers.

The streets of Utica were the perfect breeding ground for bootlegging gangs. The predominantly Italian and Irish neighborhoods of east Utica were willing markets filled with Catholic immigrants by and large uncommitted to the rural protestant prohibition movement (Kobler 1973). Local residents had been accustomed to an occasional drink after work in neighborhood bars or a glass of wine with dinner. Thus, Prohibition was not merely a disagreeable new federal policy but an assault on the neighborhood social structure as well. In fact, several scholars have suggested such an assault on the immigrant social structure to be a strong motivation on the part of the Prohibition movement (Gusfield 1963; Kobler 1973; Musto 1999). Bootleggers, within this context, merely supplied the community with a desired commodity.

The rise of bootlegging across the country was a response to this fact. There were two main developments to come about as a result of bootlegging, the first in regard to the industry's status as illicit, the second concerning the networks that were formed in the interest of bootlegging (Levine and Reinarman 1992).

Business is by nature a risky endeavor, and many of the legal protections in place in a modern society are designed to remove much of that risk. A business owner risks having goods stolen or customers refuse payment after services have been performed. Without the recourse to the legal protections available to legitimate businesses, bootleggers by necessity found different mechanisms to perform the same functions as law. When a shipment of goods was stolen, the police were of course unable to help because the result would have been that both the perpetrators and the victims of the theft would have faced prosecution. Similarly, a lawsuit was not an option when a customer refused to pay for services rendered. Without such legal recourses, those interests who are willing to perform acts of violence to both punish the offender and deter any future would-be thief are better able to conduct business. The result is that the more violent organizations are able to outcompete those less inclined to violence, and so a spiral of increasing violence ensues. It is thus not surprising that by the end of the 1920s bootlegging gangs tended to be extremely violent. Indeed, as mechanisms of social control they have today become legendary, and so have such practitioners as Lucky Luciano and "Scarface" Al Capone. (Interestingly, their gun of choice was the Thompson Sub-Machine Gun, made by Savage Arms in Utica). In Utica, by 1930 there had been several murders that would never be solved and rackets operating in gambling, loan sharking, and protection as well. Like similar operations today, they were run in a manner that resembled legitimate corporations (Padilla 1992).

The second major development during Prohibition was the forging of alliances between criminal organizations in major cities throughout North America. Whereas the manufacture, sale, and transport of alcohol was illegal in the United States, it was not in Canada. The result was that border communities, such as Buffalo and Detroit, could readily secure quality alcoholic beverages from commercial producers in Canada and then trade them with organizations in other American cities. What had developed by 1930 was a syndicate of bootleggers throughout the United States, each operating on their own in their respective cities but linked to other organizations through the network.[1] In Utica, three such figures—Joe Falcone, Salvatore Falcone, and Rosario Mancuso—would become the center of Utica's image problems in the late 1950s (OD, 6 Feb. 1958).

The networks established during the bootlegging period made Utica one of a number of cities with a local syndicate. Because it was a major center of the textile industry, it is not surprising that Utica area mobsters had ties with their counterparts in New York City who operated in the garment industry (Turkus and Feder 1992 [1951]). However, most scholars of organized crime have stressed the importance of major cities, which, as in other economic ventures, dominate the smaller communities in their shadows. Indeed, as far as the national organization of the Mafia is concerned, no major scholar has ever claimed Utica to be anything more than one of many cities with a local organization. Utica was a minor link in the syndicate, strong locally but weak within the international context of the Mafia. There is simply no evidence to the contrary.[2]

In any case, it is true that by the 1930s Utica had developed a strong local branch of the Mafia with connections with organized crime leaders in New York and around the world. Though Prohibition officially ended in 1933, the networks that had been created during the bootlegging years would remain, and criminal activities would continue.[3] And the events of the late 1950s would illuminate the details of this organization for the world to see.

A Day in the Neighborhood

Also, of course, centered in east Utica and controlled primarily by Italian and Irish immigrants and their children was the machine of Rufus Elefante and Charles Donnelley. By the late 1950s, the aging Donnelley had by and large left day-to-day operations to Elefante, who wielded an enormous amount of power in the city. Allied with many in the business community who appreciated the efficiency of the machine, but still beholden to the interests of the immigrants who gave the machine its power, the political bosses acted in many ways as power brokers in a modern urban growth machine while they still retained the bossism of a classical political machine. Although Charles Donnelley was able to deliver many of the votes of the primarily Irish and Polish west Utica wards, the machine's center of power was in Elefante's territory in east Utica.

Born in 1903, Rufus Elefante came of age during Prohibition just as the Falcones were solidifying their hold on the liquor business in the city. Living in the same neighborhoods as the bootleggers, it seems unlikely that young Elefante would not have had some familiarity with some of the local alcohol suppliers. As he was beginning his career with the local Democrats, the twenties were roaring and, in Utica as in many other cities, much of the population learned to look the other way when it came to bootlegging. Such a condition reflects a cultural trait shared by many (but certainly not all) Americans during this time—look the other way and don't get directly involved. The Utica *Daily Press* commented in 1959:

Riding the crest of the post-war boom, people were preoccupied with their own affairs—raising families, building homes, improving their economic status. Commercial sin was something for conventioneers, salesmen, and outside college students to endulge in. Gambling was considered a petty vice. As for big dice games—let the riff-raff and visiting hoodlums roll crooked dice and shoot each other, if they chose!

For many, it was easier to simply not pay attention to what appeared to be petty offenses. Indeed, assuming that Elefante himself would have had the occasion to interact with people involved in some way with the trafficking of alcoholic beverages, it would have been disrespectful at the very least to discuss the illegal activities.[4] William Lohden, an *Observer-Dispatch* reporter who wrote about the machine was quoted in 1989 as saying, "Elefante certainly wasn't Mafia, but he closed his eyes. He did his thing, and they did theirs" (see Ehrenhalt 1989, 35).[5]

What machine members were involved with was what George Washington Plunkitt (1995 [1905]) called "honest graft." The former leader of New York City's Tammany Hall political machine claimed that there was a distinction between honest graft, or the utilization of city resources for the enhancement of one's private wealth through legal means, and blatant corruption, which involves the enhancement of one's personal wealth through criminal means. Plunkitt pointed out that criminal behavior was overly risky when compared to the opportunities that were available legally through corrupt means. Leaders of Utica's machine were certainly involved with honest graft, although the legality of such operations was not as clear-cut in the 1950s as during the nineteenth century.

For instance, Elefante was a partner in the firm of Elefante & Mazza Inc., which shared a Broad Street address with Nick Laino & Sons and Laino-Fisk Tires. Deputy Police Chief James Laino was a relative of the operator of Nick Laino & Sons and a part owner of Laino-Fisk tires. Both Elefante & Mazza and Nick Laino & Sons were implicated by the Utica newspapers as being two of only four companies to receive contracts worth more than fifteen thousand dollars for snow removal after a blizzard; together with the other two east Utica firms, the snow removal cost the city thirty-seven thousand dollars without the state-mandated competitive bidding (OD, 6 May 1958; 16 May 1958). Laino-Fisk Tires and Rock's Tires were implicated by the papers in selling tires to the city without competitive bidding, costing the city about one-third more than the county paid through the same dealers (OD; 30 Jan. 1959). A state audit of city buying practices concluded that city officials had "circumvented and defeated" the law requiring competitive bidding (OD, 24 Sept. 1958). For instance, tires were bought in quantities that totaled less than five hundred dollars in order to be in technical compliance of the law, and therefore no laws were broken even though nearly fifty-two thousand dollars' worth of equipment had been bought from Laino-Fisk alone (OD, 24 Sept. 1958). This was despite the fact that the city also paid these same firms to repair used tires (OD, 20 May 1958). The newspapers uncovered numerous such practices involving, for example, coal (OD, 9 Sept. 1958), police cars (OD, 12 May 1958), and electrical supplies (OD, 24 Sept. 1958). In the latter case, the treasurer of the company that sold the city more than $4,500 worth of supplies was also on the Zoning Board of Appeals and was the secretary of the city's Electrical Licensing Board. Such conflicts of interest were seemingly common at the time, although often not technically illegal.

While the political bosses indulged in honest graft, they also failed to properly enforce the law. Prostitution and gambling had become quite common toward the end of World War II, and the Utica newspapers exerted pressure on the city administration to crack down by editorializing against "lax law enforcement." Similar outbreaks of editorial venom against poor law enforcement occurred in 1948 and 1954 as the police department ostensibly did very little to correct the vice problem in the city.

Similar charges were directed at the practices of the machine itself. In 1948, a scandal involving the city civil service commission ensued when a number of underqualified men were appointed to the police and fire departments. It resulted in the state taking the administration of civil service exams away from the city. In 1949, a voting scandal resulted in Elefante himself being implicated in bribery, although it led to no more than verbal jousting between the city administration and the newspapers. When Mayor John McKennon appointed machine-friendly officials after his election in 1955, the Utica newspapers ran eighty editorials "dealing with lax law enforcement, suspected collusion among political leaders and intimations of a conspiracy to defraud the taxpayers" (DP, 5 May 1959).

Such reporting by the Utica newspapers led to a number of embarrassments for the machine, such as a series of arrests in 1949 and continued (and warranted) charges of corruption by Republicans. Simply stated, Utica's budding urban growth machine was still beholden to the rules of bossism. Rather than the efficient development generator that similar machines in other cities eventually became (Logan and Molotch 1987), the Utica machine of the 1950s was still a cross between its former incarnation as a classical political machine based on its appeal and patronage for immigrants and a modern urban growth machine responsive to the business community, which it was striving to become. It is possible that had the machine shed its reliance on bossism earlier the press would not have exposed its excesses to the extent that it did.

Call in the Posse

With a local organized crime syndicate and a corrupt political machine that seemingly looked the other way, the stage was set for the embarrassment of an expose. The newspapers had been collecting evidence for years and regularly editorialized against machine politicians. But the national culture was engulfed in hysteria of its own, and Utica was positioned for national exposure.

The roots of what became known as the Sin City Scandals are found not only in local events prior to 1957, but also in a widespread moral panic concerning the influence of the Mafia and other organizations (e.g., communists) in American institutions (Anechiarico and Jacobs 1996; see Goode and Ben-Yehuda 1994). Concern over a national organized crime network began to grow after an eerie discovery in New York City:

Early in 1940, while digging into the source of a local felony, the District Attorney's office in Brooklyn ran head on into an unbelievable industry. This organization was doing business in assassination and general crime across the entire nation, along the same corporate lines as a chain of grocery stores. (Turkus and Feder 1992, 1)

What had been discovered was an organization called Murder, Incorporated, a branch of the Mafia that specialized in supplying trained murderers for hire. Chief among them was Albert Anastasia, considered to be the "lord high executioner" of the mob (*Newsweek*, 24 Feb. 1958). After World War II, concern over communism, immigrants, and organized crime coalesced into a series of trials, investigations, and media campaigns during the 1950s. For example, Jimmy Hoffa, president of the Teamster's union, stood trial for corruption and ties to organized crime. A general concern about the influence of organized crime led to a series of investigations at the federal level, including one led by Robert F. Kennedy, and in numerous states. In New York, two different committees, one controlled by Republicans (Legislative Watchdog Committee) and the other controlled by the Democratic administration (Reuter Investigation), competed for media attention as well as the facts. At times, witnesses would testify before the Watchdog Committee only to be questioned by Reuter a few days later.

Given the cultural atmosphere of concern over the influence of the Mafia, only a single precipitating event was necessary for the scandals that took place in Utica during the late 1950s to occur. The Sin City Scandals would be a turning point in the history of Utica.

Murder, Incorporated

The events that engulfed Utica in 1958 and 1959 were the results of activities not just in Utica but as far away as Havana, Cuba.[6] Albert Anastasia, the reputed chief assassin of Murder, Incorporated, had for several years been trying to expand his operations in the profitable (illegal) gambling rackets when he traveled to the wedding of his nephew in Utica. Apparently, while in the city he made contact with members of the Utica organization who ran high stakes gambling operations. It was reputed that games would travel from place to place throughout east Utica, and that it was not uncommon for hundreds of thousands of dollars to change hands at such games. Games operated by the syndicate were considered protected; if somebody tried to interfere with a game in some way, they would be dealt with harshly. According to the New York *Journal-American*, a "small time hoodlum" named Frank Caputo who robbed one such game in 1954 was later found dead in the trunk of a car in suburban Frankfort—the murder was never solved. Anastasia, who had connections with the Cuban Lottery (also illegal), had been able to get a ten percent share of the Utica operation and put his nephew in charge earlier in the decade.

By 1956, Anastasia wanted a stake in the gambling operations in Cuba, a country that would soon be fighting a civil war against the rebels led by Fidel Castro. But Anastasia was regarded as unacceptable by Meyer Lansky, a powerful operative considered to be the gambling front man for Cuban President Fulgencio Batista. Rejected by Lansky, Anastasia then contacted the powerful Frank Costello and offered him a 25 percent stake in the Cuban gambling operations should Anastasia get control. With the help of Lucky Luciano, who had been deported and was living in Italy, a meeting was set up between Anastasia and the developers of the Havana Hilton, then under construction. Lansky responded by bringing in the Gambino crime family as his partners in Havana, and Costello promptly backed out of the deal.

With Frank Costello no longer a partner, Anastasia turned to the Falcone brothers for help, offering them the same terms he had offered Costello. Sensing that the growing feud between Anastasia and other mobsters was becoming critical, the Falcones stalled Anastasia who, impatient, declared himself the owner of a 25 percent stake in Utica gambling. This act was considered extremely disrespectful to the Utica Mafia and was contrary to the principles of home rule that reigned in the syndicate, and the Uticans were added to the lengthy list of Mafia figures mistreated by Anastasia. An emissary was sent to try to smooth things over, who notified Anastasia that there would be a meeting of Mafia leaders in the rural town of Appalachin, New York, to resolve the Cuba issue. However, he was informed, he should stay out of Utica. In the meantime, on a yacht off the coast of New Jersey, major Mafia figures decided to have Anastasia killed.

At one of those times when fate intervenes, the wife of Anastasia's nephew died. Anastasia decided to travel to Utica in order to attend the funeral, and sent a message to the Utica syndicate that they should mind their own business. The syndicate leaders decided that Anastasia would die at the cemetery after the funeral, but he arrived at the burial surrounded by six armed gunmen. The assassins decided to avoid a bloody gunfight by letting Anastasia leave the cemetery. They then hunted him for six weeks until, on October 24, Albert Anastasia was shot to death while sitting in a barber chair at the Hotel Park Sheraton in New York City.

Visible Government

In October 1957, John McKennon was running a reelection campaign based on his "record of accomplishment" as mayor. Chosen and supported by the Elefante machine, McKennon was young and on his way up in politics. His Republican challenger, William Halpin, criticized McKennon for poor law enforcement after the American Social

Hygiene Association found Utica to have "semi-flagrant" prostitution in February. As Paul Kinsie, who testified about the report a year later, stated, "there was no solicitation from windows or doorways, but any person who sought admission was promptly admitted to brothels" (OD, 6 Feb. 1958). Similarly, Halpin continually brought up charges of corruption in city supply contracts and the bossism of Rufus Elefante. The *Observer-Dispatch* was clearly dismayed as to whom to endorse, writing just before the election,

Messrs. Halpin and McKennon are two young men well liked and we won't be alarmed by the election of either. But Mayor McKennon has the advantage of a term in office and the two years have undeniably seen construction and new life in the community. (OD, 31 Oct. 1957)

The weak endorsement of McKennon was reversed the day after the election as they editorialized,

This newspaper could not support the Mayor for re-election since it believes he has yet to achieve needed renovation of the police bureau . . . (OD, 6 Nov. 1957).

Nevertheless, McKennon was popular in Democratic Party circles, and the state committee was considering him for the senate or even Lieutenant Governor (OD, 12 Dec. 1957).

The November 6 newspaper contained more than just a public questioning of McKennon's effectiveness as mayor. In one column to the side of page one, a story entitled "How Party Came to an End at Mansion," described the scene as state troopers entered a party hosted by Joseph Barbara near Binghamton and "some of the expensively-dressed guests took off into the woods, others jumped into their cars, others called taxis, some even called private homes and asked the occupants to call cabs for them" (OD, 6 Nov. 1957). It was the same meeting described to Anastasia by the envoy of the Utica mobsters, now being held to divvy up the empire vacated by the death of the assassin. Appalachin had occurred.

Among the guest list of fifty-eight reputed mobsters were the Uticans Joe Falcone, Salvatore Falcone, and Rosario Mancuso. The meeting sparked even more intense interest in the influence of the Mafia nationwide and a renewed vigor in the existing investigations. On November 20, New York Governor Averill Harriman ordered the State Investigations Commissioner to investigate the meeting and its participants, and the Legislative Watchdog Committee would follow suit. At the Watchdog Committee hearings in December, most of those called refused to testify—one racketeer in the garment industry invoked his Fifth Amendment rights not to incriminate himself 161 times; Joe

Falcone would take the Fifth a mere eighty-four times. By the end of December, the investigation spread throughout New York State, from Vito Genovese and Carlo Gambino in New York City to Sam Lagatutta and John Montana in Buffalo.[7]

The scandal threatened important people. John Montana, for instance, invoked his connections with Vice-President Richard Nixon and Governor Averill Harriman as well as lesser political figures from both parties. As hysteria over the possible influence of the Mafia in government spread, Utica's political machine, with its penchant for looking the other way in regard to vice, stood in line for exposure. Being smaller than the other major cities in the state, Utica provided fewer votes for the Democrats but its machine had grown accustomed to asking for expensive forms of patronage. For Elefante, Utica's fate as center of the scandal was sealed not because of corruption but because of a personal dispute between himself and Harriman related to state patronage:

Elefante told Harriman that he'd promised Uticans that Harriman would help the city get a much-needed arterial highway "and we promised it in your name." The governor was livid. "Him and I got into a hell of an argument," [Elefante said]. I [Elefante] said, "I'll go back and tell the people you don't want to do it." He [Harriman] said, "Don't do that." Elefante said he got the money for the first phase of the North-South Arterial—and more: "He came after me." That, said Elefante, was a major reason Harriman started the investigation into graft and corruption in Utica. Harriman was "mad at me." That 1958–1962 investigation was "repaying me for arguments we had on the arterial highway." (OD, 28 Sept. 1986)

Although it is unlikely that the Utica sin city scandals were due to a mere personal dispute between a political boss and the troubled governor, the insistence on expensive patronage for a city that brought relatively few votes on election day certainly did not help matters. Of all the cities implicated in the Appalachin affair, however, Utica was the least powerful and thus the most expendable to state leaders. That such a calculus was not used by state officials in choosing the site of the main focus of the investigations is difficult to fathom. By December 1957, the *Observer-Dispatch* reported on rumors that Utica city officials were under investigation by Reuter, the administration's investigator.

As word of the scandal spread throughout the state and the nation, major news outlets sold papers by pandering to people's worst fears. When Rosario Mancuso, slated to testify in front of the Watchdog Committee a second time, failed to appear on January 14, 1958, the New York *Journal-American* speculated that he had fled the country or been murdered. The next day, the diabetic Mancuso had his attorney call the *Observer-Dispatch* to say:

Call up that New York Journal-American and tell them I'm not dead. . . . What do they use for reporters, a bunch of schoolgirls? I'm sick and under a doctor's care. When I'm okay, I'll come as I did before. (OD, 15 Jan. 1958)

Four days later, all of Utica would question the intentions of the *Journal-American.*

Invisible Government

The series began on a Sunday, and was one of many that appeared in the New York *Journal-American* during this time period. The language, as in tabloid papers today, was meant to evoke emotion: fear, distrust, hate, whatever. And so that series began:

An Invisible Government of the underworld today controls politically-protected rackets in parts of New York State and Pennsylvania with tentacles going in New Jersey and as far south as Cuba. (JA, 19 Jan. 1958).

Over the next two days, the series spotlighted Utica as the major center of Mafia activities in the northeast:

Murder is no stranger to Utica, a city controlled by the invisible government. Since the 1930s there have been 13 unsolved gangland type killings in this city of 100,000 people. (JA, 20 Jan. 1958)

The paper then described the murder of Frank Caputo, alleging that two police officers who tried to investigate the case were punished for their efforts and that the reporter was told by a separate officer, "The word is out that you're up here digging into mafia activities. For your own safety you'd better get out of town as soon as possible" (21 Jan. 1958).

The response from Utica power brokers was unanimous. The *Observer-Dispatch* pointed out in an editor's note that "[a] reporter from the *Journal-American* spent slightly more than two days in Utica about a week ago" (OD, 20 Jan. 1958). The Oneida County district attorney stated that "the situation as pictured about Utica in the Hearst *Journal-American* simply does not exist" (OD, 20 Jan. 1958). Members of the business community, who perceived the budding scandal as a slight on Utica's reputation and thus a threat to business, attempted to minimize the damage. Vincent Carrou, the president of the Chamber of Commerce, released a statement for the *Observer-Dispatch*:

In the past ten years there has been no city in the United states that has received more national acclaim and recognition than the city of Utica. . . . Only last October Fortune Magazine termed Utica one of the two "most wide awake cities in the United States." (OD, 20 Jan. 1958)

Aubrey Detweiler, the general manager of Sperry-Rand Corporation, stated:

I know Utica for its fine city spirit of progress and cooperation, a city among the first in New York State to offer refuge to the Hungarian patriots, a city that has undergone a revolution from cotton mills to diversified industry, a city acclaimed by the Wall Street Journal and periodicals of nationally high repute. It is up to those of us who are proud of our city to separate fact from fiction and then to be sure to make every effort we can to keep it the city of which we can boast. (OD, 20 Jan. 1958)

But despite the exaggeration and innuendo that appeared in the article, the fact was that there was corruption in Utica, there was organized crime in Utica, and there were some ties between the city administration and the reputed Mafia leaders. As a letter to the editor noted on January 24, "Well, 'the boys' have finally made headlines—national headlines—for us all. Now please sit down, all of you, and examine your consciences" (OD, 24 Jan. 1958).

Over the next four years, numerous city officials and machine leaders would be called in front of the eight various committees investigating the charges, including Rufus Elefante. Elefante had been alleged by the *Journal-American* to have told the state trooper investigating the Frank Caputo murder, "If you don't keep your nose out of other people's business, you'll wind up in the canal." However, the state trooper denied having told the reporter of the incident. Although Mafia control of the city was never established, the corruption was quite apparent. For instance, the following exchange took place between Police Chief Leo Miller and Watchdog Committee counsel Arnold Bauman:

Bauman: To your knowledge, prostitution has gone on in Utica for 25 years, and the Cuban lottery and bookmaking, and seven to 12 gangland slayings in the last twenty-five years, does that not indicate to you as chief of police of Utica that open racketeering has operated? What have you done?

Miller: We make investigations on all this, but we don't get anywhere with them.

Deputy Police Chief Vincent Fiore testified that he had been friends with Falcone for thirty years, that he had the police provide protection to Albert Anastasia when he came to Utica for the wedding of his nephew, that the bride was the daughter of one of Fiore's friends, and that he had also sent "four or five" officers to protect Anastasia at the recent funeral but not to the cemetery where Anastasia was to be killed originally. In apparent distress, Fiore proclaimed of Falcone, "He attends the same church I do. With his wife. He goes to holy Communion" (OD, 11 Feb. 1958). At one point during 1958, the *Observer-Dispatch* had the scandal on the front page every day for several months and ran almost weekly editorials against the administration, the "bossism" of Rufus Elefante, and corruption in general. Periodically, the New York *Journal-American* would reference Utica's corruption in a variety of stories. The *New York Times* and countless other newspapers also covered the scandals that started in Appalachin but soon were centered on Utica.

Utica acquired a national reputation for Mafia activities as the media utilized the city as a symbol of what was wrong with America. The case of Utica was treated not merely as the corruption of a medium-sized American city, but as involving the most corrupt of all cities and truly the most despicable. As time went on, the charges heaped on Utica became all the more unbelievable. Whereas the Utica syndicate was one of many in cities across the country, the *Journal-American* had branded Utica the "upstate headquarters of the Invisible Government which has turned the city into a cesspool of vice and political corruption" (JA, 25 Jan. 1958). A month later, *Newsweek* had magnified the claim:

Utica is the town the gangsters own. It is a wide-open town, where the brothels and the call-girls operate under the tolerant eye of the cops, where the after hours clubs flourish and it is no trick to find a dice game or a horse parlor. . . . It is a town where the gangsters know the cops and where they know the politicians. It is the headquarters town for big-time mafia operations in most of the Eastern half of the nation, with strings reaching all the way to Cuba. It is a place run by the shadowy figure of a "Mr. Big," far more important than the civic leaders who get their pictures into the newspapers. (*Newsweek*, 24 Feb. 1958)

That Utica was a headquarters town for organized crime was never established. The corruption that existed there was in all likelihood no worse than the corruption found in Albany, New York, or Chicago. Although there was reason for concern, the city did not deserve the reputation it gained. *Look* magazine stated it best:

Utica is no more a sin city than, say, Toledo, Ohio or Kansas City, Missouri. Could be that there is the same kind of five-and-ten cent corruption in all three and elsewhere as well. . . . Before the probes are finished, a few more cops may find it expedient to line up for their pensions. But I doubt anyone will lay a disrespectful hand on Joe Falcone or that Rufus Elefante will be deposed. I expect that the public apathy will return. Then, someday, maybe a thruway will start cutting its way across Utica, and there'll be something else to get worked up about. (*Look*, 8 July, 1958)

Robert Fischer was appointed as a special prosecutor in the case by Governor Harriman in June 1958, and the federal government made Utica one of seven cities to be investigated for racketeering. The other cities were New York, Chicago, Detroit, Miami, Los Vegas, and Havana. The two Utica newspapers continued to exert pressure on the city administration for better law enforcement, and in response unidentified "friends" of the administration

began a campaign of intimidation. There were dead of night calls to editor's homes. The callers made profane threats and predictions of physical harm. . . . (They) told reporters not to be out alone at night. Reporters and others discovered they were being followed on or off duty by persons not known to them. (DP, 5 May 1959)

By the time the last of the investigations ended four years later, "22 residents of the city had been sent to prison . . . and numerous city officials loyal to the machine had been forced to resign" (Ehrenhalt 1989, 35).

On May 4, 1959, in the midst of the trials that resulted from the scandal, the *Observer-Dispatch* quietly announced in a small article on page one that the paper would share the Pulitzer Prize for Meritorious Public Service with its sister paper, the *Daily Press*. The next day, the *Daily Press* acknowledged the role of the national scandal in bringing attention to its work:

The award, it should be noted, has significance beyond the bestowal of a gold medal. It means that a jury of distinguished newspapermen and educators reviewed what had been going on in Utica. They decided the steps the newspapers had taken to arouse public interest and bring about reforms were a meritorious achievement. (DP, 5 May 1959)

End of the Line

John McKennon was not to run for reelection as mayor in 1959, and the machine ran Leo Wheeler instead. McKennon's career in politics was over. But removing the figurehead from a corrupt Democratic administration did not make voters believe that corruption had ended.

Frank Dulan, a Republican who had also run for mayor in 1953, ran for mayor as the "un-McKennon": not connected with the machine, and thus honest. He ran campaign advertisements that attacked the bossism of the Elefante machine, but often not Wheeler. In one, six cartoons make the case for the Republicans, but only one discusses their plans for the future; the other five target the machine. The *Observer-Dispatch* repeatedly editorialized against the machine, reminding voters of the corruption found in the city:

[T]hese records of arrests over a 10-year period tell their own story of the laxity that resulted in the sensation reports that were bound to ensue:

1948	17 gambling arrests, 2 lottery, 3 prostitution
1949	13 gambling arrests, 2 lottery, 3 prostitution
1950	20 gambling arrests, 1 lottery, 16 prostitution
1951	6 gambling arrests, 1 lottery, 9 prostitution
1952	9 gambling arrests, 3 lottery, 11 prostitution
1953	14 gambling, 2 lottery, 10 prostitution
1954	10 gambling, no lottery, 3 prostitution
1955	No gambling, no lottery, no prostitution
1956	1 gambling, no lottery, no prostitution
1957	4 gambling, no lottery, 1 prostitution

. . . It is indeed time for a change. (OD, 1 Nov. 1959)

Voters remembered that the chief of police testified that he had kept several brothels under surveillance for up to twenty years but had ostensibly found no evidence of wrongdoing. That there were thirteen unsolved murders in the city, though most of them did date to Prohibition. That "the old man" (Elefante) called the shots. And on November 3, 1959, city voters elected Dulan as mayor as he "cut into East Utica, the foundation of Elefante's strength" (OD, 4 Nov. 1959). The machine continued its influence on the common council, but would not again win the mayoralty until 1977 (Ehrenhalt 1992). The *Observer-Dispatch* announced "Independence Declared" in a glowing editorial on November 4.

The business community, who had benefited from the efficiency of city government prior to the scandals, seemed more interested in continued economic recovery than in clean government. The newspapers were attacked for "besmirching the fair name of the city" and "driving business out of town" (DP, 5 May 1959). Although such arguments from members of the political establishment were understandable, the *Daily Press* lamented:

One protest came from an unexpected quarter—a group of recognized civic leaders, mostly Republicans, intent on selling the idea that things were no worse than in Syracuse or other upstate cities, and on sweeping the whole mess under the rug again and keeping it there. (DP, 5 May 1959)

The problem was that although the collusion between the Republican leaders, the business community, and the political bosses was quite common, the degree to which the corruption was noticeable was not. Utica's political machine had allowed its corruption to become too visible through a degree of latitude given to mobsters that was insulting to many of the city's residents. By the end of the sin city scandals, the business community perceived the machine, no matter how efficient, as more of a liability than it was worth. Rather than a collapse of the political structure, however, the scandals led to a bifurcation of political interests. The machine would continue to control the inner city and thus the common council, but could not win the mayoralty until 1977. Gone were the days when an interested corporation could just sit down with Elefante and hammer out a deal.

As the decades wore on, decisions within the city took longer and longer to implement, and many companies simply found Syracuse, Albany, and Binghamton to be more efficient communities. Business is most often hurt by the inability of a city to make things happen, not necessarily by political corruption (Anechiarico and Jacobs 1996). And so over the next several decades, Utica area politicians would take out bonds for a new firehouse in south Utica and then fail to agree on a location; bicker repeatedly about the municipal water supply; bicker over how many schools to have; bicker over what to do with empty urban renewal lots; bicker over how to fix downtown; bicker over where to build expressways; bicker over new developments and shopping centers.[8] And in time, Utica's reputation as sin city faded and a new one developed. As one resident of Cooperstown noted in 1998:

I used to think of Utica as Mafia. Hookers, drugs, parties. That's when I was a kid (in the 1960s). Now I think it's just a dump.

Chapter 6

Progress

The Utica sin city scandals impacted only the city in the short run, but in time affected the surrounding hinterland in unforeseen ways. As the 1960s opened, the expectation of progress that had developed after World War II came to fruition as communities throughout the United States began to dramatically restructure themselves to make room for the automobile and modern conveniences of every kind. In Utica, the void left by the weakening of the political machine resulted in policies that were quite different from those of the machine Democrats. And in Cooperstown and Hartwick, the prevailing discourse of what was meant by "progress," based so much on the economic and cultural lifestyles in found in cities, found a place in both communities.

The Disaffection of the Wealthy

The United States was immensely successful during the 1950s and 1960s, despite a preoccupation with the Mafia and communists across the sea. Productivity was rising, wages were rising, and the United States was investing in its infrastructure like never before. Yet something in people's everyday environment was amiss.

In many communities, the rapidity with which housing, factories, and farms had been built resulted in a landscape dominated by hastily built structures. Most cities, having been built prior to the advent of the automobile, shared a structure that was most appropriate for pedestrians. Often, buildings were built close together or even touching to maximize the number of buildings (and residents) that could live in a relatively small geographic area (Francaviglia 1996). Competition for

71

space in the city often led to buildings being built with multiple floors in order to maximize the number of functions that could take place on a given lot. In short, the physical structure of most inner city neighborhoods was high density and very old.

Small towns were often not much better. Built as small cities, they also tended to have high densities and contain many older structures. In 1960, the sheer number of older buildings nationwide that were in need of renovations was staggering. And like major cities, they were built primarily to service pedestrians. Many people felt that they too needed to be modernized.

Within this context, modernization was often interpreted as making communities more accessible by automobile (Kunstler 1993). This was the idea behind urban expressways, but it also required that there be adequate parking once the automobile was downtown. Newspaper reports throughout the late 1940s in Utica made light of the city's parking problems, and John McKennon ran for reelection as mayor in 1957 in part because of the parking lot the city had constructed by tearing down buildings between Oriskany and Liberty Streets downtown. But driving and parking was not perceived as the only problem of American communities; to many, they were simply dilapidated.

Outside of the central business district, most of Utica's inner city buildings were of wood construction. Many of the buildings dated to the nineteenth century, and most were apartment houses. In the older sections of east Utica, two and three story houses stacked apartments on top of each other—one per floor. In the areas closer to downtown, the wooden structures gave way to brick apartment buildings. Some of the brick buildings had been private homes originally built for Utica's elite during the 1820s and 1830s. With the arrival of the trolleys, the elite could quickly be transported farther away and their homes were converted into apartment houses for the burgeoning immigrant populations. In both cases, many of the buildings looked run down, with chipping paint or dulling bricks. Many had no indoor plumbing. At the time, it was considered cold hearted not to want the neighborhoods demolished.

Utica's first moves toward urban renewal occurred during the 1930s, shortly after Franklin Roosevelt became president. The neighborhood to the west of Bagg's Square, known at the time as "the Triangle" due to its overall shape, had become very run down. The oldest neighborhood in the city, its eastern fringe was home to warehouses, factories, and commercial buildings that gave way to brick row houses to the west. Many of the homes had no indoor plumbing, and almost all were in considerable disrepair. Most of the residents of the neighborhood were quite poor, the area at that time being home to Utica's small but growing African American population (DeAmicis 1994). The political machine at the time used its connections with Roosevelt to demolish several blocks of the area and construct a new rental housing complex. After World War II, another was constructed in the Triangle. The combined housing projects came to be known as Washington Courts (after one of the projects), and were the model for similar projects in other parts of the city.[1]

Electric Brains and Other Things

As the sin city scandals unfolded, other news often shared the headlines and gave the city a sense of hope. In late 1957, Remington Rand officials displayed their Utica-made line of electronic machines at the Mohawk Valley Business Show. The display included electric typewriters, printing calculators, and adding machines. But the pride of the display was the Univac File-Computer, which was "of particular interest to accountants and others who contemplate the use of electronic data processing in their business activities" (OD, 20 Oct. 1957). A year later, a monkey named Gordo survived a flight in space aboard a Jupiter rocket (13 Dec. 1958). The Associated General Contractors of America sealed predictions for the year 2000 in their new headquarters building in Washington, D.C. (8 June 1958). Among them:

- Automobiles will not be allowed downtown—above ground, at least
- Low cost housing projects built in the 1940s and 1950s will have become dilapidated and demolished
- Main highways will be double-decked, automobiles above and trucks below
- Highways will be equipped with heating elements to melt ice and snow
- Business centers will be rebuilt with spreading buildings set in landscaped malls

The predictions may seem outlandish today, but the belief in progress was absolute. For urban planners, such visions were based upon scientific realities and architectural fantasies. The two were not truly compatible. The science was new and unfortunately flawed, and some fantasies should remain in the artist's notebook.

The budding science of sociology had its American roots at the University of Chicago. Early work on urbanization tended to hold the "disorganization" of cities as responsible for crime and perceived moral decay (Wirth 1938). So certain were some sociologists regarding the moral failings of cities that they started programs to place at-risk youth in homes in rural areas (Olansky 1995). By the 1950s, most planners had studied the theories of Chicago School urbanists that believed the city to be in a constant state of growth from an older core (the central business district) to newer and nicer outer zones (the suburbs) (see Burgess 1925). Although there were various incarnations of what came to be known as concentric zone theory (see Hoyt 1933; Harris and Ullman 1945), the overall lessons were the same: cities grow outward in circular zones, and this growth is natural. If the city is not perfectly circular, the central business district will migrate to the center of the city (as happened in Utica). As the oldest area of the city, the central business district needs to be modernized or it will decline to the point of embarrassment for all involved. It was the architects who believed they knew how to save the city.

Many architects in the first half of the twentieth century entertained new designs for cities. In his *Manifesto of Futurist Architecture* (1973 [1914]), Antonio Sant'Elia imagined a city of tall buildings in a well-ordered urban core where nature was banished. The French architect Le Corbusier, in his *Radiant City* (1987 [1929]), expanded on this theme by envisioning tall buildings surrounded by well-ordered plazas and roads. In contrast, Frank Lloyd Wright (1958) called for a sprawling city of low rise buildings accessible to all by automobile. Such themes were evident in other venues, such as the "city of the future" exhibit at the 1939 New York World's Fair. Funded by General Motors, the model city contained fast and efficient expressways easily traveled during even the afternoon commute.

Other disciplines contributed to the perception of the city as well, but not always with the hopeful visions of a future utopia. Aldous Huxley's *Brave New World* (1992 [1932]) compared a dystopian city of waste and moral decay to the poverty and ignorance of a rural village—neither looked especially appealing. Similarly, Fritz Lang's film *Metropolis* (1927) also maligned the city as oppressive and dehumanizing. What each of these visions shared was a belief that the very structure of the city as then known was fundamentally at odds with the human condition and needed to be changed. Urban decay thus demanded not merely an effort to revitalize communities but the wholesale demolition and reconstruction of the city in a more favorable arrangement. Utica was among the first cities to experiment with such ideas.

Pilot Project

In 1956, Congress approved a bill that provided for pilot projects for federally subsidized urban renewal. Although officially intended for housing, urban renewal programs would extend far beyond mere housing concerns. A year later, Utica was approved as a demonstration project. The procedures developed in Utica would be replicated by cities in the one hundred thousand to three hundred thousand population range nationwide (OD, 9 Dec. 1957).

Federally supported urban renewal allowed Utica to continue policies that had been in effect for at least two decades, all based loosely on the assumptions of the Chicago School, but at an accelerated pace. Slum clearance and parking was a priority with private businesses as well as city leaders. Throughout the 1940s and 1950s, dozens of individual buildings had been demolished by private enterprise to make room for parking lots to benefit their own businesses. Public response was generally positive, as the following caption below a newspaper picture of one such lot shows:

NEW PARKING LOT—Chanatry Bros. Inc. Super Market has opened a new parking lot at the rear of the Bleeker St. building and remodeled the exterior of the structure. A three-story apartment house, two one-family houses, and a garage were razed to make room for parking. For the convenience of those using the new parking facilities, an entrance has been installed to the rear, the Jay St. side.

This scenario was repeated many times throughout the city.

State funds had also been brought into the city for slum clearance. "Site A" was the oldest of such projects and continued work started during the New Deal years. The state paid for the demolition of much of the land in the Triangle, after which the Municipal Housing Authority expanded the housing projects in the Washington Courts area. The new municipal auditorium was also built in that area. By 1959, there were also plans to demolish all the buildings on the side of Charles Street opposite the new auditorium, and in several years a commercial laundry expanded their facilities to include almost the entire block. By 1960, about 75 percent of the Triangle had been torn down. Unlike similar neighborhoods in larger cities, there were no social scientists in the Utica area willing to write a book about the death of the Triangle.[2]

The federally funded urban renewal program allowed a considerable expansion of such efforts, but along established guidelines.[3] Unlike the previous programs, urban renewal required that cities develop a master plan for the demolished area with the goal of redeveloping the area as soon as possible. A 1954 report commented:

Cumulative federal, state, and local experience with slum clearance and concomitant public housing programs has indicated that they are only a partial solution to the problem of insidious blight and decay especially since these elements threaten to engulf adjacent areas surrounding redevelopment projects and slum clearance as they are erected. (NYS Division of Housing 1954: 28–29)

Thus, the policy was to redevelop large tracts of the inner city. Cities would demolish large tracts of land with an eye toward major development projects that would completely restructure that area of the city. When it was announced that Utica would bulldoze more than twenty-two acres west of Genesee Street, many in the city greeted the news with enthusiasm. The *Observer-Dispatch* commented:

Urban renewal is a means to bring downtown areas back to life after they have lost vigor as part of the commercial community.... Unless the worst structures are removed, blight is likely to set in over a wide section in the heart of the city. (OD, 5 Feb. 1958)

With the demolition phase of what became known as Redevelopment Project 1 (RP1) set to begin in the spring of 1959, residents of the area balked at the prices offered for their homes. Although the project was publicly discussed as a housing initiative, it served to displace nearly eight hundred residents before any housing could be built. In fact, demolition started before any definite plans as to what to do with the lot had been made. The prices offered the residents were very low, especially when compared to those offered business owners a few short blocks away. While some businesses in the Triangle received between fifty and seventy thousand dollars for their buildings (OD, 11 Jan. 1959), some residents of RP1 were offered as little as three to four thousand dollars for their homes. As one neighborhood activist was quoted in the *Observer-Dispatch:*

How are the residents going to get new homes? You couldn't get a shack today at these prices. Some of them are widows, or families with children who are going to need all they can to find new homes. (OD, 5 Jan. 1959)

City officials often countered that since the houses were in a slum area, they were worth less than buildings in other areas of the city. One area resident at the time offered an analysis of the policy in 1999:

So they'd come in and declare the place a slum, and by doing that all the houses there are now worthless. Then the city comes in and offers you what they say the house is worth, but it ain't what the house is worth 'cause they called it a slum and nobody wants to live in a slum. So your house ain't worth what it was and you gotta take what they give you. If you don't, they'll just condemn it anyway.

The above sentiments expressed the notion that a neighborhood is a place to be utilized by residents in daily life. It is an expression of use value—the idea that property is to be utilized for daily life and the value of such property is derived mainly from the pleasure of its utility (Logan and Molotch 1987). For the city administration and the business community, the decaying neighborhood in the shadows of what was once the largest textile mill in the state owned by the largest manufacturer of underwear in the world was a decaying mass of blighted wooden buildings. Those eight blocks south and west of the most prestigious shopping area in the city were not aesthetically pleasing and thus served to lower property values. This not only hurt business interests but also lowered the city tax base in the area. Numerous news stories were run in which city officials discussed the "imbalance" of the neighborhood: the neighborhood provided little in the way of tax revenue, but required considerable police presence, fire department presence, and other municipal services. In other words, the administration and the business community were interested in the exchange value of the area: the idea that worth is determined by the amount of money property trades for on the open market (Logan and Molotch 1987). It is not surprising that early discussion of replacing the housing was replaced by discussion of commercial and municipal functions.

Early plans for RP1 called for a mix of retail and commercial development. The Chamber of Commerce, however, was vehement in its opposition to more retail space that could compete against established downtown businesses. The idea that the city could be a beneficiary of the redevelopment thus became more appealing (Ellis and Preston 1982). Further, "the consensus (was) that the present site (of City Hall) would be better used commercially" (OD, 25 Oct. 1958).

City Hall had been constructed in 1853 in an Italianate style. Many considered it to be a landmark of the city, with historical and architectural significance. As of 1960, modernization of the building had comprised only basic maintenance work and the installation of a parking lot behind the building—there was not even an elevator to service the four story structure. Discussion of the need for a new city hall had gone on for decades; plans were even made for a nine-story replacement before the stock market crash of 1929. With business opposed to new retail development and city leaders reluctant to place tax-free public housing projects in the site, discussion of what to do with RP1 continued into the early 1960s. And with the decline of the political machine, that was all Utica could do.

The demolition necessitated by urban renewal continued throughout the 1960s. By 1970, there were four projects underway, ranging from the small Oriskany Plaza project to the history-altering RP1 and the John Bleeker project east of downtown. Construction took longer as the Republican mayor and the Democratic common council tended to disagree. In time, however, the plans for each project were agreed upon.

In RP1, the final design took years to finalize. In 1967, a new City Hall was opened. A year later, the old, historic City Hall was demolished, but not easily. Although the building's age and structural infirmity were cited as reasons for the demolition, a witness of the demolition said in 1997:

They'd throw everything they had at that place, but she wouldn't fall. Day after day, they'd blast and hit and it came down real slow. The (clock) tower came down last—I thought that was symbolic of something.

There was a new parking garage whose roof, because of the slope of the property, formed a plaza adjacent to the new City Hall with storefronts facing Columbia Street, a major retail street. A 1970 report excitedly proclaimed, "[A]fter four and one-half years of delay on the 679 space parking garage, the grand opening was held on July 15, 1970" (UURA 1970: 8).[4] A new apartment complex consisting of a seventeen story building and two five story buildings to house middle income residents (and not the displaced poor) was also constructed. The complex would later win an award for the originality of its architecture. The centerpiece was to be the new ten-story Hilton Hotel built on the plaza (garage roof) next to City Hall. Unfortunately, the hotel was never built. By 1973, only two blocks of the original eight were not developed, but those were next to Genesee Street—Utica's main street. A series of proposals during the 1970s were suggested, ranging from simple commercial buildings to a European-inspired plaza called Le Promenade. When in 1977 a machine candidate was finally elected mayor, a Sheraton Hotel was finally built on the site and opened in 1979—twenty years after demolition began.

Similar to RP1, the John Bleeker project demolished an even larger swath east of downtown. A new boulevard was built through the area but, to facilitate automobile traffic, no new buildings were built facing the highway. The three to five story buildings were slowly replaced primarily by one story (normally, cement block) buildings surrounded by grass and parking lots. New housing was also built for those with "moderate incomes" and the elderly; utilitarian buildings, but lacking the drama of the seventeen-story tower in RP1. The centerpiece was the new Towne East Mall—an enclosed mall built on the demolished Bleeker Street shopping district. Shortly after opening, Towne East was eclipsed by the much larger Riverside Mall on the city's outskirts.

The East Arterial Industrial Park straddled the newly constructed East Expressway (New York 5S), which connected the city with the eastern suburbs (a task the New York Thruway had failed to accomplish). Making use of empty land near the city line, some of it freed up by filling in the original route of the Erie Canal, the city constructed a new industrial park with the hopes of courting out-of-town companies to build new factories in Utica.

The Oriskany Plaza project was the major downtown urban renewal effort, but was also the smallest. The city sponsored urban renewal funds to tear down an old theater that had become an annex to the Boston Store—the largest department store in Utica—and the remainder of the block, including the exquisite seven story Hotel Martin. In its place was constructed a one story tan brick annex for the Boston Store that ran the entire city block. Behind the annex was a new 280 space parking garage. The agency proudly proclaimed that the project "marked a major step forward in Urban Renewal toward assisting local businesses to expand in the downtown area" (UURA 1970: 4).

Flight of the Suburbanites

During the summer of 1952, a sign proudly proclaimed the empty field on which it stood, "Site of Whitestown Shopping Plaza: First Shopping Center in Utica Area. Parking Facilities for 500 Cars" (Preston and Hassett 1995). Of twelve businesses listed as having already secured space, seven had stores in downtown Utica, four miles away. Within ten years, there were five major shopping centers and numerous smaller centers and stores spread throughout the city and inner suburbs. The flight of the suburbanites had begun.

Suburbanization can be understood in terms of the cultural discourse of progress so prevalent at the time. Urban renewal projects had begun with the intention of modernizing the city for the automobile, but of course the suburbs held out the promise of all-new communities built especially for the automobile. So as Utica attempted to make its downtown more friendly for commuters and shoppers looking for parking spaces, the suburban plazas and stores built parking into their plans from the beginning. And of course, this new structure of settlement space was greeted as an omen of fortuity.

In 1950, Utica had a population of 101,531 and was the major center of a metropolitan area of 284,262. The city population had been stable since the 1930 federal census, but the population of the metropolitan area had increased by more than twenty-thousand (Shupe et al. 1987).

This meant that the 1930 census recorded the highest proportion of the total metropolitan area population constituted by Utica's population (38.72 percent).

While census figures gave the appearance that Utica was holding its own, the distribution of the population within the city was becoming more deconcentrated. In 1916, the city had annexed the southern portion of the adjacent town of Deerfield, but the area had grown slowly prior to World War II. After the war, however, what became known as North Utica developed rapidly as postwar housing was built in large tracts in a manner similar to Arthur Levitt's Levittown communities in the suburbs of New York and Philadelphia. They were built very rapidly, using assembly line techniques, and sold for relatively little, allowing former apartment dwellers in Utica's inner city the experience of owning their own home. Similar neighborhoods were built in other parts of the city. With such a massive level of new home construction in the city, one would have expected the city to show a dramatic population surge. It did not; the city population had dropped by about a thousand residents in 1960. The flight of residents from the older neighborhoods was actually greater than the population boom in newer portions of the city.

While the stability of Utica's population was due by and large to the ability of the city to build modern-style housing within the city limits, it also indicated an overall trend toward the automobile culture that necessitated driveways, garages, and a home away from the perceived problems of the inner city. This was especially evident outside the city. The metropolitan area population surged to 330,771 residents by 1960, due in part to the recovering economy in the city and the expansion of Griffiss Air Force Base in nearby Rome. As a result, Utica's population as a proportion of the metropolitan area as a whole dropped to 30.36 percent, and has continued to drop ever since. According to the census bureau, Utica accounted for only 20.05 percent of the total metropolitan area population in 1999 (USBC, 2000) (See Figure 6.1).

As people left the city, so did other institutions traditionally found there. In many cases, they seemed to flee the city for the greener pastures next to the parking lots in their new suburban locations. For instance, when Utica Mutual Insurance Company built a new headquarters in New Hartford in 1953, "the move into the new building was the biggest such undertaking in Utica's history" (Preston and Hassett 1995). Similarly, when Utica College proved a successful satellite for Syracuse University, the *Observer-Dispatch* ran a feature story about why the college needed a new campus. Pictures of various buildings around the Oneida Square campus near downtown were accompanied by captions

Figure 6.1. Utica's Population as a Percentage of the MSA, 1900–1999

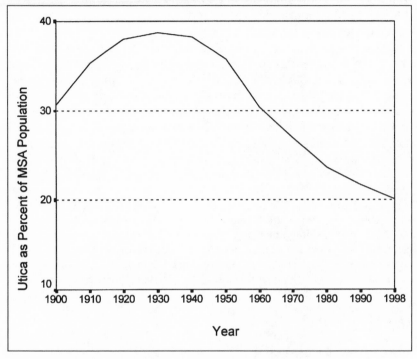

Source: Adapted from Shupe et al. 1987; USBC 2000

explaining their inadequacies and making the case for the new campus at the New Hartford town line (OD, 9 Feb. 1958).[5]

As population and jobs flowed into the suburbs, so did shopping. The opening of the Whitestown Shopping Center in Whitesboro was soon followed by the New Hartford Shopping Center, which would for years be the largest complex in the area. The stores that opened in the new shopping centers typically were branches of established downtown businesses. For instance, Woolworth's opened several stores in the Utica area to complement a large store downtown, and numerous locally owned businesses opened branches in the suburbs.

Suburbanization does not simply refer to the legal boundaries of a city, but rather can be understood as a change in lifestyle for the residents of a metropolitan area. Residents of the suburbs became more reliant on the automobile for commuting to work, doing their shopping, and merely for enjoyment (Jackson 1985). Residents of the city also became more dependent upon the automobile, and with such a lifestyle change the structure of Utica's neighborhoods changed as well. By 1960, shopping centers had opened in the "uptown" area of the city, in the suburb-like north Utica neighborhood, and amid the ethnic enclaves of east Utica.

The impact of the new shopping centers was slow but dramatic. Prior to their existence, the older neighborhoods in the city were home to secondary shopping districts that catered primarily to local residents. Often, they appeared physically similar to shopping districts in small towns and operated in a similar fashion. Local residents would do much of their everyday shopping in the neighborhood, and due to the relatively small size of the available market many residents knew or recognized others in the area.[6] As a former resident of west Utica recalled in 2000:

Why, you'd go down to Varick Street if you needed anything. Most everything you needed was there, unless of course you wanted something special that you'd need to go downtown for. And we talked to our friends there and maybe eat a sandwich and then head home. Times were different then—you knew your neighbors then, even just from the neighborhood. And every now and then I'd be over by Court Street up by the state (psychiatric) hospital and I'd stop at a store there and they'd give me a look. That's only maybe ten blocks away but it was like a different world. Now I travel farther than that when I go to K-Mart.

In east Utica, for instance, the Chicago Market Plaza opened near the shopping districts on James, South, Eagle, and Bleeker Streets and competed against all four. With larger stores and ample parking, the new shopping centers had little trouble competing with established businesses. As the presumed market for the shopping center was all of east Utica and not merely the population near each of the respective shopping districts, the economies of scale allowed businesses in the shopping center to offer lower prices and outcompete the Mom and Pop shops.

The placement of branches of downtown stores in shopping centers around the metropolitan area had another effect as well. The shopping centers were often considered ideal locations for branch locations due to their easy parking and large economies of scale. As they often defined a large area as the potential market, larger businesses and specialty stores that could not survive in a neighborhood business district stood better chances in the shopping centers. But as more businesses could be found away from the central business district, there was increasingly less reason for local residents to travel downtown. As urban renewal attempted to rebuild the inner city for the automobile during the 1960s, the presence of people, jobs, and shopping at increasing distances from the inner city made downtown appear all the more irrelevant.

Kindred Spirits

The cultural discourse surrounding the notion of progress was not limited to urban areas such as Utica. In many rural communities around the country, the idea of demolishing seemingly outdated structures and building new, automobile accessible buildings in their place was considered progressive. The automobile raised certain issues, parking being the most serious for pedestrian oriented downtown areas. Small town business districts were often the same age as those found in nearby cities and thus small town residents often shared the same perceptions of their own downtown areas that residents of urban centers did of theirs.

In Cooperstown, Bassett Hospital nearly doubled its size with a modern expansion that forever made the beauty of its brownstone front entrance and white cupola invisible from the street. Nearly forty years later, the hospital attempted to recover this lost history by placing a cupola on a back entrance that does face the street. Similarly, the Baseball Hall of Fame demolished several commercial structures for its own expansion, and a new county office building was built on the site of a demolished county office building. A new industrial park outside the village in the town of Hartwick (six miles from Hartwick village) was under consideration, although this ultimately did not occur. A new high school was built, with the old school torn down for a new apartment complex. This version of progress contrasts with the construction of a new school building in nearby Milford twenty years later; the old building was preserved and converted directly into apartments.

In Hartwick, and to a lesser degree in Cooperstown, downtown buildings were perceived as old, small, and dilapidated. Nearly all of Hartwick's downtown structures, some dating to the 1820s, were constructed of wood. Store space was limited by the relatively small size of the buildings. For instance, by 1960 one downtown Hartwick business had spread across four storefronts in two separate buildings in order to have enough space for merchandise. A small supermarket also spread into both of its building's storefronts. There were some empty storefronts by the early 1960s as the decline of agriculture and the rise of the car culture began to take their bites from Hartwick's economy, but downtown Hartwick remained a viable small town business district, and thus parking was limited. The aged wooden structures themselves required regular maintenance, which local owners increasingly could not afford. Some buildings, due to the lack of a centralized sewer system, had no indoor plumbing despite a centralized water delivery system. Like Utica, Hartwick appeared to require a major overhaul of its business district.

Although Hartwick was too small to be eligible for either state or federal funds, the cultural assumptions underlying urban renewal were at work there as well. As happened in Utica, much of the restructuring of downtown Hartwick occurred because of private interests. In the case of Hartwick, the interests involved honestly did believe that they were acting in the best interest of the community, and only later did the impact of their actions become fully understood.

In 1964, five buildings consisting of seven storefronts on Main and South Streets were demolished to make room for a modern, three store complex complete with a small parking lot. When it opened in 1966, the building housed a new supermarket, a liquor store, and a laundromat. To lose seven storefronts in a commercial area the size of Utica would have had a significant effect on a particular area, but not on the central business district as a whole. In Hartwick, the demolition had resulted in the downtown area losing 29 percent of its storefronts. It was nonetheless viewed as positive for the community. The *Freeman's Journal* (FJ, 21 Sept. 1966) commented:

This beautiful new facility is a wonderful addition to the Village of Hartwick and local residents are quite excited about having a supermarket in their midst.

Within a few years, another commercial property (two storefronts) was cleared for a new fire station, a three story hotel replaced by a mobile home, and another two storefront building torn down.

Because many village residents were commuting to Cooperstown for employment, local businesses found that once steady customers were sharing their shopping time with stores in Cooperstown.[7] As the Hartwick economy had developed with the assumption that local residents would shop in the village, even a moderate outflow of capital jeopardized the tenuous economic equilibrium. Many storeowners simply could not survive under such conditions and closed; in other cases, storeowners retired and nobody was willing to take their place. When one store closed:

He just boarded the place up. I went in there a few years ago [during the late 1980s] and the place was just like he left it when he closed. There was still candy in the jars after twenty years; it was like a time machine. He just showed up one day and closed.

With a declining number of businesses in the central business district, Hartwick failed to generate the economies of scale necessary for a viable economic center. By the early 1970s, many of those who would have become Hartwick's business elite were either in retirement or in the employ of Cooperstown businesses. Hartwick began to function as an economic satellite of Cooperstown while still struggling to maintain a tenuous sense of community. Although many worked and shopped in Cooperstown, the village still had institutions in which residents could interact with other members of the community (supermarket, diners, bank, post office, churches, and a school). Hartwick was dependent upon Cooperstown economically but remained identifiable as its own community.

While progress created variably good and bad effects for Hartwick, Cooperstown enjoyed a period of relative prosperity. With residents of Hartwick and other nearby communities forced to leave their respective villages for employment and shopping, the village enlarged the economy of scale with which to support its own businesses. Although Cooperstown has lost population throughout the period from 1950 to the present, its businesses have continued to thrive. Increasing numbers of tourists further bolstered the local economy even while the village had relatively few tourist-oriented businesses. Most businesses were community-oriented: clothing, shoes, furniture, electronics and appliances, pharmaceuticals, and food, to name a few. While such businesses to varying degrees certainly benefited from tourism, they were aimed primarily at the local market.

Cooperstown during the 1960s and early 1970s offered its own residents and surrounding communities what suburban shopping centers did: one-stop shopping with a diversified selection. For instance, there were several stores that sold clothing and shoes during this time period, ensuring a variety of styles and colors. As in urban areas, consumers increasingly perceived clothes not simply as functional, but as a statement of the uniqueness of the person wearing them. While previous generations had been content to buy clothes from a mail-order catalog or the local general store, by the 1950s attitudes had changed. Not only was clothing a fashion statement for many, if not most, Americans, the selection of the clothing was itself a satisfying diversion in its own right. Shopping was viewed as entertainment. This rise in the consumer culture was also among the variables in the decline of Hartwick's economic base and Cooperstown's rise to dominance of the local economy in the 1960s. And of course, this newfound efficiency in the local economy was considered to be a mark of progress.

The consumer culture and the dominance of the automobile for transportation amplified the ability of residents to travel to larger communities. With larger economies of scale, larger communities such as Cooperstown benefited from upscaling in retail as their neighbors suffered decline. Indeed, Cooperstown enjoyed the benefits of upscaling through the 1960s and early 1970s even as its own institutions, such as banks and grocery stores, were being bought or replaced by urban-based chains. The seeds of the village's own crisis in the face of upscaling were being planted but the fruits would not become evident until the 1980s.

As the 1970s wore on, spiraling fuel prices and economic uncertainty took a toll on all three communities. Especially after 1972, the American model of progress came into question as inflation and unemployment went up and median wages began their twenty-year tumble. Nationwide, the perception of inevitable progress fell into question and by the late 1970s many American communities were facing new challenges that to a large measure were the direct result of the "progress" of earlier generations.

Chapter 7

Slaughter of the Innocents

After World War II, the entire nation went on a spending spree emboldened by the confidence of the world's most productive economy and an inherent belief in the virtue of progress. The plans of the policy makers had been grand and the investments of the entrepreneurs had been beneficent however self-serving. Architectural renderings of the period looked futuristic and modern, even avant-garde, but when the projects were finally realized, they were lifeless. In the aftermath of the oil crisis of the early 1970s, the impact of decades of social and economic restructuring became apparent.

Earthtones

The future turned into the present with an alarming discovery. As the 1970s drew to a close, Uticans looked at their city with a disdain almost as strong as they had felt for the slums torn down only twenty years before. The disputed projects in RP1 had managed to avoid the placement of new retail establishments, but had resulted in the demolition of the historic City Hall. The new structures, such as the new City Hall, were most often rectangular in some way. Some of the buildings added height to the skyline, but shared what to one area resident was a disturbing trait:

Earthtones! Every goddam building they built was brown or tan. They had the chance to make the city look good, and they put up those God awful tan boxes. The state office building looks just like that piece of shit in Binghamton, which looks like half a dozen buildings in Pennsylvania alone. All that money, and all we have are a bunch of twenty-story earthtone buildings.

When the final segment of RP1 had not yet been developed—a patch of land fronting on Genesee Street—the city administration chose to build a new Sheraton Hotel on the site. While the hotel represented a reasonable use for the land, its design forever closed off Genesee Street from the rest of the area west of downtown. Fronting Genesee Street, an arcade pulled walkers off the street and into the building, while a parking garage fronting Broadway and Columbia Street reduced Broadway to the status of an alleyway and turned one side of the once-thriving retail district of Columbia Street into an unsightly mass of concrete. A new eighteen-story state office building on Genesee Street added an element of height to the skyline, but the concrete plaza in front of the building did little for the street life of the city. A drive-thru window for a local bank was developed on the site of the historic City Hall.

In addition, the new system of arterial roadways added to the disjunctiveness of the city. The Eastern Expressway (NY 5s) ended at Broad Street, where it became a new four to six lane boulevard through the John Bleeker urban renewal area. In order to accommodate the new width of the roadway and medians, the buildings between Oriskany and Jay Streets were demolished, along with several along Genesee Street. Due to the proximity of Jay Street, which runs parallel for five blocks, a median was constructed of asphalt and a guardrail along the length. At the intersection with Genesee Street in the heart of downtown, the boulevard was eight lanes wide with two medians dividing the various lanes. As one pedestrian commented in 1999, "You take your life into your hands there." But the physical environment was not the only aspect of downtown subject to restructuring.

Corporate Concentration

When, in 1916, the owners of the Globe Woolen Mills decided to sell their shares to the American Woolen Company, the merger marked "the beginning of outside control of local (textile) firms" (Ellis and Preston 1982: 90). The merger took place as part of the tendency of industry to consolidate competing companies in order to increase economies of scale. Prior to 1916, Utica had benefited from such trends as its firms acquired companies located in other communities, such as the Phoenix Mills and Index Mills near Cooperstown (Bohls 1991). The fact that Utica was home to the two largest textile producers in the world in 1910 was testimony not merely to the productive capacity of the city's mills but to the ability of its firms to buy other mills in other communities. The merger with American Woolen Company marked the first such merger of a Utica textile firm in which the headquarters did not remain in Utica. It also marked the beginning of the decline in the textile industry that would characterize the city until the sin city scandals of the late 1950s.

Such trends have been found in other industries as well (Kantor and David 1987; Nash 1989; Harrison and Bluestone 1988). For example, the local public utilities company has changed numerous times over the generations, due by and large to the concentration of capital into increasingly larger units. The Utica Gas Light Company formed in 1857, only to inspire competition twenty-five years later in the form of the Central New York Light and Power Company, an electric company. Owing to the overlap between the two firms, they merged to become the Utica Electric and Gas Company in 1887. Between 1887 and 1925, the company expanded greatly by acquiring other utilities and by expanding its own services into other Mohawk Valley communities. In 1927, the company built an exquisite new building as its headquarters on Genesee Street.

In 1926, the company became part of the Mohawk Hudson Power System, but maintained its identity and its headquarters in Utica. The power system was a conglomerate of local firms throughout central and eastern New York State. The system was expanded in 1929 to become the largest electric producer in the nation, serving an area from Albany in the east to Buffalo in the west. In 1950, the system was restructured as one firm called Niagara Mohawk Power Corporation. When the local firms were merged into the single larger entity, the headquarters was moved to Syracuse, and Utica lost many of the administrative functions and, hence, workforce that it once had.

A similar pattern is found in other ventures. Utica had since 1812 been a center for banking, and the city supported numerous financial institutions throughout its history. Some banks, such as the Savings Bank of Utica and the now-defunct Utica City National Bank, have graced the city with a beautiful architectural legacy. Others have served a specialized market, such as business customers or local residents. Throughout the decades, the banks have become central institutions in the social landscape of the city. And Oneida National Bank, founded in 1836, was no exception.

After World War II, Oneida National Bank took the lead in opening new branches in the suburbs to serve its increasingly decentralized customer base. Throughout the 1960s and 1970s, the bank bought several banks in smaller communities, thereby expanding its corporate presence and offering residents of those communities the services that an urban financial institution was capable of providing. By 1980, the bank had grown to thirty-four branches spread across seven different counties.

In 1981, Albany-based United Bank New York acquired Oneida National and became Norstar. While Oneida National had been a large local bank, the formation of Norstar transformed the bank into one of the largest banks in upstate New York. But it also transferred much of the administrative work to Albany, which was now the headquarters city. Within ten years, Norstar was acquired by Boston-based Fleet Bank. During the 1990s, Fleet also merged with Shawmut Bank and later with BankBoston (itself the product of a merger between BayBank and Bank of Boston) to become FleetBoston. In 2000, FleetBoston was the eighth largest financial holdings company in the United States.

Utica was the beneficiary of Oneida National's growth from the 1950s through the 1970s. Other banks also did well, notably the Savings Bank of Utica, which eventually established branches as far away as Oneonta. But others were absorbed earlier. First Bank of Trust Company was absorbed by Buffalo based Marine Midland. Marine Midland was acquired in the 1990s by London-based Hong Kong and Shanghai Banking Corporation (HSBC), one of the largest banks in the world. Similarly, Cornhill Savings and Loan was acquired by Albany Savings Bank, which was recently acquired by Cleveland-based Charter One Bank.

In every instance, the mergers were promoted as harbingers of progress. Niagara Mohawk was founded to more efficiently generate electricity throughout New York State. Each time Oneida National or its descendent merged with another bank, new or better services were promised. In every case, Utica's administrative functions dwindled as larger companies in larger cities took over and in time moved key white-collar employment out of the metropolitan area. Profits ultimately flowed out of the area as well. Utica was becoming a blue collar city.

The basic pattern found in Utica was one in which the local company grew in part by acquiring firms in other, often smaller, communities. After consolidating administrative functions in Utica, the new company would then attract the interest of another (often larger) company headquartered in a larger city, and would then be taken over. This resulted in Utica losing some or all of its administrative functions in the company.

In Cooperstown and Hartwick, business institutions were often the target of takeovers earlier in the process. On March 21, 1956, the Cooperstown *Freeman's Journal* reported the merger of the Second National Bank of Cooperstown with the National Commercial Bank and Trust Company of Albany (The Bank), a forerunner to Key Bank. Some in the community viewed the merger as a sign of progress: a bigger bank, after all, could offer lower interest rates on loans and had more capital to lend. Others perceived the merger as a loss of a vital village institution, a feeling played upon by the First National Bank of Cooperstown in the following advertisement from 1957:

Best Place to Buy and Bank: AT HOME.

Dollars that stay at home pay our taxes, support our churches and schools— make our community a better place in which to live and do business. Remember, nothing ever paid greater dividends or more handsome returns than loyalty to your home town.

First National Bank, Est. 1830

Within twenty years, there were no local banks left.

Hartwick National Bank also merged with The Bank. The Bank eventually changed its name to Key Bank and during the 1990s merged with Cleveland-based Society National Bank. Shortly thereafter, Key Bank sold many of its smaller branches (including Hartwick) to Albank (which merged with Charter One Bank shortly thereafter).

First National Bank of Cooperstown merged with First American Bank. With the BCCI scandal of the early 1990s, in which the parent of First American was accused of laundering money for international criminal organizations, Key Bank purchased several First American branches and so operated two branches next door to each other on Main Street in Cooperstown.

As with the bank mergers, new supermarkets were also greeted as harbingers of progress. In Hartwick, for instance, a shopping list consisting of meat, vegetables, and baked goods would once have necessitated a trip to three different stores. A supermarket brought nearly all of one's food needs under one roof. At first, the stores were placed in existing commercial structures in the central business districts. It was not until the 1950s that freestanding structures with private parking lots were constructed. Besides providing the advantages of larger stores and increased parking, the construction itself was greeted as a sign of progress.

In Utica, supermarkets had existed as early as the 1920s. Several chains were headquartered in Utica, including Chanatry's, Foodland, and Chicago Markets. As the supermarkets grew larger and served several neighborhoods with a single store, smaller "mom and pop" type stores struggled with the competition and many closed their doors. In addition, Utica's own supermarkets were joined by Syracuse-based P&C Markets, New Jersey–based Grand Union, and Schenectady-based Price Chopper Markets.

During the 1950s, both the Grand Union and A & P supermarket chains operated stores on Main Street in Cooperstown, as did Victory Markets. A smaller supermarket chain based in Norwich, New York, Victory Markets had gotten its start by franchising to stores in smaller communities. For example, the 1949 Hartwick High School yearbook features an advertisement for its Hartwick store. Victory grew by such franchising and eventually established its own stores in small towns throughout the region. During the middle and late 1960s, the *Freeman's Journal* reported record profits for the company. The building of a new

Victory near downtown Cooperstown, complete with a parking lot, helped to rid Main Street of the Grand Union and A & P.

Calm Before the Storm

In Cooperstown, the 1970s brought a gradual decline that, as in Hartwick, would not be apparent for another decade. Although a few stores closed, in nearly every case they were replaced by other community-oriented businesses (e.g., a supermarket replaced by a general merchandise store). In many cases, product lines were discontinued while the store continued to operate. For example, one store stopped selling carpets and concentrated instead on clothing. In most cases, such economic events were attributed to recession and the economic oddity of "stagflation." As such, local residents failed to perceive such restructuring in retail as the major structural event that it was. Cooperstown's economy was threatened not just by a cyclical downturn but by the automobile and consumer culture it had benefited from during the 1960s. As one Cooperstown resident shared:

Times were tough in the seventies. You know, people had tough times. I guess you didn't notice what was happening, though. You'd go to a store for something and all of a sudden they didn't have it anymore.

Or another:

You woke up one morning and you had to go to Oneonta because you couldn't get it here anymore. I can't say the place actually declined—just that certain things, you know, special things, you had to go to Oneonta for.

And another:

I guess it was about then that I started to go to Oneonta more. It wasn't so such that Cooperstown didn't have anything—it had most of what you'd want. But Oneonta had more stores and some things we didn't have here. Well, still don't—you know, Jamesway, things like that. And quite a bit they'd be a little cheaper too.

But unlike in Hartwick, most of Cooperstown's businesses were replaced. While Hartwick's business elite shriveled, Cooperstown's redirected its focus into more profitable enterprises. The 1970s were tough for Cooperstown, but devastating for Hartwick. The pattern of upscaling finally overwhelmed the village, one resident quipping in 1998, "If the damn disco wasn't bad enough, that's when we lost our town."

S. O. S.

The 1970s started on a benign note, when Victory Markets expanded its Peter Pumpkin supermarket to fill the entire building built on Main Street in 1966, creating a relatively large store for the time. But the decade would witness a shortage of oil and a steep recession that put pressure on federal and state budgets. A proposal for an expressway linking the Southern Tier Expressway (New York 17) to Utica, which would have run within two miles of Hartwick, was tabled indefinitely. Large businesses demanded higher rates of profit from their operations, closing or selling those that did not satisfy the heightened requirements. State aid to local school districts failed to keep pace with costs. Taxes rose as real wages began to decline.[1] In this context, it was no surprise what the Cooperstown Central School District planned for Hartwick.

The bicentennial year of American Independence was particularly bad for Hartwick. In June 1976, what local residents and state officials believed to be a tornado, not a common occurrence in Appalachia, damaged numerous buildings and trees in the village. In November, fire destroyed the Highway Department garage and much of the snow removal equipment. As one resident quipped, "God, not November. May, maybe. But it snows in November!" It was also 1976 that turned Hartwick from a merely declining to a defended community.

On February 25, 1976, the *Freeman's Journal* ran a story about the school district's intention to bus grades four through six to Cooperstown Elementary School from the Hartwick Grade Center. The Hartwick School had no gymnasium on the premises—students had to walk a block to the gym on Main Street for physical education classes. The original intent of the school board was for fourth through sixth graders to go to Cooperstown so the gymnasium could be closed. Students in kindergarten through third grade could have physical education classes in the school cafeteria. During the following months there was little comment either way in the newspaper, an editorial rather cautiously noting:

The Board of Education has not yet seriously considered the proposal. When it does, members should seriously consider its costs in terms of the system's education.

Some Hartwick residents now report having heard rumors of the school's imminent closing, but others felt that the proposal made considerable economic sense. Many others seem to have forgotten entirely the original proposal.

The first official indication of the possible closing of Hartwick's school was not until September 1976. School officials announced the application for a grant to enlarge Cooperstown Elementary School so that they could abandon Hartwick altogether (FJ, 22 Sept. 1976). Within weeks, a group of Hartwick parents and community activists mobilized to fight the school closing, the *Freeman's Journal* (13 Oct. 1976) reporting that "many people in Hartwick are upset that the community was not consulted." At a meeting of the Board of Education, school officials argued that the move would save money and reduce taxes. Members of the Hartwick delegation countered that the school was a focal point for the community. One resident declared, "If you take away our school, you'll kill our community" (FJ, 20 Oct. 1976). The group would name themselves S.O.S.—Save Our School.

In November, S.O.S. presented the school board with a petition and a list of requests (FJ, 7 Nov. 1976):

1. Creation of a school polling center in Hartwick. Citing a low voter turnout in Hartwick, S.O.S. requested a polling place there. Committee members claimed that the single polling center in Cooperstown put an undue burden for Hartwick residents to vote in school district elections.
2. Making Hartwick students study in Hartwick. The school district allowed Hartwick residents to send their children to Cooperstown Elementary School, thus lowering attendance figures for the Hartwick Grade Center. S.O.S. requested a stop to this practice.
3. Conducting an independent cost-benefit analysis of the proposal. Figures circulated at this time were generated by a school board member not from Hartwick.
4. Scheduling improvements and repairs at the Hartwick Grade Center. This request more than likely reaffirmed the decision on the part of the board to close the school as it listed needed repairs, further demonstrating the building's old age.

S.O.S. again cited a concern for the fate of the community. A new element was also introduced: Hartwick parents felt that their children were being discriminated against in Cooperstown schools. One 1970s-era student shared his feelings in retrospect in 1999:

AT: You were a Hartwick kid going to Cooperstown school. How was that?
RE: Oh, it wasn't any fun.
AT: How so?

RE: There was a high degree of discrimination and alienation as a Hartwickian.

AT: In what way?

RE: You were from Hartwick, and they weren't. And they made sure you knew that . . . you were a second class citizen.

School officials argued that having Hartwick students attend Cooperstown from kindergarten would ensure a greater level of integration among all students and put an end to such discrimination. A Hartwick parent with young children in the system during the middle of the 1990s said:

What I see of (my children), when I talk to them, they don't feel the discrimination that we did graduating from sixth grade to go over to join the junior high school there. There seems to be less of that.

The main issue in 1976 was not discrimination but saving the school. Many residents viewed the school as the last symbol of the village's autonomy. In January 1977, the school district was denied the grant to expand Cooperstown Elementary School, but the board still pressed to close Hartwick. The board's desire was bolstered by an independent cost-benefit analysis released in February that predicted savings of $107,000 per year if Hartwick was closed. Exasperated, S.O.S. discussed a possible consolidation with Laurens Central School, to the village's south, a move that would have required the dissolution of Cooperstown Central School. A new plan was presented to the Cooperstown School Board less than two weeks later which resembled the original Board plan of a year earlier. The last-ditch efforts were made in vain. At the March Board of Education meeting, the Hartwick Grade Center was voted closed in June. On April 20, S.O.S. announced plans for protests at the April Board of Education meeting and at the school the first day after spring vacation (FJ, 20 Apr. 1977). The protest at the school attracted fifty people, 8.3 percent of Hartwick's population. A similar proportion in the city of Boston today would number more than forty-five thousand people. At the Board of Education meeting, board members were apparently nervous enough to request the presence of the sheriff's department (FJ, 27 Apr. 1977). In June, the Hartwick Grade Center closed. For the second time in twenty years, Hartwick students started a year not realizing it would be the school's last.

Downward Spiral

The years following the closing of the Hartwick Grade Center were marked by continued dispute. The former school properties in

Hartwick—the school, the gymnasium, and the athletic field—were topics of some debate. Although discussion in 1957 about school consolidation actually used the word *consolidation*, the final legal terminology utilized the word *annexation*. This meant that the Hartwick School properties belonged to the school district, the town having no legal claim on them. Perhaps because of the bitterness of the school closings, school officials decided to sell the gymnasium and athletic field to the town for one dollar each. The district later sold the school itself for ten thousand dollars. But Hartwick's problems were becoming more serious.

On April 1, 1978, the town closed the landfill. Hartwick residents now had to haul their trash to the Otsego town landfill, one mile from Cooperstown, a relationship that would continue until the formation of a regional waste authority fifteen years later. While this may seem a minor circumstance, town residents perceived the closing as just the latest assault against the struggling community:

It wasn't the dump. I mean, who wants a fuckin' dump in their town anyway? It's that you had to go to Cooperstown for the dumps, too. I mean, you buy your shit over there and then you had to throw it out there, too. Maybe we should've moved there. Why did we need Hartwick?

On April 8, the Peter Pumpkin closed, with four years remaining on the lease. The Oneonta *Daily Star* commented tritely in the news brief, "The closing brings to an end Victory's connection with Hartwick that began before the 1960s" (DS, 6 Apr. 1978). On June 30, the Agway farm supply store closed, a victim of the decline in the local farm population. Rumors spread that the local branch of The Bank was also planning to abandon the village, and a petition was started to save a bank whose headquarters said they would not close (DS, 3 Jun. 1978; 24 Jun. 1978).

During June 1978 Hartwick again mobilized. A meeting was called for all interested residents to discuss the village's future. Many residents today identify the closing of the Hartwick Grade Center as the key event in the community's decline. Despite more than two decades of decline prior to that event, the period between 1976 and 1978 is especially significant due both to the rapidity of the collapse and to the mobilization to save the village. The previous two decades had seen much misfortune, but it had occured slowly. The 1970s witnessed the final evisceration of Hartwick's economic base, depriving the community of its most crucial secular institutions in which everyday social interaction occurred. Not surprisingly, the basic sentiment at the first meeting was that Hartwick's downfall had begun with the school closing. It was the rapid progress of the village's last gasp that brought about the mobilization, however. The first meeting witnessed the following speech by Leonard Wright, a businessman and the principal organizer (DS, 8 Jun. 1978: 15):

Events which happened in the town since the closing of the Hartwick Grade Center in 1977 have seemed to start a trend, which must be changed. The landfill closed on April 1, followed shortly by the Peter Pumpkin store on April 8th and now the closing of the Agway at the end of June. . . . The greatest loss was that of the closing of our largest food supply—Peter Pumpkin, which closed with little notice or concern of the Victory chain for the community.

The closing of the supermarket seemed a particularly bitter event. Supermarkets throughout the area had grown in size over the previous two decades. In 1976, Victory Markets built its second Cooperstown store—the Great American. The new store was almost twice the size of the Cooperstown Victory and the Hartwick Peter Pumpkin, and so quickly won loyal customers from both villages. The Hartwick store, like earlier stores in earlier years, raised prices, forcing more customers to travel the eight miles to Cooperstown. With declining business in Hartwick, Victory had a financial reason for closing the store. The company owned the only two supermarkets in Cooperstown, so that closing the Hartwick store would raise profits in the other stores while cutting the costs of operating the Hartwick store. Hartwick residents were more or less forced to shop in Victory's Cooperstown stores.

The meeting in June led to the establishment of the Hartwick Business Association (HBA), open only to members of the business community. It is possible that this may have deprived the association of non-business talent, but there is no way of knowing for sure. The HBA did make some early steps toward the village's revitalization. After receiving the petition requesting a commitment to the community, the chief executive officer of The Bank "pledged the support of The Bank in any 'meaningful endeavor which will result in the revitalization of Hartwick's economy'" (DS, 24 Jun 1978, 3). Hartwick would not only keep its only bank, but also get help from the economic development office of The Bank.

At a covered dish dinner in August 1978, experts from The Bank delivered their recommendations. The Bank suggested a coordinating organization to market the village to outside investors, a task the HBA accepted. The group would identify existing and potential sites for businesses and compile a database of such sites. Recruitment of a major employer, likely in assembly work, was a top priority. At various points in late 1978 and early 1979, a plant for processing cheese, a small Bendix assembly plant, a photographic processing center, an elderly housing complex, and an I.G.A. supermarket were all discussed as possible projects. Only one would occur: the HBA endorsed a plan to move the Otsego County Association for Retarded Citizens into the former Peter Pumpkin as a satellite center in September of 1979.

The End of Innocence

As the 1980s began, the citizens of Hartwick were forced to drive elsewhere for even the most basic goods and services. The demise of retail shopping and other community institutions meant that residents no longer interacted in local stores on a regular basis; there were simply very few places where residents could interact. Some institutions, such as the volunteer fire department and the three churches, continued as vital centers of community integration, but local residents also interacted as much or more in institutions outside of Hartwick. As the 1980s went on, many Hartwick residents came to see themselves as part of the community in Cooperstown as well as Hartwick. Still others, especially those who moved into the area, viewed themselves as part of the Cooperstown community and sought out relatively little interaction within Hartwick. Both within the village and in neighboring communities, Hartwick came to be viewed as a "bedroom community" of Cooperstown. Hartwick had been untowned.

Chapter 8

Extended Communities

It took decades for the dynamics that untowned Hartwick to coalesce, but less than three years for the final collapse of the economy to take place. In its wake, Hartwick became dependent upon other communities to provide employment, goods, and services.

When community vitality is involved, size matters. Hartwick collapsed as an independent entity because it was smaller than Cooperstown, and thereby unable to effectively compete when technological changes permitted greater contact between residents of the two villages. As Cooperstown became the dominant social and economic center in northern Otsego County during the 1970s, it did so because of the decline of its neighbors. Cooperstown had benefited from upscaling, whereas Hartwick residents faced a new reality in rural America.

Historically, Hartwick residents, like those in many rural communities, perceived their village as a self-reliant economic and social system (see Vidich and Bensman 1968). In her research on central New York, Janet Fitchen (1991) commented:

Rural communities are presumed by their members to have individual identities, each different from the next. Uniqueness is an article of faith, an untested assumption, in fact, an assumption that should not be questioned or tested. The ingredients of uniqueness are not always clear, yet people just "know" that their community is unique. (253)

With an inability on the part of Hartwick to be autonomous, many residents shifted at least part of their community loyalties to nearby Cooperstown. By 1980, Cooperstown and Hartwick were part of an Extended Rural Community System (ERCS): a system of villages and their hinterland dependent upon one another for economic and social functionality (Thomas 1998: 17).[1]

An ERCS is formed of two or more formerly autonomous communities. The system is organized around a primary center (e.g., Cooperstown)—the economic and cultural focus of the Extended Rural Community System. In such systems, the primary center is the largest village in the system, its size being the attractor for the centralization of economic functions in the village. Surrounding the primary center are a number of secondary centers (e.g., Hartwick). At times, as in the case of mobile home parks, a secondary center may be a fairly recent addition to the environment. In most cases, however, a secondary center is a formerly autonomous place that, through the processes of economic restructuring, has been subsumed as a part of the ERCS. Secondary centers are, typically, dependent upon the primary center for most economic functions, although this varies with the size of the village and its geographical location within the system (Thomas 1998).

If the ERCS represents the centralization of economic and social forces, it should be understood that the pattern is unique to sparsely settled rural areas. In rural areas generally, population has become more deconcentrated, but economic and social functions have become more centralized than those typically found in urban areas, such as Utica.[2]

Cooperstown had in common with Utica its status as a primary economic and social center within its system of community. Utica, however, still had a greater population than the entire county of which Cooperstown was the seat, and so the ways in which restructuring affected the two communities were quite different. Similarly, the available options for community revitalization and the ability to attract and retain capital were also quite different between the two communities. So as Cooperstown, the economic and social center of central Otsego County, began to struggle with the erosion of its own economic base as a result of further upscaling, Utica struggled against the loss of its institutions to the increasingly dominant suburbs.

Expected Surprises

Urban renewal in Utica brought with it an expectation that the overall value of the city in terms of tax assessments would rise as it was modernized. In each project, city officials projected that the value of the property involved would rise considerably as new modern buildings replaced the slum structures of the past. With this in mind, many local officials took the news of the 1970 census to be a mixed blessing. The overall population of the metropolitan area had risen to about 340,000 residents, although the city population fell to only ninety thousand. City officials were concerned about the 10 percent drop in population, but were comforted by the prospect of increasing valuation in the center city and continued progress to make up the shortfall. The news was, if anything, a blow to the city's collective self-image: Utica was no longer a city of one hundred thousand.

By the end of the 1970s, the state had lost almost seven hundred thousand residents, mostly in upstate New York. As the hard times of the 1970s dragged on, Utica was at a disadvantage due to the gridlock in its political system, high unemployment rates that lingered from the loss of the textiles industry, and its proximity to larger cities. Manufacturing began to leave upstate New York cities in increasing numbers, and Utica again was hard hit. Sperry Rand, still building the descendents of the Univac, scaled back operations in Utica as Silicon Valley became more important in the computer industry. In 1986, Sperry Rand and Burroughs Corporation merged to form Unisys and pulled out of Utica entirely. Such companies as General Electric, Bendix, and the few textile firms still in the area also scaled back production, resulting in more layoffs in manufacturing. In addition to factory layoffs, many companies began to consolidate their service divisions in Syracuse. Located less than an hour from Utica, Syracuse contained twice the number of residents and was within easy driving distance for sales personnel and insurance claims adjusters. In many cases, metropolitan Utica lost jobs; in others, Utica simply never gained the jobs that went to Syracuse instead.

Given the troubles afflicting the metropolitan area during the 1970s, it was not altogether surprising that the 1980 census brought unequivocal bad news: Utica was home to only 75,632 residents (USBC 1980). In regard to population loss, Utica was similar to other major cities. But the suburbs lost population as well, and the metropolitan area population fell to only 320,000 (USBC 1980). Only Buffalo, dealing at the time with the loss of the steel industry, fared worse. Progress was over.

Questionable Costs

Two new skyscrapers rose over downtown Utica in 1970, one to house state offices and the other to contain county offices. Across the street from the new state office building, an empty lot of grass stretched for two blocks to give a view of the new Kennedy Parking Garage and the buttress upon which the new Hilton was supposed to have been built (but never was). A visitor to the city in 1977 commented, "It was like Boston Common done bad; it looked really dumb." The new route 5s, a six-lane boulevard, slashed through the city and condemned any building north of its path to putrefy. Every building on the east side of Genesee Street from Oriskany Street (NY 5s) north to Bagg's Square, a three-block stretch, was demolished to build a new bridge; it condemned the historic center of the city to wear a permanent concrete umbrella. Given the view of the concrete approach to the bridge across the street and the general isolation of the area from the rest of downtown, the decay of the area north of Oriskany Street accelerated and today no longer functions as a viable economic environment.

As the 1970s turned to the 1980s, the character of Utica's decline changed.[3] In 1947, most of the central business district as then defined was oriented toward pedestrian traffic. More than 80 percent of the city's blocks presented the pedestrian with either a building or a park.[4] On the Block-Quintile (BQ) scale, a measure of the pedestrian friendliness of an area, downtown Utica scored a 14.03 out of a maximum of fifteen (see appendix A). The pedestrian friendliness of the area was fairly uniform, whether on Genesee Street or on the side streets.[5] But as the city demolished large tracts of land, some of which were officially in the central business district, the pedestrian friendliness of the area diminished considerably. Further, private businesses bought buildings and replaced them with parking lots in a good example of private benefit unintentionally translating into social harm. In other cases, buildings became the property of the city due to nonpayment of taxes and were eventually demolished. The net effect was that by 1995, the BQ score for the area had dropped to 9.79. Most of the decline was on the side streets, as a six-and-one-half block stretch of Genesee Street was maintained as the showpiece of the city.

With so much of the south side of Columbia Street demolished for RP1, it is not surprising that the shopping district along that street also entered a period of decline. It had been a viable shopping district since the late nineteenth century when a trolley line was built there, and along with Bleeker Street formed the heart of downtown Utica's shopping district.[6] The demolition of its south side hindered economic activity on Columbia Street almost immediately. Economic activity was curtailed by 1970 and did not recover. Urban renewal effectively destroyed the Columbia Street shopping district.

Bleeker Street, perpendicular to the east of Genesee, was lined with stores as it stretched into the heart of Italian east Utica. Along with smaller specialty shops, Osber's Department Store, and several restaurants, Bleeker Street was known especially for its furniture stores. The John Bleeker project, named after the nineteenth-century developer of the neighborhood, bulldozed much of the area, replacing numerous stores with apartment buildings, a new fire station, and several parking lots. The Towne East Mall, considered the centerpiece of the project, attempted to divert pedestrians from the street into the enclosed mall. With parking below the building and in a large lot next door, city officials hoped that the mall would bring shoppers into the city from the suburbs. Within only a few years, however, Towne East proved itself to be a failure; Utica's Riverside Mall, on the city line in suburb-like north Utica, proved to be the first truly successful enclosed mall.

The impact of the physical restructuring of downtown was noticeable in the local newspaper.[7] An analysis of the locations of businesses advertising in the *Observer-Dispatch* reveals that from 1899 through 1964, the majority of advertisements were bought by downtown businesses. It also reveals the impact of the automobile. In 1899 and 1904, all of the advertisements were run for downtown businesses. It was not realistic to expect residents of particular neighborhoods to travel to business districts in other areas of the city, as they were accessible to the majority of city residents, primarily by foot or by trolley, so many shopkeepers did not advertise in the *Observer-Dispatch* as it was not necessary to reach the mass market of the entire city. Instead, neighborhood newspapers, several written in languages other than English, were better avenues of advertising due to their lower rates. By 1909, however, there had appeared an advertisement for Central Auto, an automobile retailer. The automobile allowed retailers in neighborhood business districts to invite shoppers to drive directly to their stores, given that the right product was for sale. It also allowed retailers of specialty items such as phonographs and coal to operate in less costly areas of the city with the expectation that customers would seek them out. As a result, the percentage of advertisements run by downtown businesses declined from 82.5 percent in 1944 to about sixty percent between 1959 and 1964 even as the downtown businesses were prosperous and advertising more than in the past. The rise of suburban shopping centers also impacted downtown advertising. By 1974, the percentage of advertisements for downtown establishments had fallen to little over 20 percent, whereas suburban businesses accounted for about one-half of the ads found in the newspaper.

Within the central business district, a similar pattern was evident. In one issue in 1949, eleven advertisements were for businesses on Columbia Street, whereas there were twelve for those on Genesee Street. Not surprisingly, the demolition of much of the south side of Columbia Street in 1959 and 1960 had reduced the number of advertisements for businesses on Columbia Street to three in 1964. Bleeker Street also showed a reduction in the number of advertisements. By the 1970s, the downtown Utica shopping district consisted primarily of Genesee Street, with businesses on the side streets struggling with the physical decline of the buildings around them in the form of empty storefronts, empty lots or, in winter, unshoveled sidewalks. Of thirty storefronts photographed by Przybycien and Romanelli (1976) on the north side of Liberty Street in 1975 and 1976, twenty-one were vacant. By 2001, twenty-three had been demolished. In contrast, of eighteen photographed on

Genesee Street, all were occupied in 1976. In 2000, there was only one vacancy in the storefronts pictured. (Four storefronts were demolished when the Devereax Building burned in 1990 and was replaced by a public square and fountain).

The physical decline of downtown was the visible result of the shifting of employees out of downtown and the concentration of former Utica companies into larger companies headquartered in other cities. As the usable portion of the central business district shrank to a few short blocks of Genesee Street, many in Utica perceived the decline to be a problem of its retail economy. As one resident stated in 1999:

I miss the stores. You could go downtown and walk all afternoon from store to store, look in the windows or buy a knick-knack. And then they were gone. They tore down some; some they needed for, well, something. But they closed, and downtown got quiet like it is now, and nobody wants to go where it's quiet like that.

Still others believed the problem to be a lack of adequate parking:

I knew the place was dead when the New Hartford Shopping Center put up a billboard right on the Busy Corner with a picture of a parking meter with a line through it. No meters there; free parking and lots of it. That's what killed downtown Utica, no damn parking.

Concern for the business district often centered on the visible indicators of health, such as cleanliness and occupied storefronts. Several efforts to "clean up" the city and increase retail activity were attempted from the 1970s through the 1990s. To some, this still seemed the obvious problem:

Nobody wants to go there—it's filthy. The street's a mess and funny looking people walk around. If they cleaned it up and put some good places in there, people might go back. But me, I'd rather go to the mall.

Attempts to improve the aesthetic appearance of downtown have centered on Genesee Street, with full-scale efforts being made between 1973 and 1975, 1979 and 1981, 1989, and from 1995 through 1999.

These efforts have functioned as cosmetic remedies to deeper structural problems, and as such have had a minimal impact on the overall decline of the central city. The demolition of the residential areas surrounding downtown, once decried as slums, had the effect of shifting the population that remained in the city away from downtown. The movement of office buildings to other parts of town or to the suburbs had the effect of sending away the workers who provided the daytime economy of the area. The opening of new stores in the suburbs made it all too easy for most residents of the metropolitan area to forget that there was a shopping district downtown. And the definition of downtown primarily as a district for shopping has precluded any meaningful policy to try to bring back to the area the other necessary functions, such as residential areas, manufacturing, and office employment.

By 1980, the last of Utica's downtown department stores, the Boston Store, had left the city. For many, it was the last reason to go downtown. In 1982, Sangertown Square Mall was built in suburban New Hartford. Larger than Riverside Mall, the enclosed mall provided a retail anchor that had greater economies of scale than downtown. The decline of the central business district that had been slowly taking place throughout the 1970s finally culminated during the 1980s. Not only was there competition from New Hartford, it was stronger than downtown. On the first Saturday of December in 1954, the *Observer-Dispatch* ran twenty-nine advertisements for downtown stores; on the same date in 1984, the paper ran five. The only conceivable benefit is that it is difficult today, at even the busiest time of day or night, to not find a parking space within a block or two of any downtown establishment.

As an industrial city facing competition from newer suburbs and nearby metropolitan areas, Utica has had few weapons with which to stem the tide of urban decay. During the same time period, however, Cooperstown faced competition from merchants in Oneonta, twenty-five miles to its south, and the very same Utica suburbs to its north. As Cooperstown faced the same economic pressures, the village was privileged with a different set of options that had been developing since World War II.

Economic Supplement

From the end of World War II through the 1970s, the local market in Cooperstown was profitable and as such Main Street contained businesses aimed primarily the local community. In Cooperstown, as in Hartwick in previous years, the vast majority of businesses relied upon the local market for economic survival. One Cooperstown resident recalled:

There were stores you could use; that you really needed. You could get clothes and shoes and a good meal if you wanted it. You didn't really have to leave.

To be sure, there were businesses directed at the tourism market, but the tourist-oriented businesses were greatly outnumbered by community-oriented businesses. Another resident remembered:

There was Wood's on Main Street—they had souvenirs and jerseys and other baseball shit. And the batting range, and a tourist shop next to that. Maybe one or two others—not many.

A business owner shared:

In the seventies, this place was a real town. There were clothing shops and barbers and whatever else you wanted. We didn't get all the (baseball) card shops 'til the eighties, and then they took over.

The orientation of the economy toward the resident population, both in the village and increasingly in surrounding villages, limited the impact of the growing tourism economy. The local market was profitable, so merchants did not feel the need to cater primarily to visitors. As one business owner shared:

I don't think there was ever a time when the tourists weren't important here. I mean, a lot of places sold post cards and maybe some gum cards. But you focused on the locals—you didn't want to alienate them. The tourists gave you a little extra income, but the locals kept you going.

The museums, the art scene, and the Glimmerglass Opera Company gave Cooperstown "a ritzy feel; we're a high class town." But the tourism economy was a supplement to the community-oriented economy, as one resident stated:

Baseball was big, but it wasn't the only game in town. We had our own (community-oriented) stores, and the other museums mattered, too. Then it changed. Not overnight, but real slow.

The Baseball Hall of Fame helped Cooperstown maintain a tourism economy even after the resort patrons looked elsewhere for a leisurely vacation.[8] The end of World War II brought an almost immediate boom to the museum, attendance jumping from 8,266 in 1945 to 22,066 in 1946. From 1946 to 1951, attendance increased roughly four and one-half times, to 97,645. Throughout the 1950s and 1960s, American hegemony in the world economy and ever-larger stadiums allowed large numbers of the working and middle classes to partake of the national pastime (Reiss 1989). As baseball grew, so did the Hall of Fame. From 1955 through 1965, attendance averaged over 144,000 per year. But the stability of the local market, growing with the centralization of the local economy in Cooperstown, meant that community-oriented businesses were still profitable. As a result, such businesses continued to dominate the business district and only a small number of businesses catered to the growing tourism market.

Often overlooked, Cooperstown's other museums also experienced a period of steady growth. The *Freeman's Journal* yearly praised the gains of the village's museums. The museums of the New York State Historical Association, Fenimore House and the Farmer's Museum, completed a trinity of village attractions. By 1970, there were five museums, and Cooperstown dubbed itself the "Village of Museums." The museums all had a common theme: history. Historical folk art, carriages, Native American artifacts. The Farmer's Museum moved buildings from throughout the region to a simulated "village cross-roads." Even the Baseball Hall of Fame was regarded as much history museum as sports shrine. Cooperstown assumed a new identity: Historic Cooperstown. The village actively marketed itself as a center for historic architecture and values, emphasizing its role as the home of James Fenimore Cooper and the mythological birthplace of baseball.

Tourism continued to grow throughout the late 1960s and early 1970s, as Baseball Hall of Fame attendance rose from 146,454 in 1965 to 230,836 in 1971 (NBHFM 1997). Attendance at the Hall grew faster than at the other museums, and by the early 1970s the *Freeman's Journal* was announcing attendance figures for the Hall of Fame first and the other museums second—an implicit acknowledgement of the Hall's role as the primary tourist draw. Except for the peak of 260,763 in 1973, the Hall's attendance was relatively stable from 1971 to 1985, averaging approximately 221,000 visitors per year.

From the early 1970s through 1990, the composition of the tourist population changed dramatically. As the village tried to bolster the historic Cooperstown image, the tourists were increasingly likely to be interested exclusively in baseball, to the detriment of the other museums. By 1985, only the NYSHA museums and the Baseball Hall of Fame were left. Attendance figures for the NYSHA museums tell the story.[9] At both the Farmer's Museum and Fenimore House, attendance peaked in 1973 at 141,624 and 63,065, respectively. By 1980, attendance at the Farmer's Museum had dropped to 92,716, and slowly declined to 64,430 in 1997. Whereas the average yearly attendance during the 1960s and 1970s was 120,483 and 121,868, respectively, attendance averaged only 77,798 during the 1990s. Figures are similar for Fenimore House, which after averaging 57,202 visitors per year during the 1960s, dropped to 40,544 and 39,712 during the 1980s and 1990s, respectively. As the Baseball Hall of Fame became more popular, Cooperstown acquired the reputation as "Baseball Town," as more than one tourist noted.

It is a reasonable hypothesis that as this reputation developed, likely visitors to the other museums found the village less attractive, although more study is needed on this point. What is certain is that through the combination of ease of shopping in Oneonta and Utica and the increased attendance at the Hall of Fame, Cooperstown business was able to concentrate on the niche market rapidly becoming dominant in the community. This conflicted with the image of the "quaint, rural town" area residents had of the village, and so the infrastructure not in accordance with this image came to be resented by many local residents. When the Corvette Americana Hall of Fame opened in 1992, the museum quickly developed a stigma for being "out of character," a euphemism that presupposed that the Historic Cooperstown model had not been altered during the 1980s. A similar reaction was on display when a baseball camp opened several years later, and the addition of a shopping center not only violated the cultural ideal of Historic Cooperstown, but posed an economic threat as well.

Pride

Throughout the 1970s and 1980s, the village government passed a series of laws meant to reinforce the rural character of the "Historic Cooperstown" model. Many local residents believed their village to have an idealistic rural charm. As one resident shared:

This is the cutest town in New York. How many other towns have flowers on Main Street? Sure, some do. But none of them compare to what we do in Cooperstown.

To at least some degree the decline of surrounding villages contributed to this perception. As residents of other communities shopped in Cooperstown, their own business districts fell into disrepair. Economic decline was evident in nearly every community for a thirty-mile radius, and in comparison Cooperstown's quaint streets were rather exceptional. One resident summed it up nicely:

I don't understand why anyone wants to live anywhere else. There aren't any other towns quite like this in the world. You go up to Fort Plain or Herkimer and they look so run down. Oneonta's too big; I mean, it's a city. A little city, but a city. No, Cooperstown is about as ideal a town as you can get . . . it's like a town right out of the fifties.

The fact that tourists came to the village served as a confirmation of the quaint "Historic Cooperstown" model that many residents had accepted. One resident expressed this sentiment:

There are times that I'm sick to death of all the tourists. But can you blame them? Cooperstown is the prettiest village in the state. We have the lake and great houses—where else do you find towns as cute as Cooperstown?

In order to preserve the Historic Cooperstown model against an emerging "Baseball Town" model, legislation followed attitudes that sought to limit development and control the aesthetics of the village. During this period, ordinances were adopted meant to enhance the

quaint, historical character of the village. The entire village was eventually designated as historic and placed on the National Registry of
Historic Places; vinyl and aluminum siding was prohibited from older
structures; mobile homes were prohibited; and signs were required to
meet certain specifications. Ideally, signs would be small and hung
perpendicular to the building, with another larger sign over the door.
While not required, newer signs were often of wood and with antique
designs. Subdued colors were also ideal. For businesses on side streets,
small "sandwich boards" listing all of the street's businesses could be
placed at the corner. Early photographs of Main Street, such as those
in the Smith and Telfer collection at the New York State Historical
Association, actually showed a greater variety of signage—most not
nearly as elaborate as the new signs, and some very large indeed.
Many residents disliked the modern signs of plastic with interior light-
ing, and sought a more historic character for the village. Historical
accuracy was not the primary goal, but rather the conformity with the
cultural iconography of small town America. Cooperstown's Main
Street evolved into the cultural image of a historic small town rather
than a previous incarnation of itself. Both in the minds of locals and
tourists, the village was a "cute little town" worth a visit.

In the surrounding countryside, this image of rural life began to
inform new architecture. While many low-income residents moved into
mobile homes, many members of the middle class built homes on subdivided farms that sought to replicate the idealized image of the farm.
In many cases, the homestead portion of a farm was purchased, the
house restored, and the barn treated to a new coat of red paint. In other
cases, new homes were built that seemed to match the rural image.
Soapbox houses, not an architectural style indigenous to the area, are
one such example of the new rural ideal becoming a part of the local
reality. In most cases, however, a five to ten acre parcel of land was
treated to a double-wide mobile home or a modular home (OCPD 1997).

Businesses catering primarily to urban dwellers seeking a weekend
excursion to the country have also sprouted. Bed and breakfast inns,
an apple cider mill, antique dealers, and numerous craft shops invite
the urban visitor to partake of simple rural pleasures and handiwork—
but the products are of commercial and symbolic importance rather
than utilitarian. In most cases, such items were produced in distant
(often urban) locales and are marketed as authentic rural paraphernalia. As one business owner commented in 2001:

You know, sometimes I think that the people who buy our food products
actually think that (my wife) slaves away all day in the kitchen just so they
can have that jar of jam ... We actually have it made to order with our own
label from a company in New England.

During the 1970s, the growth of such tourist-oriented businesses was limited by a downtown Cooperstown catering to the local population, and so such growth often occurred in smaller villages such as Fly Creek or in the hinterland.

Transformation

In 1980, community-oriented businesses in Cooperstown relied not only on area residents but also on consumers driving from as far as twelve miles away. Those consumers living outside the village made suburban-style commutes everyday, and as such had a variety of choices available to them once in their cars. During the 1980s, many began to drive to larger communities for goods they once bought in Cooperstown. For residents of Milford and Hartwick, the small city of Oneonta was only five minutes more distant. Regional discounters, such as Ames and Jamesway, had located near the city, often under-cutting prices in Cooperstown while providing a greater selection. With the opening of Southside Mall in 1980, residents of Cooperstown and its satellites shopped increasingly in the Oneonta area and Cooperstown faced competition in its community-oriented economy. A trip to one of the malls in the Utica area not only provided the goods and services being sought, but also provided a day of entertainment. By the middle of the 1980s, many merchants in Cooperstown were forced either to close or redirect their merchandising in directions that were more profitable.

It was during the 1980s that tourism assumed the role of the most visible economic activity in the village. The vast majority of the tourists arrived to visit the National Baseball Hall of Fame and Museum, and the village's other museums, having completed their relative decline, maintained stable admissions from the middle of the 1980s to the present (CAP 1993).

Not only was the tourist economy growing, it was a niche market. Many local merchants began to sell baseball-related merchandise, even in such establishments as pharmacies and hardware stores. By 1990, many of the village's staple community-oriented businesses had either closed or by and large converted into tourist shops. Many of those that closed were replaced by tourist-oriented businesses. Area residents wanted the selection and pricing available in urban areas, and as such money flowed out of the village. But rather than decline like Hartwick and downtown Utica, Cooperstown became transformed from a community-oriented to tourism-oriented economy. Even the movie theater, facing fierce competition from Oneonta theaters twenty-five miles away, began to show baseball-related films daily during the summer before finally closing in 1987.

By the end of the decade, many area residents held ambivalent views about the benefits of tourism. Parking was a serious problem and many of the staple stores of Main Street had been taken over by baseball card shops and restaurants only open part of the year. But Cooperstown had not declined; its BQ score of 14.2 in 1947 was unchanged in 1997. In contrast, Utica's score had fallen to 9.79 in 1997 (from 14.03 in 1947) and Hartwick's had fallen from 14.16 in 1947 to 10.83 in 1997. Cooperstown had retained the appearance of a quaint little town with full storefronts and a lively street life. It was only on closer examination that one noticed that the quality of life so cherished by its residents had escaped them in large part due to their sharing it with others.

Chapter 9

Deconstructing Utica

The despair of the 1990s approached that of the 1970s. The region lost thousands of jobs, residents fled the area, and entire communities were forced to question the function they served in the global economy. A general pattern emerged in which children graduated not only from high school but from their hometowns as well. And the patterns established during the 1980s served as the basis for continued adaptations to an increasingly marginal position in the world. The region that contributed so much to the establishment of the information age and the consumer economy found itself enmeshed in that system without an obvious role of its own.

No Rest for the Weary

During the time that Utica lost many of its administrative functions and struggled to retain its industrial base, its sister city of Syracuse was continuing its trend of growth and regional dominance. With a larger and more educated population than Utica, Syracuse had distinct advantages over Utica as early as World War II. So despite a metropolitan area population of more than three hundred thousand, Utica suffered the same trends of upscaling as its smaller neighbors to the south. Not because of population, but because of its proximity to a city of even greater population. Located less than an hour apart, the two often competed against one another for increasingly important investment by non-local firms.

Home to Syracuse University and two smaller colleges, Syracuse was poised to dominate the region to a degree it had not before. In contrast, Utica had only Hamilton College in nearby Clinton as an educational institution prior to the establishment of Utica College after

World War II. Despite government investment in the city, Utica remains the only major metropolitan area in New York State without a major university, doctoral programs, or a professional school. Machine leaders during the 1950s recognized the competitive disadvantage this represented and worked to establish Utica College, Mohawk Valley Community College, the main campus of the State University of New York, and even to move Ithaca College to Utica. The most promising opportunity seemed to be the establishment of SUNY Institute of Technology (SUNY Tech) during the 1960s, but opposition to a full-fledged technology university by cost conscious politicians and representatives of the two-year Agriculture and Technology colleges resulted in SUNY Tech becoming an "upper division" college that offered only the last two years of a bachelors degree. Instead of becoming a public version of Massachusetts Institute of Technology, the college instead became what a Cooperstown High School graduate referred to as "a freak school. Spend two years at Morrisville and transfer to (SUNY) Utica/Rome. Right! If I'm gonna spend two years at Mo-ville, I'll transfer to (Rensellaer Polytechnic Institute)." This also prevented SUNY Tech from developing into a major research institution that might have attracted both employers and employees to the region and could possibly have helped to retain the computer industry that had been nurtured in the city and then moved away. A SUNY Tech competitive with other universities would not have given Utica a competitive edge over other metropolitan areas with their own universities, but neither would the area have been at a competitive disadvantage. In contrast, Syracuse was comnpetitive.

The expressway system similarly put Utica at an ultimate disadvantage vis-à-vis Syracuse. As the demise of the emergent urban growth machine became apparent, the ability of area officials to win funds for the metropolitan area became hampered as the mayor and city council tended to bicker amongst themselves. The 1960s witnessed competition among metropolitan areas to secure interstate highways that connected them to other cities and local expressways that connected the cities to the growing suburbs. Syracuse did well in the competition, eventually winning not only Interstate 81, which ran north to Canada and south to Binghamton, but several other expressways that crisscrossed the area. Although the grand vision of Syracuse engineers was never fully realized, a substantial proportion was completed and thus the city embodied an aura of progress into the 1970s. In contrast, Utica planners envisioned an arterial highway through the city that, due to the opposition of some residents, was built with traffic lights in the heart of the city—the only major metropolitan area in New York where the major expressway does so. Additional plans for expressways running from the New York Thruway in Westmoreland (to the west) through the Sauquoit Valley (to the southeast) and from Utica to Rome were only partially completed. Other plans, such as a continuation of the arterial highway beyond the suburb of Clinton and additional connectors to the Thruway were never even attempted. When during the 1970s plans were touted for an expressway to the south, through Otsego County via Hartwick and Oneonta, to meet with the Southern Tier Expressway (New York 17), area officials were lackluster in their support. A connection to Binghamton and I-81 was deemed more important, but neither was ever built. By the 1980s, Syracuse rightfully promoted itself as "the crossroads of New York State" while Utica was forced to highlight its single Thruway exit and second-rate expressway system. A visitor from Boston commented in 1998 that "real cities have real highways . . . that's why Utica's a wanna-be city."

Albeit unintentionally, the United States Census Bureau contributed to Utica's increasingly harsh image problem. Prior to 1960, the Census Bureau classified the Utica-Rome metropolitan area as consisting of Oneida and Herkimer counties. Syracuse, located as it is in the middle of Onondaga County, was classified as consisting of only Onondaga County as its metropolitan area. The result was the appearance of statistical parity: metropolitan Utica-Rome contained 263,163 residents in 1940, whereas metropolitan Syracuse contained 295,108. In 1960, however, the definition of the Syracuse metropolitan area was changed to include Onondaga, Oswego, and Madison Counties. Metropolitan Utica-Rome contained 330,771 residents; Onondaga County contained 398,203 but the new definition meant that the Syracuse metropolitan area was reported at 563,781 residents. For potential investors and marketers, Syracuse was now considerably more attractive the Utica. After the 1990 census, the definition for metropolitan Syracuse was changed once again to include Cayuga County, so the 1990 census reported Utica-Rome with a population of 316,633 compared with 742,237 in Syracuse.

Utica's own economic problems cannot be ignored, however. After the flight of the textile industry during the 1950s, the metropolitan area had an unemployment rate higher than the New York State average until 1990. Not surprisingly, metropolitan Utica grew at a slower rate than the rest of the state during the same time period. Had the growth rate for the metropolitan area simply mirrored that of New York State as a whole, the 1998 population would have been 381,001. Instead, the population was 294,677—22.7 percent lower. In contrast, metropolitan Syracuse gained population as many of the administrative and white-collar jobs once or potentially found in Utica were created in Syracuse instead. Onondaga County's population in 1998 was 458,301, 7.3 percent higher than what would be expected if the metropolitan area had grown only as fast as the state.

As the 1990s opened, this dynamic between the two cities and the relative position of Utica in the world economy as a whole constituted an ominous omen.

Defending the Nation I

Griffiss Air Force Base in nearby Rome had become a key part of the Strategic Air Command. For decades throughout the Cold War, warplanes circled the region ready to traverse the Artic and drop their payload of nuclear weapons on Soviet cities and bases (Arkin and Fieldhouse 1985). For Rome and Utica, the thousands of Air Force personnel stationed in Rome translated into a stable economic force amid the chaos of the civilian economy. Home to Rome Cable and Revere Copper-Brass, Rome's main industry after World War II became the military. Located twelve miles from Utica, area residents found jobs at the base and the other businesses that serviced base personnel. It was because of the presence of Griffiss Air Force Base that the American Social Hygiene Association sought to gauge the level of vice in Utica. The report helped to fuel the sin city scandals of the 1950s. It was similarly the presence of the base and the high technology Rome Air Force Laboratory that aided local companies like General Electric, Bendix, and Sperry-Rand.

Area leaders had fought to keep the base since the end of World War II. Besides geographic advantages, they often pointed to the effect a base realignment would have on the local economy. For instance, in 1974 they fought a Pentagon plan to trim nearly fourteen thousand military and civilian jobs from the base on the basis that such an action would cost the region one hundred million dollars per year and aggravate the 10 percent unemployment rate of the area (NYT, 23 Nov. 1974). The result was that restructuring of the base was often relatively minor, such as the 1987 elimination of the fighter interrupter squadron (NYT, 7 Jan. 1987). But as the Cold War came to an end, legislators looked for a "peace dividend" derived by cuts in the number of military bases.

The Military Base–Closing Commission was formed in 1992 and voted in June of 1993 to close two major Air Force bases and downsize operations at three more. In order to minimize opportunities for political malfeasance, the recommendations were sent to President Clinton as a group that could only be rejected together (WP, 25 Jun. 1993). Griffiss Air Force Base would lose four thousand jobs, leaving only Rome Air Force Lab and a new Accounting Center announced by President Clinton in 1994 (NYT, 4 May 1994). As a result, the city of Rome lost almost ten thousand residents between 1990 and 2000, half of what the metropolitan area lost during the decade.

Competition for the dwindling number of defense related jobs was fierce. Supporters of Hanscom Air Force Base near Boston attempted to bring the jobs at Rome Lab to Massachusetts in 1995. One of the arguments made was that Boston had a stronger high technology economy. As a Boston area professor opined in 1995, "We have Route 128, M.I.T., and major corporations. Do they even have computers in Rome?" Faced with tough competition in the form of Senator Ted Kennedy and the companies and universities at the heart of the "Massachusetts Miracle," Oneida County officials retained a public relations firm that challenged the numbers and ultimately won the day. The *Observer-Dispatch* proclaimed that the rebuilding of the area economy was to begin (OD, 25 Jun. 1995). The *New York Times* tritely called the decision a "reprieve" (NYT, 23 Jun. 1995). The *Boston Globe,* in contrast, decried the commission's decision that "denied Hanscom Air Force Base in Bedford a gain of 585 civilian jobs . . . as a blow to supporters of Hanscom" (BG, 23 Jun. 1995, 3).

Griffiss Air Force Base is now Griffiss Park, a technology park with a runway capable of landing some of the largest airplanes ever built and the Space Shuttle. According to area officials, the park is filling and acting as a generator for new jobs. Once the site of anti–nuclear weapons political demonstrations, Griffiss is today best remembered for the last incarnation of the Woodstock Music Fair in 1999. Drawing over two hundred thousand people, the three days of peace and music ended in a riot. The Pittsburgh *Post-Gazette* commented, "with an acute self-consciousness, (this generation) made Woodstock memorable" (PPG, 1 Aug. 1999, B1). That same day, an area resident worried, "this is what people will remember about Rome."

Defending the Nation II

The expansion of General Electric in Utica after World War II was greeted with much fanfare.[1] Even after the company had transferred the manufacture of clock radios to Kentucky, area residents took pride that General Electric left much of its most advanced operations in the old Mohawk Valley Cotton Mills, former producer of Utica Sheets, and its new facility on French Road. Advanced radar and electronics technology was developed in Utica as the defense industry enhanced the city's position as the first Silicon Valley in the 1950s and 1960s. At that time, Utica's economy, focused as it was on the new aerospace and computer industries, appeared similar to that of California. But as with the realignment of Griffiss Air Force Base, General Electric's officials saw a downside to the end of the Cold War. As one official stated in the New York Times, "The world's changing political outlook will result in a smaller, more intensely competitive worldwide defense market" (NYT, 28 Apr. 1990). In addition, the center of the high technology industries had moved to other states. On April 27, 1990, GE Aerospace announced the elimination of 4,200 jobs at five plants, including in Utica. It was only the first round.

In April 1993, Martin Marietta acquired GE Aerospace. In May 1994, the company announced plans to move the infrared sensors operation in Utica to Orlando, Florida. In 1995, the French Road plant, the only remaining facility, would lose two hundred employees (BS, 21 Jan. 1995). In March, Martin Marietta merged with Lockheed and began investigating ways to eliminate duplication in its facilities; the Utica plant was among twelve to be closed (Lockheed Martin, 26 Jun. 1995). Sensing such action, Senator Al D'Amato had reportedly "flared up on the phone . . . hollering and cursing at (President Norman) Augustine" in an attempt to save the jobs in Utica (WP, 27 Jun. 1995, D01). An area resident at the time commented:

Talk about the market being bullshit! We have engineers and computer scientists for a dime a dozen here, and no company will touch us. They'd rather pay fifty grand a year to people in San Jose.

The sentiment was not uncommon, and the observation that major high technology companies ignored the area was by and large valid. For the most part, the unemployed had to move.

The result of the restructuring of the local defense industry sent the region once again into a spiral of population decline. By the 1990 census, the metropolitan area had posted its third population decline, dropping from 340,670 in 1970 to 316,633 in 1990. The 1990s resembled the 1970s, however, when the region lost twenty thousand residents. By 2000, the population of the metropolitan area had dropped to 299,896 (USBC 2000). Even as political leaders in Washington praised the booming national economy, Utica dropped to only 60,651 residents in the city and there were no major building projects even in the suburbs (USBC 2000). Whereas as late as 1989 Alan Ehrenhalt (1992) described Utica as "little more than the depressed core of its reasonably healthy metropolitan area" (121), the 1990s called even that assessment into question. The city itself had fallen into disrepair, the suburbs were lethargic, and the global economy appeared to have passed the area by.

An Air of Desperation

By the middle of the 1990s, the hemorrhaging of the economy and the flight of the population gave the city what an area social scientist termed "an air of desperation. We'll try anything, trust anyone." The *New York Times* compared the situation in Utica and other upstate cities to the fiscal crisis in New York City during the 1970s (NYT, 25 Mar. 1996).

The success of Cooperstown in maintaining the appearance of community viability was an inspiration for residents of other upstate communities struggling with increasing assaults upon their own hometowns. As early as the 1970s, communities throughout the region attempted to replicate Cooperstown's formula with halls of fame of their own. In Oneonta was built the Soccer Hall of Fame, the (horse) Trotting Hall of Fame was built in Saratoga Springs, and the Boxing Hall of Fame in Canastota. Other towns, such as Little Falls and Cherry Valley, attempted to remake themselves into stereotypic images of small town America through historic districts and new festivals. In Utica, the success of the Boilermaker Road Race—the largest fifteen kilometer running race in the United States—inspired their own plans for tourism notoriety.

When the National Distance Running Hall of Fame inducted its first members in 1998, the ceremony took place at the campus of Hamilton College, eight miles from its future location. In short order the museum opened in an abandoned shoe store on Genesee Street across from the approach for the bridge covering Bagg's Square. News reports throughout the decade posited the Bagg's Square area, roughly three blocks in each direction from the birthplace of the city, as a historic area that could be used for economic development. A New York Mills resident commented in 1999:

It's like they don't know there's a bridge there. I feel like saying, you tore it (Bagg's Square) down you dumb shit. Nobody's gonna walk under that scary freakin' bridge to get from a running museum to a train station because the area's disgusting. But they gotta know that.

Historic preservation and economic development projects in the city were spread throughout the historic expanse of the downtown area, and thus none of them created a sense of health in any one area. The renovation of the fifteen-story Hotel Utica begun in 1998 was two blocks from the Running Hall of Fame, which was three blocks from the restored Union Station train station. In between, urban decay continued to grasp the city and acted as a limiting factor in community revitalization. Even the thousands of employees who commuted downtown daily were spread over a wide area and thus did not produce the economies of scale necessary to produce even a small area that most urban dwellers would consider "healthy."

As the Running Hall of Fame opened, local officials were faced with the irony that one of the vices for which Utica was chastised during the 1950s had become the county's largest employer: gambling. Twenty miles to the west, the Oneida Indian Nation attempted to fight the poverty in their midst by building Turning Stone Casino. Within two years, the casino attracted more annual visitors than Cooperstown. For local officials, the development and jobs created by Turning Stone signified hope for the future. For others, the Oneida Nation was a powerful force who had added individual landowners as defendants in a land claim lawsuit against the state and controlled large shares of tax-exempt property. (Landowners in the land claim area were dropped from the suit in 2001.) The tribe also opened tax-exempt gas stations and convenience stores throughout western Oneida and northern Madison Counties. In response, a group called Upstate Citizens for Equality called for the revocation of the nation's tax-exempt status. The passions in support and against Oneida Nation activities has generally made any venture with them what one area scholar called "a political firecracker."

In Utica itself, a three-way race for mayor in 1995 led to the election of Ed Hanna—a former mayor from the 1970s who had made headlines at that time for removing the door to his office and requiring employees at City Hall to answer the phone, "People's Government" (NYT, 20 Sept. 1980: 22). Hanna had been parks commissioner during the McKennon administration and the sin city scandals, but had also become associated with reform during the 1960s (Ehrenhalt 1992). In short order, Hanna made headlines again as he moved to close the Utica Public Library, a move that would have made Utica the largest city in the country without such a library, and then to close a fire station in a neighborhood with one of the highest arson rates in the country. At the same time, he spent city funds to renovate a park in front of City Hall that had been named after him shortly after he left office the first time. He told the *New York Times* that the "city government should be closed down" in an article subtitled, "Utica's Leader Relishes His 'Lousy' Job in a 'Lousy' Place" (NYT, 24 Sept. 1997: B1). In 1997, the CBS newsmagazine *Coast to Coast* (15 Jan. 1997) portrayed him screaming obscenities into his car phone and referring to his city as less than the ideal place to live.[2] And many Uticans agreed.

Hanna had a vision for the city, and it sometimes takes an eccentric to make a vision seem accessible. He recognized that the city was in need of drastic action and that its overall appearance acted as a deterrent for potential investors. Therefore, Hanna sold buildings taken over by the city for as little as one dollar, built new public squares, and enacted new works of public art. At the historic Busy Corner (Bleeker and Genesee Streets), he erected a replica of the Liberty Bell on an empty lot of formerly burned-out buildings and renamed it "Liberty Bell Corner." On a highway median near John and Oriskany Streets, a very large Aluminum sculpture evoking imagery of the American flag was erected. Even the trees that lined Genesee Street, dedicated as Utica's "five-star" main street, were decked with a permanent display of white Christmas lights that served to make the city seem more exciting and "uptown." For a time, it seemed that Utica was on the verge of a renaissance.

Beneath the surface of the new lights and pedestrian plazas was the sad reality that many of the jobs located downtown had moved either to the city-built Utica Business Park three miles from downtown or to the suburbs. With those companies went the population meant to enjoy the amenities of the urban environment. The workers left behind were spread throughout downtown and tended to drive elsewhere for lunch and dinner rather than stay downtown. Special events, such as the Good Ole Summertime festival and Utica Monday Night did succeed in bringing people back into the city, but only for a short hiatus from the suburban lifestyles now shared by city and suburban residents alike. State and federal aid to rebuild the city was only a fraction of what was needed, and private enterprise chose the broad expanses of shopping malls and suburban office complexes over the inner city. Utica was a city of broken windows.

The View from Afar

Increasingly, attention on Utica from the national media has tended to be negative. On a visit from the C-Span tour bus commemorating the journey of Alexis De Tocqueville through the United States in the early nineteenth century, much of the discussion of Utica concerned the problems afflicting the city. Several stories in the *New York Times* and *Buffalo News* have highlighted the financial problems of Utica and other upstate cities. The former mayor, regardless of admirable motives, portrayed the city as a dump. Even in the cartoon *The Simpsons,* a spoof on a film clip from the 1950s admonishes, "better look out Utica, Springfield's a city on the grow." But perhaps the most bitter insult was the city's portrayal as a "backward hick town" (as one resident stated) on the short-lived NBC sitcom *Jenny.*

Utica in itself was not important—the two characters portrayed could have come from Portland, Maine, Burlington, Vermont, or Erie, Pennsylvania—metropolitan areas of similar or smaller size. For the purpose of the show, Utica was only a symbol of small town America.

The first scene was set fifteen years ago. A nun asked two girls why they skipped class to go to a 7-11 convenience store—a chain not present anywhere in Utica. The following scene showed Maggie (a main character) expressing her desire to go to Rome to meet Italian men, although

Utica is home to a large Italian-American population and known regionally for Italian cuisine. She continued: "What is it about Utica that grows a man's butt?"

Later in the same episode, when Jenny and Maggie first arrive in Los Angeles and consider moving there, a Hollywood lawyer advises them to "go back to your little burg; marry a couple of nice local boys named Buck and Bo; join a bowling league; and start poppin' out babies, because this town will swallow you whole." When the two express a certain apprehension about moving, the lawyer states, "L.A. is a very scary town . . . Ooo, scary!" The two decide to move because, in the words of Jenny, "What happened to all the talk about getting out of Utica; leading exciting lives?" The message is clear: small town life is unexciting, and can only be made interesting by leaving one's boring community and moving to Los Angeles, which is big and exciting. Small town people, however, are too naive or stupid to thrive in a large city; too easily intimidated by living in a "scary" place.

In the following episode, the two are invited to a party in Malibu. To Jenny, it means that they will be able to meet with people apparently superior to those in their hometown:

Jenny: We are finally going to be with really hip, cool people.
Maggie: So what are you going to wear?
Jenny: Floral top denim skirt.
Maggie: Oh.
Jenny: What?
Maggie: Well, this is a cutting edge party. I mean, if we want to fit in, we need clothes that say, "L.A."—and that floral top kinda screams "Utica."
Jenny: Teal mini-dress?
Maggie: Utica.
Jenny: Navy blue jump-suit?
Maggie: Utica Prison.

The subtext again contains the message that people in Utica, and by extension small-town America, have decidedly "un-cool" populations. That they are bland. That in Utica, people dress in nonfashionable, unsophisticated, stereotypically rural, attire. This conceptualization of fashion rests on the assumption that what is popular in large cities is fashionable, because the tastes of urban dwellers are inherently superior to what is found in rural America. By extension, one might presume that urban people are superior.

During the same episode, the two go to a body-piercing establishment. Although there were several in the Utica area (two in downtown alone), Jenny and Maggie are ostensibly in this type of shop for the first time. Jenny decides to have her tongue pierced, because "it's about as far from Utica as you can get; no one back there has their tongue pierced . . . our days as small town dorks are over."

The show's presentation of small town life was based largely on popular stereotypes. Small town residents were understood to be simple and naive, and therefore would have trouble "fitting in" with the trendy and sophisticated Los Angeles crowd. Ruralites were symbolic of mundane human existence, and Los Angeles was a remedy for such a life. But ruralites were also cast as deviant—able only to thrive in their own subcultures, somehow immune to (urban based) social constructions of good taste, and incapable of living within the main currents of society. Such a presentation of small town life is indicative of the fact that popular culture carries with it attitudes and beliefs hostile to the reality of small town existence. That a metropolitan area of nearly three hundred thousand residents was portrayed as a small town is indicative of the cultural domination enjoyed by residents of large cities and their suburbs. Perhaps through the perception of a resident of New York, Boston, or Los Angeles, Utica is a small town. For residents of rural communities, Utica is a large city indeed.

While *Jenny* showcased two culturally dysfunctional women ostensibly from Utica, the differing perceptions of this one city illustrated how cognitively distant urban and rural areas are from one another. Two Cooperstown people, after viewing the show, commented:

Re. 1: Utica was used solely as a word. There's no connotation of place attached to the word whatsoever.
Re. 2: Or a lifestyle or a way of life.
Re. 1: Well, they're trying to attach a certain lifestyle to it; but, there's nothing based in reality whatsoever. Utica was just a word.

Another local resident made this comment:

They seemed very white bread for being Catholics raised in Utica. Whether they're Polish Catholics or Italian Catholics or Irish Catholics there would be a lot more ethnicity to them.

There was a latent resentment as many residents viewed a show that claimed to be about them but made no attempt to authenticity. One woman stated, "Except for the term 'hicks,' I don't think they used any local expressions." Another simply stated, "It just plain hurts." Utica was symbolic of the cultural gulf between those in large urban areas and those in small, rural towns. To a person from Los Angeles,

Utica may have seemed a "white bread, boring little town." To a resident of Hartwick, the perception was considerably different:

Seems they don't know what the place is like. They actually call them a bunch of hicks. Shit; every time I go up there I see a bunch of freaks—all nose-rings and purple hair and shit. If they're hicks, what's that make me?

The View from Nearby

The relatively low population of Otsego County, especially in Cooperstown and Hartwick, was manifest in a dearth of services and products that many people in metropolitan areas would consider "basic." A former resident of metropolitan New York said the following:

Beautiful country, you know. But shit, I wish they had just the basics here. You know how long it's been since I had a good bagel? But that's the price you pay. I'd rather live here, so I just have to do without some of the good stuff, like good restaurants, movies, even Taco Bell.

As many newcomers moved into the area for a relaxed lifestyle, they found that their new lives included new stressors, such as narrow roads, inadequate shopping, and limited entertainment options. However, many locals consider their flight from the cities as evidence of urban corruption and decay. Perceptions of urban areas evoked mixed emotions, as they were simultaneously places of refinement and awe while also representative of the problems of mainstream America. While rural life was considered to be an alternative to city life, it could not have continued as it did without the proximity of urban centers.[3]

Otsego County had no television stations, so "local" news was broadcast from Albany, Binghamton, Syracuse, and Utica. In general, it was the Binghamton CBS affiliate (WBNG) and two Utica stations (WKTV, WUTR) that covered the area most often, but even then only sporadically. While a Utica or Binghamton city council meeting would have been covered regularly, meetings of the Otsego County Board of Legislators most often were not. The county was home to one daily newspaper, the Oneonta *Daily Star*. In popular media, the domination of urban interests was nowhere more apparent than in radio. In Cooperstown, 27 FM radio stations could be received at Lake Front Park with little or no static.[4] None of the stations originated in either Cooperstown or Hartwick. In fact, only 14.8 percent of the stations originate from within Otsego County, as shown in Figure 9.1.

Most of the radio stations (62.9 percent) were located in the two nearest metropolitan areas: Utica (40.7 percent) and Albany (22.2 per-

Figure 9.1. Source of Radio Stations Received in Cooperstown, by County of Origin

County of Origin	Number of FM Stations Received	Percent of Total FM Stations Received
Albany	3	11.1
Chenango	2	7.4
Delaware	1	3.7
Fulton	1	3.7
Herkimer	3	11.1
Oneida	10	37.0
Otsego	4	14.8
Rensselaer	2	7.4
Schenectady	1	3.7

Additional source: RadioStation.com (1997)

cent), when stations located in both the central city and contiguous suburbs were counted. The remainder of the stations were broadcast from nonmetropolitan communities.

Utica was the nearest community where the mainstream urban culture was lived and could be experienced. With tall buildings, multilane roadways, expressways, a comprehensive bus system, and other aspects of urban life to which the majority of the American population was accustomed, Utica itself became the interface between the rural lifestyles that were lived in the city's hinterland (such as in Cooperstown and Hartwick) and the mainstream culture that pervaded the media. In this way, Utica also became a symbol for what area residents perceived to be wrong with American society generally.

As in many American cities, the evening news from Utica frequently carried stories of fires, crime, and the occasional political scandal. This influenced how rural residents perceived the metropolitan area. One Hartwick resident commented, "I could never live in a place where they have a crime every day." Another resident stated:

All you ever hear in Utica is that some place burned down or someone got shot. How many houses they got up there? They keep goin' like this, they ain't gonna have any left. The whole goddam place is burnin' down.

Or as a Cooperstown resident commented:

They had another murder up there this week. Boy, I'm glad I don't live there. I wouldn't want to have to watch my back every time I leave the house. Hell, you're not even safe there.

Even as Utica was demonized as just another example of what was wrong with the nation, Utica brought the mainstream urban culture to the isolated villages of northern Otsego County. To varying degrees, many area residents traveled to Utica for, as one resident stated, a "better shopping experience than you can get here or in Oneonta." There were many more stores, more competition in the same economic market, and prices were often lower (Thomas 1998; Thomas et al. 2002). Items found with much difficulty or not at all in Otsego County were normally found in metropolitan Utica. Some residents even perceived the constant traffic volume as stimulating. Entertainment options included several small theatrical companies, several cinemas, nightclubs and bars, and many of the other entertainment options available in any moderate sized urban center. To urban dwellers, these things were rather commonplace. To those living in rural areas, these things were quite special. The options simply are not there at such a level in Hartwick, Cooperstown, or even Oneonta. To find them, one must drive to a metropolitan area. For many in Cooperstown and Hartwick, Utica is that metropolitan area.

Chapter 10

Reconstructing Hartwick

The Cooperstown *Freeman's Journal* had been reporting the story for nearly a year, but it was on November 2, 1989, that the Utica *Observer-Dispatch* finally took an interest. Beneath a picture of President George H. W. Bush holding Jessica McClure—a little girl recently saved after falling in a well—ran a story perhaps equally as emotional for the residents of Cooperstown in the question it posed: whether or not a Pizza Hut restaurant should be allowed in the village (OD, 2 Nov. 1989). The debate was symbolic of the debates of the 1980s and embodied the schizotypal image of the village. The *Observer-Dispatch* editorialized that, as it was not in an historic area, Cooperstown should be open to the restaurant, opining:

As members of a community that makes much of its living from hundreds of thousands of annual visitors to the baseball museum and other attractions, Cooperstown citizens sound a little hollow when they object to commercial development. (OD, 21 Nov. 1989: 10A)

The newspaper then invited comment from its readers.

By a two-to-one ratio, the readers sided with the village. One reader wrote, "Let in one of these fast-food concessions and it will open the door for all the others and then you will have just another commonplace town. Never! Never!" Others begged that developers not "ruin the uniqueness of the beautiful village of Cooperstown" and "Wake up, fat, soft, lazy Americans. We're getting just what we deserved if we don't stop destroying the beautiful creation God gave us" (OD, 28 Nov. 1989, 7A). Like many Cooperstown residents, metropolitan Utica residents valued the village as a bastion against the "modern world" and for its bucolic charm. The encroachment of chain restaurants and other such "modern" institutions seemed to be an assault not only on the village but upon the mythology it embodied. One letter to the editor (in the *Observer-Dispatch*) captured the belief:

Tourists come to Cooperstown, Williamsburg, Mt. Vernon, for example, not only to see national attractions but to escape a commercial atmosphere. . . . It was disturbing to see a big city newspaper being highly critical of the wishes of the people of a small village by stating they sound a "little hollow" objecting to commercial development. (OD, 4 Dec. 1989L: 12A)

Pizza Hut was ultimately not allowed in the village, but the debate foreshadowed others during the 1990s.

Like Disney?

By the late 1990s, the effects of tourism on downtown Cooperstown were quite apparent (see appendix C), and the change continued unabated. In 1997, 18.5 percent of the retail establishments in downtown Cooperstown were community-oriented, such as clothing stores, shoe stores, or pharmacies; by 2001, 12.7 percent were oriented primarily toward the local community (Thomas & Cardona 2002). Specialty stores represented 59.3 percent of the downtown establishments in 1997, one-third of which were specifically oriented toward baseball. In 2001, 65.8 percent were specialty stores, forty percent of which were baseball-oriented (Thomas & Cardona, 2002). During the 1997–1998 winter season, twenty-one of the eighty-one retail businesses closed for one month or more, including five of the downtown restaurants. Given that most tourists arrived during the summer, this was not surprising. But it did make life uncomfortable for local residents during the winter, as one resident shared:

Try and find a cup of coffee in this place during the winter. There's nothin.' Half the restaurants are closed, and the others are only open 'til five (o'clock). Can't blame them, though. Not enough people here to make a livin'—the tourists keep 'em alive.

As tourism grew more dominant, the quaint signs and niche stores turned the village itself into an attraction. Many visitors even spoke of the village in this way:

I've always wanted to see Cooperstown . . . You know, the museums, the lake, the shops. And in the fall! This place is beautiful in fall. This is when people should see it.

The point was not lost on the local residents, who viewed visitors' attitudes as rather humorous, if not annoying. One waitress shared:

I had a family ask me what time Cooperstown closes. Like it's Disneyland. You'd be surprised how many people ask me things like that. Some of 'em really think the town closes.

It has been suggested that the Doubleday baseball creation myth has served to promote a pastoral and idyllic theme for baseball despite wide scholarly agreement that the roots of the game are decidedly urban, specifically in the New York City area (Springwood 1996). As so much of its economy was reliant upon this mythology, Cooperstown developed a symbiotic relationship with the game in promoting such an image. The village and its attractions supported pastoralist ideals by presenting exhibits (including the village it-self) that reinforced those ideals. Baseball, and perhaps more importantly, the Hall of Fame visitor, could cling to a vision of small-town America as it should have been but in reality was not. To this end, Cooperstown projected an image of idyllic rural life via each attraction, and it was this common theme that united a base-ball museum, an art museum, and the small shops that composed the streetscape.[1]

At the Farmer's Museum, buildings throughout the area had been disassembled and reassembled at the museum in order to construct the Village Crossroads. While the presentations and exhibits did seem to portray the local customs and practices fairly well, the architectural flavor of the museum might have led some to assume that ornate stone and brick structures were prevalent in the past. In an area of relatively few natural outcroppings of stone but an abundance of wood, it is no real surprise that stone and brick buildings were most often either public spaces, such as commercial and governmental buildings, or the private homes of the wealthy. Indeed, a large percentage of the historic commercial buildings in downtown Cooperstown are con-structed of wood.

Fenimore House, with one of the largest American folk art collec-tions in the world, served as an anchor for the arts. Several smaller galleries and organizations, such as Gallery 53 and the Cooperstown Art Association, filled out the local visual art scene.[2] The Glimmerglass Opera Company, which had recently constructed a new opera house near Springfield Center at the northern end of Otsego Lake, as well as some small theater companies spread around the area, provided an eclectic performing arts scene.

It was with American folk art that Cooperstown truly excelled: the area was justified in claiming to be a national, if not international, center for such art. Like the buildings of the Farmer's Museum, much of the art tended to portray a rather idyllic rural lifestyle. This was in part a reflection of the local culture—the works of art juxtaposed the purity of country life against the problems associated with city life, resulting in what an art teacher referred to as

happy art. You don't see the type of criticism that you see in New York or Chicago. It's like they're thinking, "Things are good here, and that's what I want to show."

Such a focus also played well with tourists, many of whom traveled to Cooperstown to escape the problems of urban life rather than confront the problems associated with rural life. It was the bucolic past that interested the tourists, not the less glamorous realities of the present.

The business district was subject to a number of regulations that governed any number of aesthetic details from the size of store signs to the placement of street vendors (none allowed). In conjunction with local business, flowers were planted along Main Street each year and a small park was maintained with benches and a tourist information center. The intended image was one of bucolic beauty that reinforced the "small town character," as many residents were fond of saying.

To Find Some Reeboks

The commodification of village life indicative of dominant tourism spawned conflict between competing interests in the area. Whereas many business owners supported the tourism economy as good for the area, many local residents who did not directly benefit considered it to be a nuisance. Parking in the village was especially difficult, but area residents had competing views on how to control such problems. For instance, a downtown merchant commented in 1997:

The big problem with parking is that these people think they should all be able to park downtown. If you live in the village, you should walk to Main Street. If you live outside the village, you should park in the lots and take the trolleys in.[3] The tourists should get the spaces downtown—they need them more.

A Fly Creek resident replied in 1998:

We live here. Where are all the tourists in February? We're here! Some of these places close up when it's just the locals—I guess we don't mean much to them.

Many residents claimed that the village should build a parking garage, but many others argued that a parking garage would breed crime. Some believed a garage was necessary, but that the village should not have to pay the costs of building it:

They're [the tourists] here to see the Hall of Fame, so they should put it up. They [the village] shouldn't give them any new permits until they agree to build a garage. They can put it right behind Newberry's (store) and it would probably make that dumpy parking lot look better than it does now.

Despite the fact that linking building permits to the provision of infrastructure to support a new building is common practice in many municipalities across the country, Cooperstown officials chose not to do so. One resident commented, "That's too much 'big government.'" In the end, the village decided against a new garage in lieu of a "trolley" system. Visitors to the village could park free in one of three public parking lots at the edge of town and for a minimal fee take a bus painted like a trolley downtown. The solution did help the situation, but it did not fully remedy it.

Many other residents expressed a sense of siege, as one resident explained in 1998:

The worst is Hall of Fame weekend. Ten thousand people show up in a town of, what, twenty-five hundred people. And there's no parking, and traffic doesn't move. For those three days a year, it's like living in the city. I don't want to live in New York City.

Another concurred:

There's no parking. People are grumpy. I try to stay away if I can. You can't go anywhere anyway. . . . So I go up to Utica or Albany for the day, do some shopping. Anything to get away.

Those who worked directly with tourists often had a range of complaints. Many tourists seemed to allow themselves and their children latitude not considered appropriate in their hometowns, as one waitress explained in 1999:

These people come in, every night, and they let their kids run wild. I got kids running through the restaurant, playing baseball, screaming up a storm. And if you say something, the parents get pissed; "Give them a break, lady, they're on vacation." Oh yeah, why don't you give me your address so I can fuck up your town for a day.

A retail manager commented further:

Some of them, not all, but enough, will use standards of behavior they wouldn't use at home. I catch kids, even adults, they're doing things like screaming in the street or getting drunk or just being an asshole generally. That's the problem with Cooperstown; they come here, they get relaxed, they turn into assholes.

Tourists generally perceived the situation from a different perspective:

Our (children) have piano, baseball, soccer, and swimming. They have to study all year, and you know school is hard work . . . so when we're on vacation, we let our guard down a little and let them be kids. When we get home, they gotta behave.

Most residents also recognized the dependency of the village economy on the annual influx of visitors. As one employee shared:

No, I don't like them. I don't think anyone really does. But they're our bread and butter. You take them away, and half these storefronts would be empty. What's the point in having parking if there's no place to go?

Such sentiments were a tacit acknowledgement of the village's predicament in the face of upscaling: in order for the village to survive, tourism was deemed necessary. A business owner commented:

Summer here is nuts. No parking, people all over the place, people from Massachusetts doin' ten miles per hour. And I love it: they keep me in business.

The ambivalence shared by many residents reflected the central contradiction of the area's high-impact form of tourism: Cooperstown had a healthy retail economy that did not adequately provide for the needs of the community. One resident explained:

You can get a beautiful painting here or a five-hundred-dollar baseball card, but try and find a simple pair of Reeboks (sneakers). Good luck!

Nearly every area resident left the village for shopping several times per year, and many of those under age thirty-five left several times per month. Many residents claimed that selection was better in other communities and also perceived that goods and services purchased outside the village were superior to those in Cooperstown:

I don't want the welfare clothes they sell in town—I want Eddie Bauer and The Gap. And you have to go to Utica or Albany for that. Cooperstown's good for knickknacks and baseball stuff, and maybe the things you need everyday (although they're expensive), but not for clothes.

As a result of residents' dependency on other communities, many were sentimental for Cooperstown as it was before tourism was such a potent force in the economy:

You know, I love it here. But the tourists move into town, and a lot of us have to move out. This town's just not the same as it was when I was a kid. It's all baseball, and no one seems to know each other anymore.

Residents were also realistic about the possibility of a return to the past, and instead sought a balance between the rural character of the village and the commodified tourist town it had become:

I wish I could have the town back the way it was. But that'll never happen. So I guess we need to balance things: we have to tolerate the tourists, but we have to hold onto our rural character, too.

The desire to balance the village's rural character with the realities of the tourism economy led to considerable conflict. The Historic Cooperstown model that was preferred was a construction of the local culture, but many residents continued to perceive the village through this lens.

This idealistic perception was challenged during the 1990s by the arrival of two new attractions, both started by outside investors. The Corvette Americana Hall of Fame attracted disdain by claiming on billboards, "Now you have two reasons to visit Cooperstown." Many local residents felt insulted that the New York State Historical Association museums were discounted:

They claimed that they and the Hall of Fame were the only places that mattered. It sounds like Cooperstown's just baseball—we're more than just baseball!

Similarly, the Cooperstown Wax Museum focused on figures from baseball history, and thus also attracted similar ire:

Can you imagine anything more tacky than a wax museum? Why would anyone want to see Babe Ruth melt? And it's all baseball—it just doesn't fit what Cooperstown is!

The new institutions were representative of how many tourists increasingly perceived the village: as a mecca for baseball fanatics. But they also signified an assault against the Historic Cooperstown model. Although many communities would welcome such investment, such attractions were seemingly at odds with the perception many residents had of the village. Cooperstown's fame had necessarily involved the forfeiture of the ability to control its own image, and many residents wanted that ability back.

The Many Villages of Cooperstown

The pattern of settlement found during the 1990s was the result of decades of economic restructuring in the area. Since 1970, much of the residential growth had been in the form of five to twenty acre "mini-estates." Former farmers subdivided and sold parcels of their land in order to gain income or lower their yearly tax burden. This practice allowed area residents to own homes in the country from which they could drive to work in town. As property values could be prohibitive, this option was open primarily to middle and upper income residents. The Otsego County Planning Department (OCPD 1997, 6) estimated that:

Most (building) lots (were) five acres and above, with the average size between 15–30 acres. Lots of this size sell for $20,000 to $40,000, clearly out of line when the median household salary is $25,000 to $49,000.

In other cases, landowners created mobile home communities. Tenants rented land on which to place their own mobile homes or rented preexisting mobile homes, and this guaranteed the property owner income without the need to sell the property. They tended to be densely settled despite their locations away from older, established communities. There were, of course, few if any employment opportunities in the new communities, and residents necessarily commuted to nearby villages. The opening of the first of these parks was greeted with some enthusiasm, the *Freeman's Journal* (23 Sept. 1964) printing the following caption below a picture:

Shown here is the beautiful new "Oak River Mobile Estate" at Index, located two miles south of Cooperstown. . . . Tenants may rent mobile homes or rent a lot if they now own their own mobile home. The lots are attractively landscaped and the estate is indeed a fine asset to the area.

The mobile home parks functioned as secondary centers within the extended rural community system.

Almost from the beginning, mobile homes were perceived as a way of providing modern housing for those who could not afford conventional housing. Three other large parks, and several smaller parks, had been built by 1990. The parks quickly filled with the elderly and the working poor, now subject not only to government regulation but the whims of the property owner as well. As the well-to-do built mini-estates on former farms, many of the area's poor were being concentrated on land parcels little larger than the new middle-class properties. Parks ranged up to thirty-five mobile homes, all removed from the most popular middle-class areas of the Fly Creek Valley, Middlefield, and Hartwick's Christian Hill. Due to the aesthetic and socioeconomic qualities of the parks, Cooperstown had already enacted legislation forbidding the placement of any mobile homes in the village. As a result, mobile homes tended to be located in municipalities with weak, or in the case of Hartwick, nonexistent zoning laws.

As the economy centralized and many poor people began to live in established secondary centers and mobile home communities, Cooperstown was becoming a more desirable location in which to live for those who did not desire a country home. Rents and property values in the village climbed faster than in the surrounding area, gradually ensuring that working-class residents would increasingly look elsewhere for housing. Always more exclusive than the surrounding villages, Cooperstown became even more so.

The three postal districts—Cooperstown, Hartwick, and Fly Creek— are useful for illustrating the trend.[4] For instance, while the Hartwick zip code contained 17.9 percent of the area households in 1990, it accounted for only 4.4 percent of those earning more than one hundred thousand dollars in that year. In contrast, Cooperstown village contained 49.7 percent of the households earning that much, but accounted for only 31.9 percent of all area households. Among households with incomes below fifteen thousand dollars, the Hartwick and Fly Creek zip codes were proportionate. However, Cooperstown village accounted for 5.4 percent less than would be expected, whereas the rural portion (outside the village) of the zip code had 5.4 percent more low-income households. This is likely because of the four mobile home parks within the Cooperstown zip code but outside the village limits. Moreover, inequality between communities was widening.[5] Simply stated, class segregation in the area was becoming more pronounced (Thomas 1998).

Although the formation of the Extended Rural Community System (ERCS) during the 1950s and 1960s provided the impetus for higher property values in the village relative to surrounding communities, tourism further aggravated price differentials among the towns. Cooperstown's (village) median property value was $141,400 in 1990, compared to $89,200 in Fly Creek and $56,100 in Hartwick (USBC 1990a; 1990b). This is in part due to the impact of tourism: of the 921 tax bills Otsego County sent out for the village, only 80.9 percent were sent to the Cooperstown zip code; 13.3 percent were sent to urban areas. Of the 174 nonlocal tax bills, one in five were sent to zip codes where the median property value was twice that in Cooperstown.

Enter East Hartwick

Area residents had become accustomed to driving for employment, goods, and services, and this set the stage for the major environmental change of the 1990s. Six miles east of Hartwick village, the eastern fringe of the township of Hartwick was within two miles of Cooperstown and along the major road into the village from the south. Three small hamlets—Index, Hyde Park, and Hartwick Seminary— composed a corridor that stretched for approximately four miles. Due to the decline in the business base in Hartwick, town leaders were in need of a source of revenue. The East Hartwick corridor provided the answer.

By the early 1990s, many Cooperstown area residents were calling for the preservation of the "village character" and local officials felt constrained to act on such pressures. Development projects in the village were sometimes stalled in committee for years. A condominium project was debated for several years and ultimately never built; houses built on lakefront property the village had declined to buy created a bitter controversy; a downtown baseball shop, technically lying in a residential zone, was denied a "sandwich board" sign on Main Street and went out of business a short time later.

By the early 1990s, many developers from outside the area had been watching the controversies over seemingly small building projects. From the perspective of urban developers, a single fast food establishment seemed inconsequential. As one developer said:

What's the big deal about a McDonald's? It's a McDonald's! Every place has a McDonald's. No, I see that, and I'm glad it's not me!

Village residents had a very different perception:

You let in one, I don't care, McDonalds, Pizza Hut, Taco Bell, and you'll have 'em all here. And our businesses go down the tubes. Jesus; we can't compete against McDonald's.

The debate over the Pizza Hut in Cooperstown was for many people just another example of the village being too restrictive. In contrast, the town of Hartwick was in need of ways to increase its tax base and so tended to be more open to new development. And due to the conservative leaning within the town, there were no zoning laws, as they were deemed "big government," as more than a few town residents summarized them. Because the town does not directly benefit from the tax base in Cooperstown, it was in its best interest to allow such development.

By the early 1990s development had begun along the East Hartwick corridor. Although the development was minor at first, Cooperstown merchants began to recognize the threat to their interests. As one resident said:

I think Cooperstown's problem is that you got people in Hartwick more concerned with their taxes than with having a nice community. They don't seem to realize that what's good for Cooperstown is good for them. . . . They should keep all the businesses in Cooperstown. We don't need them down there.

Another said:

If the Hartwick town board would just realize that they shouldn't have that kind of development. We shouldn't have it anywhere around here, but if we do, it should be in Cooperstown. Hartwick's a bedroom community, and it should stay that way.

Hartwick residents had a different perception:

You should see what those stores do to my taxes. I don't think the town taxes have even gone up; just county and school. Hell, I wish they'd build more.

And another:

Cooperstown thinks we should all go into Cooperstown. You try parking in Cooperstown in the summer. You just keep driving around Main Street looking for a space. They want us all to shop there, but they wouldn't put up a [parking] garage, would they? I'm glad The Commons [Shopping center, in Hartwick Seminary] opened. Serves 'em right.

By 1993, at least two different petitions had been circulated in Cooperstown calling on Hartwick to restrict growth even though there is no overlap in legal jurisdiction. One Hartwick resident commented at the time, "If they want us to help their businesses, maybe they should help our taxes." When The Commons shopping center, which included a Pizza Hut, a McDonald's, and a Best Western Hotel, opened amid picketers in November 1993, the *Freeman's Journal* (16 Nov. 1993) commented:

The Greater Cooperstown area has entered a new shopping era with Saturday's grand opening of The Commons Shopping Center.

Originally to be called "Cooperstown Commons," Hartwick officials urged "Hartwick Commons" instead. After some debate, the developers opted to call the shopping center simply "The Commons" rather than identify the complex with any one place.

Other proposals in the East Hartwick corridor met with similar opposition from local residents from both within and outside of the town. When the Cooperstown Dreams Park—a youth baseball park— opened in 1995, area residents were alarmed not only by the nightlights that illuminated the sky but also by the sheer boldness of the association with baseball. "It's gaudy," said one resident. Several similar proposed camps were also greeted with relentless opposition. Town officials felt compelled to strictly enforce subdivision and environmental impact regulations, but there was no generic environmental impact statement or zoning regulation to aid the process. The result was that the process to gain a permit frequently took up to a year or longer, during which time critics could organize opposition to the project. Such opposition often dismayed developers. For instance, when developers of Cooperstown Baseball World faced unforeseen difficulties in obtaining the necessary permits to build in the town of Hartwick, the city of Oneonta aided them in starting temporary operations there. In a letter of appreciation to the city, a representative wrote in dismay to city officials:

As you know, we have had a constant battle to get our approval in Hartwick. . . . We have worked very hard to save the program despite the very risky economic and political climate being fostered by people north of your county. (Oneonta Common Council Minutes, March 17, 2000)

In addition, many property owners raised the asking price for land in the corridor. As a result, the high costs associated with buying and developing property likely drove away potential community-oriented developers and thus made the corridor profitable primarily for those who could develop tourism-oriented ventures. Paradoxically, between community opposition and the high costs associated with development, the prospect of future development in the corridor was sharply reduced (although not alleviated completely) by the end of the decade.

The development along the East Hartwick corridor was simultaneously the result of tourism and the rise of the extended rural community system. Were it not for the restrictive policies in Cooperstown, the town of Hartwick would likely not have been as attractive for developers. Were it not for tourism, local government would likely have had a more open attitude toward development, as the threat of "over-urbanization" would have been reduced. The development of the East Hartwick corridor was also a symbolic acknowledgment of the growth of the extended rural community system: the development was meant to serve the entire area, and not just the villages in which it was located. In the new system of community, "The Commons" were just what they claimed to be.

Chapter 11

Different Strokes

As the new millennium began, central New York seemed different. Metropolitan Utica had lost more than twenty thousand residents between 1980 and 2000, and the racial and ethnic balance had changed. More than 36 thousand whites had left the region during that time, whereas the area gained almost fifteen thousand blacks, Latinos, and Asian Americans. The black population had nearly doubled during those twenty years, the Latino population grew by 182 percent, and the Asian American population grew by 287 percent (Lewis Mumford Center 2001). Otsego County gained slightly more than a thousand residents; with a population of 61,676, the county contained more residents than Utica (60,651) for the first time since the 1890 census (Shupe et al. 1987). But the biggest change was not to be found in census records.

Noblesse Oblige

Residents of Cooperstown may be surprised to learn that tourism is not the largest employer in the area; rather, it is Bassett Hospital. Located three blocks from downtown, the hospital had little impact on the character of Main Street shopping and restaurants as most employees could easily travel to and from work without going downtown. The result was that tourism became the most visual element of Cooperstown's economy, with the hospital acting in the background. Beneath the high visual impact of tourism and the economic generator of the hospital, many residents perceived the common thread holding the village economy together:

Look, I don't care if they say the hospital is bigger. It may be, but baseball is what you see. But there's really no difference between the two: they're run by the same crowd. The engine behind Cooperstown is the Clarks—you want to understand Cooperstown, you have to untangle their web first.

With a family fortune rooted in Singer Sewing Machines, the Clark family has had a tremendous impact on the fortunes of Cooperstown through two major mediums: Leatherstocking Corporation and the Clark Foundation.

Leatherstocking Corporation was the "for-profit" segment of the local Clark empire. Headquartered in New York, the corporation ran the historic Otesaga Hotel, the Cooper Inn, as well as numerous smaller functions throughout the village.

Larger and more pervasive was the Clark Foundation, the nonprofit arm of the family. The Clark Foundation, as of 2000, held assets of about $450 million. Also headquartered in New York City, the foundation spent about $8 million in the Cooperstown area during 2000, including about $4 million spent performing such community functions as operating the Clark Sports Center (a health and fitness center), the Clark Scholarship Program (for local college students), and a beautification program for the village. In addition, the foundation has been influential in the creation and financing of Bassett Hospital, the New York State Historical Association, and the Baseball Hall of Fame. The family also owned, in conjunction with other local families, a greenbelt of undeveloped land that completely surrounded the village.

In the Clark fortune was found a form of elite patronage that helped to link the community to outside sources of capital and talent. Such patronage was uncommon among rural communities, and for this Cooperstown was quite unique. It was through the continued efforts of the Clarks that Cooperstown was able to gain some of the unique institutions that enabled the village to prosper even as the region suffered: the Baseball Hall of Fame, the New York State Historical Association, and Bassett Hospital. As Cooperstown faced the trends of upscaling and agricultural decline, these institutions helped to keep the village afloat. Nowhere was this more apparent than in the rise of Bassett Healthcare.

A Modern Health Care System

Bassett Hospital was named after Mary Imogene Bassett, a local physician who counted Edward Severin Clark as one of her patients. Popular belief suggests that Clark had heard of Bassett's desire for a good lab facility in the village, "and granted her wish, building not only a laboratory, but a fully-equipped 100-bed fieldstone hospital building" (Bassett Healthcare 2001). The Clarks were heavily involved in the success of the hospital throughout the years, turning it into one of the better-known rural hospitals in the country. The hospital also started education and research facilities, and by the 1980s was advertising its affiliation with Columbia University.

In 1988, O'Connor Hospital of Delhi, more than forty miles from Cooperstown, merged with Bassett Hospital. In time, Schoharie County Hospital in Cobleskill also merged with Bassett and the enlarged health care system opened nineteen outpatient clinics. The mergers and new clinics made the Bassett system the largest in the region, stretching over eighty miles. The expansion helped to bring new patients to the Bassett system by moving into new markets. A Bassett employee commented in 1999:

We're a small, rural hospital, and there are, you know, only so many patients here in town. And you go out into the country, and there aren't any of those old country doctors who run clinics out of their homes. You know, like old Doctor Baker over in Hartwick . . . she had an office in front of her kitchen. There aren't any of those anymore, so Bassett needs to fill in the gaps. Luckily it works for all of us.

But as the expansion worked for Bassett and some of the communities served, some of the new clinics were placed in locations that directly competed with other health care systems. In nearby Oneonta, the A. O. Fox Hospital found that it had new competition as Bassett opened two new clinics, Bassett Healthcare Oneonta and Bassett Healthcare Oneonta Specialty Services, in the city. A mere twenty miles apart, the two hospitals had always competed for patients from the towns in between, but the new clinics in the city, "meant that all of a sudden we had to worry about losing Oneonta patients as well," as one Oneonta physician commented.

Bassett also expanded into metropolitan Utica by building a new clinic in the eastern suburb of Herkimer, directly next door to a clinic owned by the Mohawk Valley Network,[1] a coalition of hospitals in the metropolitan area centered in Utica. Despite Bassett billing itself as a "rural healthcare system," some area residents perceived the move as an attempt to attract new customers:

They have a clinic in Richfield Springs [twelve miles south of Herkimer]— that's rural. Here in Herkimer, there's Little Falls Hospital five miles up the road, Mohawk Valley Hospital just two or three miles up in Ilion, all the hospitals in Utica. They're only fifteen miles away. I think Bassett just can't find enough patients in Cooperstown so they're raiding Herkimer.

It was over cardiac care that Utica and Cooperstown would finally meet.

The three Utica hospitals had applied for permission from the State Health Department to begin cardiac care numerous times throughout the 1980s and 1990s. The Health Department rejected the applications, citing interhospital competition and questioning the ability of the program to perform the required five hundred surgeries per year. It took the cooperation of the hospitals and the 1994 election of George Pataki as governor for Utica to finally receive a cardiac unit at Saint Elizabeth Medical Center. The Mohawk Valley Heart Institute was a collaborative effort between the hospitals. The first surgery was performed in 1997 (SEMC 2001). It thus came as a surprise when Bassett Hospital announced plans to open a clinic in Cooperstown.

Hospitals in Binghamton, Schenectady, and Utica all opposed the plan. Not only would Bassett cut into the patient base of the three urban hospitals, but also the ability of Bassett to perform the required five hundred surgeries per year was in doubt. The strongest opposition came from the Mohawk Valley Heart Institute, which sent a letter to the Health Department criticizing the plan on a number of points (DS, 8 Dec. 2000). Bassett responded that the required five hundred surgeries placed an undue burden on rural hospitals, especially given that eleven of the state's thirty-four programs did not meet the criteria. In a letter to the State Health Department, Otsego County Chamber of Commerce President Rob Robinson asked, "Why should rural residents of Otsego and surrounding counties be deprived of convenient access to angioplasty and cardiac surgery, which is routinely and conveniently available to our urban counterparts?" In December 2000, Bassett's application was approved.

The significance of the conflict was not in the development of a cardiac care unit in Cooperstown as much as it symbolized the differences between the two communities. But in some ways, it showed the similarities as well.

Non Noblesse Oblige

By 2000, Utica once again seemed to have a relatively stable political structure. Moderate Republicans controlled the city and the county alike, and the area's Congressional representative, Sherwood Boehlert, was a typical example. In 2000, Boehlert generally voted for moderately conservative economic policies and moderately liberal social policies. He supported expanded free trade agreements such as the North America Free Trade Agreement (NAFTA) and General Agreement on Tariffs and Trade (GATT), and the World Trade Organization (WTO). Yet he also received a rating of 70 percent from the League of Conservation Voters, 100 percent from both Planned Parenthood and the National Abortion and Reproductive Rights League (NARAL), and voted with the pro–gun control Brady Campaign to Prevent Gun Violence fourteen of sixteen times. Such a record is indicative of neither a right wing conservative nor any significant liberal tendencies. As one Utica resident commented:

Boehlert isn't one of those Nazis that seem to have taken over his party—he seems to represent New York Republicans pretty well. You look at guys like Newt Gingrich, a family values guy who dumped his wife on her deathbed, and you know that Boehlert ain't like that. But he's no liberal either.

When challenged by both Democratic and Conservative Party opponents in 2000, Boehlert won by dividing the opposing vote. A Cooperstown resident commented:

He's right down the middle. He's sane: he's for choice and gun control, but he's not for high taxes and lots of welfare.

In Utica politics, the two parties seemed very similar. In fact, Ed Hanna, mayor during much of the 1990s, had been an Independent, a Democrat, and a Republican during his administration. But despite a more stable political structure, area leaders inherited a metropolitan area that had lost much of its population and prestige during the previous three decades, and many business leaders were unwilling to invest in the city.

In 2001, there had not been a major building project in downtown Utica in twenty years. Some existing landmark buildings, such as the sixteen-story Adirondack Bank Building and the fifteen-story Hotel Utica, had been completely refurbished. A few new parks had been built on the sites of buildings that had burned. But overall, numerous brown fields dotted downtown and many buildings needed a facelift. While it was undeniable that some progress had been made, it was apparent that Utica could no longer count on the local elite to revitalize the city.

Part of the problem Utica was experiencing was that many of the institutions that had been headquartered in Utica were now headquartered elsewhere. For instance, of the nine banks in the central business district in 2001, only four were headquartered in the city. Of the four largest banks, Charter One, FleetBoston, Key Bank, and HSBC, all were headquartered outside of New York State. Mergers between banks that had been based in Utica and subsequently taken over built three of these: Charter One, FleetBoston, and HSBC. For instance, Charter One's local branches had once been owned by Corn Hill Savings and Loan. HSBC, when it was Marine Midland, maintained a regional headquarters in the city. FleetBoston had grown, in part, from Oneida National Bank. Of these, only FleetBoston maintained a significant level of administrative functions in Utica.

Corporate concentration was not solely to blame for the lack of investment in the city center. Of the largest non-financial companies, only one (ConMed Corporation) is headquartered in the central business district. Some residents see this as the heart of the problem in the city:

Look, most companies don't even think of Utica. Utica National [Insurance] uses the name, but they're in New Hartford. Utica Corporation—they're in Whitesboro. Oneida Research—Whitesboro. Metropolitan—Oriskany. And you know, it's a shame. If some of these companies would just say, "I'll go down-town," and all do it together, Utica could be something. But they just don't care.

In July 2001, boosters of Utica received gratifying news. Two local companies, Utica National Insurance and polling firm Zogby International were competing for the same downtown lot. Located only two blocks west of Genesee Street, the vacant lot comprised an entire city block placed between the city's two downtown hotels. Upon discovery of the competition, Utica National dropped its plans for a new downtown building, leaving just Zogby International. Zogby planned a $10.5 million office complex complete with "a world-class atrium benefiting a global corporation based in Downtown Utica" (Zogby International, 25 July 2001).

Zogby International had been founded by native Utican John Zogby. His polling firm had grown dramatically, and by the late 1990s Zogby was a staple figure on the cable news stations. In this regard, both John Zogby and the firm he grew were exactly what economic development officials in cities all over America hope for: a local entrepreneur who starts small and stays local. It thus came as some surprise a month later when Zogby announced that the company was also negotiating with the Oneida Indian Nation, whose reservation was about twenty miles west of Utica, for land on which to build the new headquarters. For some local residents, the news was not surprising:

Zogby's doing what all Utica boys do when they get successful: they leave. And why not? This place is a slum . . . I'd leave, too, if I made it big. Who can blame John?

A New Hartford resident also commented:

It's just part of the business cycle. Start your business, get big, and move your shit somewhere else. It was nice seeing "Utica" on MSNBC, but you knew it couldn't last. Utica's not big enough to keep these guys, and they're too big, or they think they are, to help out their hometowns.

Even as many local residents were split as to why Zogby might leave the city, the Utica *Observer-Dispatch* placed any blame firmly on the city:

Talks ran into some kind of snag toward the end of summer, however, and Zogby now says he's considering other options including on tax-free Oneida Indian Nation land, or even outside the Mohawk Valley. . . . If the city cannot keep a successful company spawned here by a native son, what hope is there that it can attract and keep other significant companies? You can bet The Associated Press, which sends news stories worldwide, would quickly visit and write a story about "another blow to the decaying city of Utica," or something like that. That certainly is not the publicity Utica wants or needs. (OD, 14 Oct. 2001)

Indeed, such a story had already been written a month earlier, appearing among other places in the Boston *Globe* (BG, 7 Sept. 2001). Despite intentions to begin construction in December 2001, the location of the ten story building that Zogby himself called "the signature building for a genuine downtown (Utica) renaissance" (BG, 7 Sept. 2001) was still in doubt in the middle of 2002.

The episode highlighted the inability of the city to fix the problems left by years of inactivity. Zogby International, as one of the city's premier businesses, offered to invest in downtown in order to help revitalize the urban core as well as provide the company room for expansion. Although Zogby announced the project in late July, it was not until September 12 that the city's Urban Renewal Agency approved an option for sale to the company. Zogby had reason to question why it took the city a month and a half before approving even the most basic element of the project. But Zogby International also showed a disheartening impatience with the city, reminding city leaders and residents alike that Utica was of secondary importance to the company. A spokesman for the Oneida Nation commented, "Zogby is a high-profile, international business. They could operate anywhere. What's important is that these jobs will stay in Central New York" (BG, 7 Sept. 2001). The president of the Mohawk Valley Chamber of Commerce similarly remarked, "We are the Mohawk Valley chamber so our position is that Verona is better than South Carolina. As long as he stays in our region, the residents here will have their jobs." Zogby could leave, area residents knew it, and no matter the outcome the episode reminded the community of its vulnerability. In the end, Zogby remained loyal to his hometown: in late 2002, the company announced plans to move temporarily into an old textile mill in anticipation of its new downtown headquarters.

Power Structures

The significance of the Zogby affair contrasts sharply with both the involvement of the Clark family and other village elites in Cooperstown and the Elefante political machine of years before.

In Cooperstown, the potential existed for new projects to be acted upon reasonably quickly if village leaders approved. As one area resident commented:

I don't think there's any doubt that an expansion at the Hall of Fame or at (Bassett) Hospital would have any real problems. People would just sit down, choose a design, and it would get through in a few months and probably get built within a year or two.

This reality contrasts with the image of sluggishness the village acquired after a proposed Pizza Hut was stalled and ultimately defeated in the late 1980s. However, it is true that other major projects had passed fairly easily, such as a new Clark Sports Center just outside the village, a recent expansion of the Hall of Fame, and a new clinic building at Bassett Hospital. While all three projects had detractors, they also were passed without the fierce opposition that faced Pizza Hut. Indeed, many of the controversies around development issues during the 1990s were not in the village at all, but rather in the surrounding townships where political power is not as concentrated. Cooperstown thus enjoyed a political and economic efficiency not experienced in Utica since the days of the Elefante political machine.

There were other parallels among the power structures in Cooperstown, Utica, and the old Elefante machine. Many of the complaints lodged against the political machine in Utica revolved around a lack of democracy in the city. One city resident commented, "They did their thing, and when the deal was done they'd tell us about it." Many Cooperstown residents made similar comments:

Basically, what the Clarks want, they get. Want a lowered speed limit somewhere, they get it. Want to expand the Hall of Fame, it happens. And no one ever thinks to say, "Hey, build a parking garage with that thing." I don't think it's a matter of actual corruption, though; just a matter of not wanting to step on anyone's toes.

But such a perceived lack of participation was not limited to the concentrations of power experienced in contemporary Cooperstown or 1950s Utica. Even with the relatively less concentrated power structure of metropolitan Utica in the late twentieth and early twenty-first century, some area residents perceived a lack of consultation:

I remember even during the late eighties when the Common Council just couldn't agree on anything, it was about them. It was the politicians fighting with each other—they didn't actually represent anybody in those debates except their own special interests.

The sin city scandals of the late 1950s weakened the political machine, and this created a vacuum in the city as the machine controlled Common Council and both Republican and Reform Democrat mayors struggled for power (Ehrenhalt 1992). Some in Cooperstown worried about a similar fate in their future:

Jayne Clark isn't going to be alive forever, and I'm not sure that there's anyone to take her place. She's been awful good to the town, and I don't know if someone new would take care of Cooperstown the same way. The Clark Foundation might decide that its money is better spent in the city [New York], or the flowers on Main Street should be done by the village.

The political structure in Cooperstown was one that was concerned with the local community, and in this way was also similar to the concerns of the Elefante political machine. A former Utica resident suggested:

Say what you will, but those guys got things done back then. They created the colleges, brought new jobs, and helped make the city look decent. They wanted to make sure that the city didn't fall apart. They [the politicians] don't seem as concerned about Utica anymore.

In contrast, the past twenty years demonstrated a remarkably low level of commitment to downtown Utica. The city constructed a business park on the outskirts of the city where some downtown businesses could move, ostensibly because "it kept those taxes in the city—that's the most important concern." The city also failed to utilize development opportunities to their best advantage. When ordered to construct a handicapped accessible courtroom, for instance, the city chose to merely add to the decades-old courthouse rather than construct a new one in a location that could spur further development. The city also failed to invest in its own infrastructure so that it could compete with other cities: there is no convention center in the city, although there is one in suburban New Hartford, the hockey arena dates to the 1950s and the Mohawk Valley Edge, the main economic development agency for the metropolitan area, did not even list downtown Utica as a potential development site on its website (Mohawk Valley Edge 2001). Some projects had been completed, the redevelopment of the sixteen-story Adirondack Bank Building and the fifteen-story Hotel Utica two blocks away the most notable, but with the exception of Zogby International Utica's business community was by and large disinterested in the urban core. Although some area political and business leaders professed to be concerned with the fate of Utica, actions suggested a complete lack of regard or even understanding for the symbolic center of the metropolitan area. Given the differences in political structure, it is not surprising that a casual walk through Cooperstown provided a more delightful urban experience than a walk through downtown Utica. Cooperstown's elites remained committed to a healthy Cooperstown.

The help given Cooperstown carries some disadvantages. The extensive holdings of Clark-affiliated institutions are often nonprofit. The Baseball Hall of Fame, Bassett Hospital, and the Clark Foundation were very large property owners in the area, but due to their nonprofit status paid no taxes. As a result, the local solid waste management authority introduced a "user fee" that was applied to nonprofits as well. One local official commented:

They do a lot of good for the area. But there's a cost. Every time Clark gets a piece of property, it seems to come off the tax rolls a few days later. So we have all this property that no one's paying taxes on, and we have to push it all on other taxpayers.

Many of the community institutions were also highly dependent upon Clark patronage. One resident, having recently moved to the area, commented:

You know, there are some things that communities just build on their own. Here, it seems like the Clarks do everything. You know, like a gym—in a lot of places, the school makes it, or there's a Y [YMCA], and the community holds bake sales to keep it going. Or the swim team—other places, it's called the name of the town, but here, it's the "Clark Sharks." I mean, it's nice that they support the town like this, but I don't know if anyone here realizes that in other places the community itself makes these things happen.

In the midst of such privilege, some residents (certainly not all) perceived that it limited the community's ability to create its own institutions.

Different Folks

The political structure of metropolitan Utica had changed dramatically since World War II, whereas that of Cooperstown had simply gained new actors in a fairly stable regime. The elites of each community reacted to external conditions that affected the local community, and in doing so created the conditions under which they would react to future conditions. Cooperstown's elite was able to build on the successes of previous decisions regarding the village's infrastructure and economy. As the village was comparatively small, local leaders did not demand nor require the types of public and private investment to keep the village competitive.

Utica, in contrast, won much more public and private investment than Cooperstown, but it was not sufficient to compete effectively against similar cities both in the northeast and around the nation. For instance, Utica received an arterial highway, but it paled in comparison to the modern expressway system won by metropolitan Binghamton, a smaller city seventy-five miles south. Indeed, the major expressway between Utica and Rome was not even scheduled for completion until 2003. As a result, Utica has had trouble maintaining symbols of major city significance. In 2001, the professional hockey team declared bankruptcy midseason, and the owner of the professional baseball team announced that he was negotiating the sale of the team to business concerns in Pittsfield, Massachusetts—a metropolitan area considerably smaller than Utica.

To compare Cooperstown and Utica is to compare apples and oranges. Cooperstown appears healthier because the area no longer competes for institutions today found primarily in urban settings. Cooperstown does not seek to develop new shopping centers, business parks, and housing developments. Many local residents have recognized that Cooperstown, a community that today includes the village and numerous surrounding villages such as Hartwick, cannot compete on the terms demanded by urban society. The case of Bassett Hospital notwithstanding, the area attracts tourists because it has attempted to preserve its landscape and recreate itself in an image of small town America that urban residents long to relive. By its sheer size, Utica is too large to be a rural tourist town, but performs its function as a retail center quite well. It is doubtful that any one family could ever exert the kind of power over the city's affairs that the Clarks exercise in Cooperstown, but the complexities of governing a diverse and widespread metropolitan area require a more complex form of governance anyway. It is with these characteristics that central New York enters the future.

Chapter 12

Gotham's Shadow

The letter arrived in January 2001, the return address on the envelope featuring a picture of the closed Hartwick Seminary and the line "Town of Hartwick Historical Society." The seminary had closed decades earlier, moving its resources from the rural town to the more urban Oneonta and reopening as a secular college of the same name. Just as the closing of the Cooperstown-area textile mills had only a few decades earlier, the abandonment of Hartwick by Hartwick College authorities embodied the dynamic of upscaling: larger places are considered more important, more exciting, more sophisticated. Smaller places are expendable, except as they may be important as commodified versions of a pastoral ideal that never truly existed. The college today overlooks the many houses of Oneonta, the remnants of its seminary roots demolished and replaced by a trailer park. Hartwick residents still take pride in the seminary founded by their eccentric founder; it is unlikely that the college community shares the same pride in Hartwick.

All that remains of the once proud buildings of the oldest Lutheran Seminary in the United States is the Lutheran Church and a brick monument set amid the mobile homes. There are many similar monuments in central New York, not so deliberate and none so obvious. Tourists stop their cars and photograph the tranquility of an abandoned barn not thinking of the parallel with the crumbling bricks of shuttered factories. Little towns and urban slums turn empty storefronts to their citizens. Real estate signs dot the landscape and forests are reclaiming their lands. The monuments surround us, and there is a logic to their creation.

A New York Minute

A curious story appeared in the Oneonta *Daily Star* in the aftermath of the attacks on the World Trade Center. Realtors in Delaware and Otsego

151

Counties were reporting that property sales were up, one realtor commenting, "They want a place they can go to get out (of the metropolitan area). They are looking at this area as a refuge, a safe haven" (DS, 23 Oct. 2001). It was testimony to the perception that central New York is somehow removed from the problems facing New York City.

The global economy has, of course, made such notions of a safe haven from New York and the economy it commands a comfortable illusion and nothing more. Although many of New York's corporations will not invest in central New York, many global corporations do have a presence here. Even in the midst of this once great agricultural area, beef from Latin America, fruit from Florida, and vegetables from California are sold in the supermarkets and restaurants. The best selling maple syrups are those produced in distant corners of the country and sold in molded plastic bottles, not those collected and prepared by local craftsmen seeking to preserve a way of life. The global economy is entrenched in central New York, and it is unlikely that many local residents would seek a return to the past. But what is globalization?

In the media and even in the social sciences, globalization is too often treated as a new phenomenon. While it is undeniable that the extent of economic integration found today is quite unique in global economic history, the dynamics that make it so are neither unique to our times nor new.

Many of the more distressing issues associated with the global economy today are merely updated forms of yesterday's problems, experienced on a larger scale and more visible than in the past. Utica's textile companies grew through corporate concentration, but they did so during the late nineteenth and early twentieth centuries. Not surprisingly, many of the conditions associated with corporate concentration today were found then as well. The mills bought by the Utica firms were run for some time and then closed, the companies taking advantage of the lower labor costs and easier social control of the immigrant populations found in the more urbanized Mohawk Valley. Cooperstown and Hartwick were deindustrialized. Similarly, the concentration of banking in central New York resulted in less community control of those institutions in smaller communities such as Cooperstown and Hartwick as administrative functions were transferred to the cities.

The issues associated with these basic dynamics of corporate concentration, deindustrialization, and economies of scale were recognized as serious social problems only after they began to affect larger cities, such as Utica. Such works as Bluestone's and Harrison's *The Deindustrialization of America* (1982) and Michael Moore's classic film *Roger and Me* (1989) concentrated on the effects of globalization on urban America because it was there where the dynamics of capitalism were more visible. In both urban and rural communities, the dynamics had been building for years.

The concept of "macro level forces" masks the observation by Randall Collins (1975) that such macro level events are rooted ultimately in "micro" level interactions that have widespread ramifications. Such interactions often take place at a distance from the affected communities, the effects often taking on emergent characteristics that magnify the initial interactions to global proportions.

Economic decisions are based upon the embedded relations of the relevant social actors (Granovetter 1985). As Utica, like other cities, became more dependent upon state and federal funding during the twentieth century, the ability of the city's elites to network with and influence state and national leaders became vital to its interests. The Elefante machine was capable of this from the 1930s through the 1950s as city leaders were on comfortable terms with other Democratic leaders. When, during the late 1950s, the state Democratic leadership was in the hands of a different set of elites, Utica's demands were seen as out of line with the city's importance at a state-wide level. While it is unlikely that Governor Harriman ordered the investigation into corruption in Utica because of a personal grudge against Elefante (see chapter 5), the lack of a positive personal relationship between the two leaders certainly did not help the city.

The embeddedness of economic relations in social networks brings about another major consideration. Social groups generate cultures, and the subculture of social and economic elites often determines their willingness to invest in a community. Although upscaling as a dynamic of capitalism may be considered as an economic pattern, it is a cultural pattern as well. Local leaders in many communities recognize the importance of maintaining a positive image for their cities, and this is ultimately because a positive image can often attract the attention of non-local concerns. When the Utica *Observer-Dispatch* editorialized that the city needed to keep Zogby International in the city, the prestigious effect of people worldwide hearing the name "Utica" was one of the cited concerns (OD, 14 Oct. 2001). Similarly, the structure of urban renewal projects during the 1960s and 1970s were more the result of the cultural discourse of progress prevalent at that time than rational economic decisions. Such designs were not without critics, but the critics were ultimately not the ones making the decisions (see Jacobs 1992).

Upscaling is the dynamic associated with urban/rural relations. Rooted in economies of scale, it is tempting to consider upscaling as a deterministic quality arising from the cycles of capitalism. But the size of a city and its market is not ultimately determined by some unseen hand, but rather through very human politics that decide where development will take place and what policies to pursue. New York is not larger than Utica simply because of a particularly good harbor. Charleston, South Carolina, also has a fine harbor, but is closer in size to Utica than to New York. New York grew to its great size due in part to a fateful decision to build the only inland water route from the Atlantic to the Midwest, the ability of farmers from hundreds of miles away to create a surplus of food, and the ability of the city to trade not only products from its own factories but from the factories of hundreds of cities and small towns that chose to export their goods through the great port of New York. The global economy means that New York no longer relies on its hinterland for raw materials, food, or products to trade: the world is New York's hinterland. As new trade agreements and technologies make the world smaller, central New York has discovered that its workers demand too much pay for their labor compared to those in the non-union South and the peasants of South America.

The ability of communities to adapt to economic change has been dependent upon the accumulation of past decisions regarding infrastructure and other types of economic factors. Cooperstown has been able to adapt reasonably well to change due to past decisions on the part of its elites that created the infrastructure and mythology that today serve as the basis for its tourism economy. The village has also benefited from the continued presence of elites that integrate the community with the larger society, enabling the local hospital to compete against others that have not had the same level of patronage. And such dependency upon past events is not limited to local decisions, but also upon events in distant locales. Tourism is based on the automobile, a technological development that took place quite independent of Cooperstown but has nonetheless affected the community.

In Search of Community

One hundred years ago, central New York was part of that great industrial region of the northeastern United States. Spread along the major transportation corridors connecting the Atlantic Coast to the Great Lakes, the area was at the heart of this region and enjoyed the privileges of its position. The region's manufacturing dominated the world economy, and its agriculture supported the largest city in the world (New York) and one of the most heavily urbanized corridors in the country.

It was the dialectic between technology and public policy that ultimately brought central New York's privilege to an end. Improved transportation, refrigeration, and processing technology made it possible to import food from other regions of the country and, more recently, the world. Such technology ultimately benefits urban capitalists as it enables them to lower food costs and thus the "fixed" cost associated with keeping their labor alive. For rural areas in upstate New York, however, their proximity to the great metropolitan areas of North America is suddenly of dubious benefit. Urban-based companies now buy agricultural products from the least costly source and then resell them to their customers in urban and rural areas. Upstate farmers are today exposed to competition never felt before—many simply cannot compete against the productivity of the Great Plains or the low overhead of Mexico or Guatemala.

It is a familiar scenario but one normally associated with urban and suburban factory workers. More visible and dramatic, the rubble of the inner city is a powerful image that evokes no feeling of posterity. Similarly, technology has enabled business to take place nearly anywhere, enabling companies to seek out the "most favorable business climate" (Markusen 1987; Storper and Walker 1987). Increasingly, as companies leave and those left behind must make up the difference with higher taxes, upstate New York is not that place.

Public policy interacts with these dynamics. Whereas the automobile deconcentrated the population, it was policies favoring the automobile (road building, etc.) that accelerated the process. Federal agriculture policy has similarly favored larger, often corporate, agriculture concerns: a boon for urban consumers but devastating for New York farmers. The reluctance to enforce antitrust regulations has produced fewer and larger corporations headquartered in large cities; many policies have made it even easier for companies to merge. Trade policy has increasingly made it more attractive to shift production and even corporate headquarters out of the nation entirely. And all these policies make smaller communities all the more irrelevant to the overall functioning of the world economy.

Research and development is increasingly concentrated in large metropolitan areas as the same process of upscaling that so devastated Utica benefits the global cities where the companies are headquartered. Despite the Mohawk Valley's role in the early computer industry, the scale economy of knowledgeable people found in California's Silicon Valley was never equaled in the Mohawk Valley, so Unisys is no longer there. State and local officials today attempt to market the area as a high technology haven apparently oblivious to the fact that the basic conditions in existence when the area lost its initial prominence have not changed. SUNY Institute of Technology was recently given permission by the state to offer the first two years of a bachelor's degree, but it is still not a public MIT. There is still an inadequate transportation infrastructure: southbound automotive shipping must either travel miles out of the way for an expressway or traverse the two-lane highways of Otsego and Chenango Counties, the airport is struggling to compete with Syracuse International Airport forty-five miles away, and rail has been forced to compete against heavily subsidized automotive and air travel. Perhaps most important, there is still not the concentration of industry found in Silicon Valley. Home to Xerox, IBM, General Electric, and the forerunner to Unisys, perhaps New York could have had California's economy, but there is no way to know for sure.

Increasingly, corporations based in global cities control the fate of central New York as they export administrative and manufacturing employment in order to make their own firms more efficient. Niagara Mohawk is now a subsidiary of London-based National Grid Group, Fleet is headquartered in Boston, and WestPoint Stevens in New York. The income generated by Utica Gas & Electric, Oneida National Bank, and Utica & Mohawk Cotton Mills no longer stays in the area but rather benefits those living in London, Boston, and New York. Like other cities its size, Utica clamors for the dwindling number of manufacturing and back office jobs that can be placed in any city willing to slash the tax bill for the company. Tourism itself relies upon the scraps of global cities as their residents choose from an array of communities desperate for their entertainment dollar.

Connections

A community's connections with outside capital has always helped its economic health, especially in smaller communities with relatively little productive capacity of their own. As the global economy continues the trend of great concentration of capital in fewer and larger cities, a community's ability to draw on its connections in such circles becomes even more important. Utica once supported itself on its own productive capacity, and one hundred years ago that capacity was impressive indeed. By midcentury, it was reliant upon the large-city owners of its corporations who gradually left the city in search of more profitable venues. In the 1990s, Utica's economic and political power was so weakened that it struggled for several years to win approval from the state health department for a cardiac unit. State officials were content with Uticans having to travel to Syracuse for open-heart surgery. It took the election of George Pataki to finally win Utica a cardiac surgery unit.

In contrast, Cooperstown has utilized its elite connections to great benefit. As rural hospitals faced bankruptcy during the late 1980s and early 1990s, Bassett Hospital, backed by many of the same interests that brought the Baseball Hall of Fame to Cooperstown, was able to take over their operations. In addition, the hospital built several clinics and is now one of the largest health care providers in the region. By building clinics in West Winfield and Herkimer, the hospital now competes for patients against metropolitan Utica hospitals. When in 1999 Bassett applied for a cardiac care unit, the hospital faced little opposition outside Utica area hospitals and will likely gain all the needed permits.

In contrast, Hartwick never generated a significant level of production and was thus dependent upon its own productive capacity for survival. When the automobile made it possible for its residents to leave the community in search of selection and prices, there was no corporation, foundation, or individual willing to work on the village's behalf (the experience of Key Bank during the late 1970s notwithstanding, although that bank eventually sold its Hartwick branch to Charter One Bank). As the smallest and least powerful of the three communities, Hartwick has also experienced the most total decline. Many residents today consider the village a "bedroom community," which is to say that self-sufficiency no longer even enters the discourse of the community.

The political and economic dynamics found in these three communities are not limited to central New York State. Upstate New York is littered with communities sharing similar stories, as are many other regions throughout the United States. The coal-producing Appalachian Mountains, the agricultural Great Plains, and the rust belt of the Great Lakes are all summoned to mind when one considers the story of central New York. They all share in their subordination to global interests that have increasingly looked beyond their borders. Living in the shadows of the world's greatest city no longer confers the benefit it once did. As the world economy marches on, upscaling will continue to benefit larger cities at the expense of their smaller neighbors. How long will it be before Columbus and Hartford lose ground to Detroit and Boston? Or Philadelphia and Baltimore to New York and Washington? As the concentration of capital favors the largest cities among us, how long will it be before sociologists talk of primate cities in modern societies? Like the warriors of Aztec foes, many more communities will ascend the altar of the global free market.

Appendix A
The Block Quintile Measure

In order to compare the health of the central business districts in all three communities, a measure was necessarily developed with the intent of circumventing the problems associated with comparing communities of such disparate sizes. The definition of the central business district was coterminous with the extent of contiguous business buildings in Cooperstown and Hartwick. In Utica, the definition was taken from a 1950 report on arterial highways for the city (DPW 1950).

The Block Quintile (BQ) Score is based on the assumption that a healthy city is also a pleasant environment in which to walk. Downtown areas in older communities typically developed to serve a predominantly pedestrian population, and Utica, Cooperstown, and Hartwick are no exception. As a result, all three communities had pedestrian-oriented central business districts in 1947 that contemporary news accounts and interviews indicate attempted to beautify the streetscape and lure pedestrians into shops. In most cases, the streetscape included buildings in close proximity to one another (or touching) that met the sidewalk in a line with other buildings. Occasionally, buildings would contain small plazas but this was not the norm. Especially in Utica, small parks and plazas were strategically placed in different locations around the downtown area and these functioned as places of rest and tranquility from the city. Based on these assumptions, the central business districts of each community were divided into blocks. A block was defined as one side of a street between two side streets. Each quintile was then coded as follows: Empty lots=0; parking lots=1; ordinary lawn and parking garages=2; buildings, parks, and plazas=3. The score is then summed for a block score with a maximum of fifteen.

A weakness of the BQ score is that it fails to account for the individual characteristics of buildings, and as such it is theoretically possible for a rather dilapidated area with few demolished buildings to have a high BQ score. Similarly, it is only appropriate for use in areas where the dominant form of urbanization includes buildings built next to each other and at a common building line.

Figure A.1. BQ Scores for Utica, Cooperstown, and Hartwick

	Utica	Cooperstown	Hartwick
No. of Blocks (1947)	240	15	6
No. of Blocks (1997)	209	15	6
Mean (1947)	14.03	14.2	14.16
Mean (1997)	9.79	14.2	10.83

Appendix B
Newspaper Advertisement Data

The type and location of retail advertisements was coded for specific dates at five-year intervals in the Cooperstown *Freeman's Journal* and the Utica *Observer-Dispatch*. This allowed tracking of the location of newspaper advertisers throughout the communities over a long period of time, thus allowing an analysis of the impact of the automobile and suburbanization.

For the *Freeman's Journal*, the first Saturday in July at five-year intervals between 1899 and 1984; after 1984, the location of advertisements was quite sporadic as the newspaper had redefined its market during the 1970s from being a "Cooperstown" newspaper to a "Otsego County" newspaper, thus allowing it to sell advertisements all over the region. By the middle of the 1970s, any clear pattern as to where advertisers were located was overshadowed by the regional nature of the newspaper. However, the advertisements provide a good record of the types of goods and services for sale in the Cooperstown and, in a more limited way, Hartwick areas prior to 1980. Newspaper accounts, high school yearbooks, telephone books, and interviews provided information from the late 1950s through 2000.

Advertisements in the *Observer-Dispatch* were coded for the first Saturday in December at five-year intervals between 1899 and 1999. Data for the 1990s is of questionable value due to the scarcity of advertisements in the downtown area and the dominance of national-brand and chain-store advertising. Also, retailers increasingly advertised on television. Data from 1899 through the 1980s is quite good, however, and shows very clearly the dominance of downtown stores earlier in the twentieth century and the rise of the suburbs. Locations were coded as either in the central business district, city neighborhoods, or suburban locations.

In addition to locations, advertisements were classified as 1) clothing or department stores; 2) specialty shops; 3) whole or supply companies; 4) food and drug stores; 5) transportation (horse, buggy, or automobile dealerships).

161

Appendix C
Retail Functions Study

A survey of businesses in contiguously urbanized areas in which twenty-five or more structures, excluding agricultural, storage, and warehousing buildings, are located within one-tenth (0.1) of a mile of the nearest building was conducted during the summer and fall of 1997. Cooperstown, Fly Creek, and Hartwick are natural centers for economic activity. A fourth area, consisting of an agglomeration of three contiguously developed urbanized settings—Hartwick Seminary, Hyde Park, and Index—are here classified as the East Hartwick corridor due to their location along New York Route 28 in the town of Hartwick. As the survey was limited to businesses in urbanized settings, it does not represent every business; it does, however, represent a substantial majority of retail and food service establishments in the area.

The survey was further limited to those establishments specializing in retail and food service, as it is in these sectors of the economy that the most social interaction takes place. Antique dealers are particularly difficult to classify as some are professionally operated retail establishments and others are operated from the proprietor's barn on weekends or by appointment only; as such, these businesses were excluded.

The remaining businesses were classified into six categories: 1) general; 2) general-swing; 3) general-fuel; 4) specialty, non-baseball; 5) specialty, baseball; and 6) food service.

Businesses classified as "general" sell goods that are of use to the general population on a regular basis. This definition is inclusive of grocery, pharmaceutical supply, and other such general merchandise. Such businesses often sell items related to tourism, but the primary purpose of such stores is the sale of general merchandise. In those cases where a significant portion of the store is given over to the sale of tourism related goods, it is designated as "general-swing." General merchandise businesses normally rely on tourism to sustain revenues; for example, a grocery store often sells food and supplies for picnicking, camping, and other similar activities, but the primary purpose of the store is the provision of groceries. In contrast, a "general-swing" business sells general merchandise as well as a significant number of souvenirs and other tourism related merchandise. General stores that supply automotive fuel are designated "general-fuel." This category does not include businesses that sell fuel as the primary source of revenue.

Specialty stores sell goods that are intended for aesthetic or symbolic use, such as works of art or souvenirs. Boutiques that sell clothes in addition to a number of other specialty items were classified as specialty stores, although the store selling only clothes is classified "general." Businesses that do not have as a primary orientation baseball related merchandise were classified "specialty, non-baseball." A "specialty, baseball" designation is applied to those stores that do have a primary orientation toward baseball related items.

Food service establishments include businesses whose primary purpose is the preparation and service of food for consumption.

Businesses were also coded by type of owner. There are four categories: chain; full year resident; part year resident; and nonresident. A full year resident is defined as a person who resides locally eight or more months of a given year. A part year resident is defined as a person who resides locally less than eight months a given year. A nonresident is a person who does not reside in the local area. Residency is considered to be local if the person resides in Otsego County. A chain is defined as a legal entity that operates two or more businesses in differing markets.

Notes

Chapter 1. One Summer Day

1. The city has dropped from a stable population of slightly over one hundred thousand residents between 1930 and 1960 to 58,750 residents in 1999 (USBC 2000).

2. Rome is a city of 39,696 residents, in 1999, twelve miles west of Utica (USBC 2000). Although of more strategic importance early in American history, Utica quickly overtook Rome in terms of population and influence early in the nineteenth century. The census bureau classifies Rome as a central city in the Utica-Rome Metropolitan Statistical Area, and metropolitan area figures thus include Rome as well. However, due to its dominance of the metropolitan economy and culture, this work will concentrate on Utica.

Chapter 2. An American Story

1. The confederacy is also known as the League of the Five Nations. In 1710, the Tuscarora joined to form the League of the Six Nations. There were a number of other tribes considered to be Iroquois but not members of the confederacy, such as the Hurons, Neutrals, and Eries. It is interesting to note that Deganawidah, who with Hiawatha was instrumental in the formation of the confederacy, was a Huron.

2. For a detailed discussion of the early settlement of the Croghan (Otsego) Patent, see Birdsall (1925) and Taylor (1995). It should be noted that Cooper started with Andrew Craig, whom he soon bought out.

3. For further reference on this point, see Arndt (1937); Birdsall (1925); Gjernes (1972); Strobel, (1867); and Taylor (1995).

4. It should be noted that Hartwick first purchased the territory from the Mohawks, and then sought a patent for the land. This was his second attempt at land acquisition. With the first such deal, he purchased land from the Mohawks but failed to receive a charter from the king.

165

5. Speaking in 1861, Reverend Henry Pohlman alluded to such settlers, but official records list none. See Strobel (1867), 20–22.

6. The Jewish population grew slowly but steadily (Kohn 1959). The African American population grew in the early and middle nineteenth century, but then declined during the late nineteenth and early twentieth century (DeAmicis 1997). After World War I, the African American population grew more steadily.

7. For a discussion of early industries in the area, see Bohls (1991), Vaughn (1978), and Weeks (1964; 1981).

8. For an expanded discussion of community integration, see Warren (1978).

9. It is worth noting that some members of the elite chose not to live on the outskirts of town, but rather to build large houses on Genesee Street that were also displays of wealth.

Chapter 3. Loom to Boom

1. It should be noted that the two metropolitan areas developed differently, however. The Utica-Rome MSA includes the City of Rome and numerous small towns that extend from Utica through the river valleys, meaning that the character of the metropolitan area was of numerous industrial communities in close proximity with one another. In contrast, Syracuse followed more of a concentric zone pattern as the area expanded from the oldest part of the city. The result was that although City of Syracuse was considerably larger than Utica, the metropolitan areas were relatively close to each other in overall population. In 1940, the Utica-Rome MSA had 263,163 residents and in 1950 had 284,262 residents (Shupe et al. 1987). By comparison, the Syracuse MSA had 295,108 residents in 1940 and 341,719 in 1950 (Shupe et al. 1987). For this reason, Utica's leaders at the time considered themselves to be more similar to Syracuse than to other metropolitan areas.

2. All of the preceding statistics are found in Shupe et al. (1987).

3. This is similar to the experience of other cities. See Oestreicher (1988) for a discussion.

4. It is interesting to note that a generation earlier, Theodore Roosevelt launched an investigation into the influence of New York City's Tammany Hall political machine when he did not receive the support of Boss Richard Croker in 1899. See Allen (1993) for further discussion and an analysis of the experience of the New York City political machine.

5. Basically, Utica and to a lesser extent Rome were given over to the Democratic Party, whereas the rural and suburban towns in the county were given over to the Republicans.

6. The connections between the two groups can be discerned from several works from the period. Stuart Witt (1963) *The Democratic Party in Utica* and

Robert Sheehan (1949) *Take Utica, For Instance* both discuss various local leaders, although not with the goal of comparison. In addition, Bean (1989, 1991, 1993, 1994) and Ehrenhalt (1992) are extremely helpful in piecing together the elite structure of the time.

7. The following statistics are derived from USBLS (1984) unless otherwise noted.

8. This figure includes those employed in textile mills (9,700) and in the apparel industry (2,400).

9. In fact, some of the strikes were considerably violent. The east Utica strikes against several mills in 1919 resulted in several riots and the police firing upon the strikers in order to reassert their control.

10. Data gathered from County and City Databooks and State and Metropolitan Area Databooks (USBC 1947, 1952, 1957, 1962, 1967, 1972, 1977, 1982, 1987, 1992, 1997).

11. Utica's approach may be understood as progressive due to its emphasis on building on the city's strengths. See Clavel and Kleniewski (1990) for more information.

12. The central business district was considered at the time to be the heart of the metropolitan area and still the ideal location for a business. For instance, when the six-story Gardner Building at Genesee and Columbia Streets burned in 1947, the owners promised "speedy repairs" the very next day (OD, 2 Feb. 1947).

13. The level of success is subject to debate. Although there are today five colleges in the area, census figures show that the metropolitan area has consistently lagged behind the state average for education since that time (USBC 1947, 1952, 1957, 1962, 1967, 1972, 1977, 1982, 1987, 1992, 1997).

14. Two things are interesting about this perspective. The first is that the Utica machine is ignoring the fact the Binghamton, only moderately smaller, also had no colleges at the time. Second is that although city leaders claimed that Utica was a natural location due to its location near the center of New York State, the state university already had a campus within five miles of the exact geographic center of the state: SUNY College of Agriculture and Technology at Morrisville. If centrality was to be an issue, then Morrisville would have been the natural location for a new university.

Chapter 4. On the Road

Portions of this chapter have been adapted from an earlier article in the *Electronic Journal of Sociology* with permission from the publisher. See Thomas (1999).

1. It should be noted that Hartwick is not an incorporated village under New York State law, but most local residents refer to the "village" in order to

distinguish between the urbanized community and the rural township of which it is part. It should also be noted that the other major villages in the region, Milford, Cherry Valley, and Laurens, are all about the same size or smaller than Hartwick.

2. See Francaviglia (1996) for a discussion of the development of small town business districts.

3. See Kunstler (1994) for a discussion of the development of the automotive infrastructure.

4. In metropolitan Utica, the Thruway was placed so far from urbanized settings that there are parallel expressways that serve the Mohawk Valley to the east (NY5s) and the west (NY 49). At one point, NY 49 actually straddles either side of the Thruway in order to serve the area that the Thruway does not.

5. The Thruway is similar in other urban areas. There are two exits for Albany, for example, and the drive is for the most part comfortable through the city. As a college student once commented about driving to New York City, "you're in Yonkers before you know you're even near a city."

6. The following analysis is based on statistics gathered during several Censuses of Agriculture (USBC 1946; 1977; 1989; 1994).

7. For the first year, only Hartwick grades nine through twelve were sent to Cooperstown. With the new Cooperstown Central School, grades seven and eight were also sent to Cooperstown. The Hartwick Grade Center would serve Kindergarten through Grade Six.

8. Parce, Mead. 1957, "Spring." Column entitled, "Era Comes to an End." On display at the Hartwick Historical Society.

Chapter 5. Sin City

1. Alliances tended to lack a central organization, although major figures were influential in settling disputes. See Reuter (1985) and Levine and Reinarman (1992) for a discussion. This is similar to what has been found in similar ventures, such as cocaine and opiate trafficking. See Inciardi (1992) and Adler and Adler (1997) for more details.

2. For representative work, see Balzamo and Carpozi (1991), Jacobs (2001), Lacey (1991), Nelli (1990), Reuter (1985), and Smith (1990).

3. The Falcones had been convicted of conspiracy to defraud the government of liquor taxes in 1939, but the conviction was set aside in 1940 (OD, 21 Nov. 1957).

4. A Utica resident commented that at that time, "even if ya knew what they were doing, you didn't bring it up. There were just certain things the uninitiated didn't say."

5. It is possible, of course, that Elefante and other machine leaders took an active involvement in Mafia activities. However, despite some accusations, no evidence ever surfaced about a more direct involvement on the part of most machine leaders than mere civil inattention.

6. The following account is based upon personal interviews and articles appearing in the Utica *Observer-Dispatch* between November 16, 1957, and November 3, 1959, and in the New York *Journal-American* between October 16, 1957, and March 5, 1958, unless otherwise noted.

7. Lagatutta was questioned while riding in a car with the Falcones near Barbara's Appalachin home.

8. See for a discussion Ehrenhalt (1989; 1992). The condition also became common in the suburbs. For instance, a shopping center in the town of New Hartford proposed in 1988 had still not been built in 2000 due to citizen complaints and political infighting.

Chapter 6. Progress

Portions of this chapter have been adapted from an earlier article in the *Electronic Journal of Sociology* with permission from the publisher. See Thomas (1999).

1. The Washington Courts projects were the last major housing project to take place as a result of demolishing sections of the downtown area. Later low-income housing projects were built on the outskirts of development, in north Utica and east Utica, in order to control costs. Further demolition downtown was used primarily to serve transportation needs or corporate interests.

2. Urban sociologists may immediately recall the case of the West End in Boston discussed so eloquently in Herbert Gans' *The Urban Villagers* (1962) or the critical pen of Jane Jacobs *The Death and Life of Great American Cities.* (1992 [1961]).

3. The federal government paid two-thirds of the total cost with the rest being contributed by the state and city governments. See DHCR (1961; 1963) for more details.

4. There had been several proposals for the site, the most ambitious being an enclosed mall to stretch five blocks, but each had met with resistance and legal complications (Ellis and Preston 1982).

5. Actually, although the campus was, technically, built in Utica, this is because the city annexed the land. The location itself is very suburban in character, bordered as it is by two four-lane highways and post-war tract housing.

6. See Gans (1962) for a description of similar neighborhoods in Boston.

7. Similar trends of "inshopping" and "outshopping" have been found in other rural communities throughout the United States. See Miller et al. (1998); Pinkerton et al. (1995), and Brown et al. (1996) for more information.

Chapter 7. Slaughter of the Innocents

Portions of this chapter have been adapted from an earlier article in the *Electronic Journal of Sociology* with permission from the publisher. See Thomas (1999).

1. For an enhanced discussion of the impact of taxes on American's social well being, see Barlett and Steele (1994).

Chapter 8. Extended Communities

1. It should be noted that I previously referred to this concept as simply a Rural Community System. The name is changed here both because of its relationship to the previous incarnation of rural communities as comparatively independent and because of the relationship to similar patterns found in metropolitan areas. See Thomas (1998) for an earlier discussion.

2. This may be a misstatement. In many metropolitan areas, retail and other economic functions have become increasingly centralized in suburban "nodes." See Garreau (1992).

3. The following analysis is based on a study of advertisements appearing in the *Observer-Dispatch* at five-year intervals between 1899 and 1999, contemporary newspaper reports, aerial photography, contemporary photographs contained in Hassett (1992), Preston and Hassett (1995), and Przybycien and Romanelli (1976).

4. For analytical purposes, a city block is defined as one side of a street between two side streets. A Block Quintile Score is scored by dividing a block into fifths and then coding each fifth as such: Empty lots=0; parking lots=1; ordinary lawn and parking garages=2; buildings, parks, and plazas=3. The score is then summed for a block score with a maximum of fifteen.

5. This is measured with a ratio of the total score to the main street score, in this case being Genesee Street (BQ=0.98).

6. It should be noted that Columbia Street becomes Elizabeth Street when it crosses Genesee Street, but it was the west side of Genesee (Columbia Street) that was affected by urban renewal. Running parallel one block north is Lafayette Street, another important shopping area that becomes Bleeker Street when it crosses Genesee (Bleeker is one block north of Elizabeth). Bleeker Street is named here because it too was affected by urban renewal. These streets composed the most prestigious areas of the shopping district.

7. See Appendix B

8. The following analysis is based on data provided by the National Baseball Hall of Fame and Museum (NBHFM 1997).

9. The following analysis is based on figures provided by the New York State Historical Association (NYSHA 1998a; 1998b).

Chapter 9. Deconstructing Utica

1. It should be noted that although General Electric is an obvious and perhaps the best example of the restructuring of the defense industry in Utica, there were other firms in the area that also underwent restructuring.

2. At the time, I was living in Boston. The day following the episode, I encountered numerous Boston residents who laughed at the humor of the situation. Several described the city as it was portrayed as quite undesirable, and a friend commented to me, "Living there must have been Hell!"

3. For further discussion of this theme, consult Vidich and Bensman (1968) and Fitchen (1991).

4. This figure is based on stations tuned 8 Nov. 1997, utilizing a Pioneer KEH-P7400 automobile receiver with 11dBf usable FM sensitvity, selectivity=70 dB, and a signal to noise ratio of 70dB.

Chapter 10. Reconstructing Hartwick

1. For additional information in other communities, see Kirshenblatt-Gimlet (1998), Handler and Gable (1997), Judd and Fainstein (1999), and Ringholz and Muscolino (1992).

2. Gallery 53 closed in 1999.

3. The trolleys are actually buses painted to look like trolleys and were meant to solve the downtown parking problem. Three lots were built at the edge of town and visitors could pay one dollar to take the bus downtown.

4. The following discussion is based on 1990 Census Data (USBC 1990a; 1990b).

5. This claim is based on data from CACI 1987; USBC 1980; 1990a; 1990b).

Chapter 11. Different Strokes

1. The Mohawk Valley Network is a coalition of hospitals in the Utica Area that share in purchasing and coordinate services.

References

Suggested Reading

There have been many sources of information utilized in these pages. The following is not a complete listing, but rather a partial list of some of the better resources for those who may be interested in further reading.

The impact of the global economy on cities is a relatively large research literature. The interested reader may consult Logan's and Swanstrom's (1990) book of readings *Beyond the City Limits* for a good introduction to the topic. Several scholars have chosen to look primarily at smaller cities. Rabrenovic's (1996) *Community Builders* examines Utica's neighbors to the east, Albany and Schenectady. Similarly, June Nash's (1989) *From Tank Town to High Tech* examines economic restructuring in Pittsfield, Massachusetts. Kantor's and David's (1987) *The Dependent City* is a more general examination of cities' dependency upon outside forces. Other authors have examined the areas where metropolitan areas and rural places meet. Jackson's (1985) *Crabgrass Frontier* and Garreau's (1992) *Edge City* both look at the issue of suburban sprawl , whereas Daniels's (1998) *When City and Country Collide* more closely examines issues of preservation of rural space from a rural perspective. For an overall critique and populist overview of recent changes in urban America, Kunstler's (1993) *The Geography of Nowhere* concentrates on the automobile and the urban environment.

The restructuring of rural communities also has a sizable literature, though not as much as that as urban areas. Lyson and Falk's (1993) *Forgotten Places* provides a good overview of issues affecting rural areas. Similarly, Neil and Tykkylainen's (1998) *Local Economic Development* examines the fate of rural communities from an international perspective, placing the fate rural America in a global context. Both Barlett's (1993) *American Dreams, Rural Realities* and Davidson's (1996) *Broken Heartland* focus on the demise of farming in the United States. Griffith's (1993) *Jone's Minimal* examines factory workers in the rural south and Tauxe's (1993) *Farms, Mines, and Main Streets* chronicles

173

community change in response to a new mine. Fitchen (1991) *Endangered Spaces, Enduring Places,* Greenhouse's (1986) *Praying for Justice,* and Young's (1999) *Small Towns in Multilevel Society* all examine community change in a broad context yet have differing approaches to the topic. Ames and Ellsworth's (1997) *Women Reformed, Women Empowered* examine the difficulties encountered by rural women.

As in central New York, tourism is big business and a hopeful messiah to communities around the world. Kirshenblatt-Gimlet's (1998) *Destination Culture* examines the role of museums as tourist attractions involved with marketing as much as exhibition. Handler and Gable's (1997) *The New History in an Old Museum* examines the museum's role in the social construction of history by focusing on Colonial Williamsburg in Virginia. MacCannell's (1999) *The Tourist* analyzes "tourists" as an institution and a class in modern society. Judd and Fainstein's (1999) *The Tourist City* examines tourism in urban settings, whereas Ringholz and Muscolino's (1992) *Little Town Blues* does so in rural towns in the western United States.

Information about metropolitan Utica comes from a variety of sources. White's (1999) *Exploring 200 Years of Oneida County History* provides a good overview of Oneida County's history, whereas Ellis and Preston's (1982) *The Upper Mohawk Country* does the same more specifically for Utica itself. Clarke's (1952) *Utica, for a Century and a Half* and Walsh's (1982) *Vignettes of Old Utica* are somewhat more detailed. Utica's ethnic and immigration history is discussed well in Pula's (1994) *Ethnic Utica* and Noble's (1999) *An Ethnic Geography of Early Utica, New York.* Good histories of specific immigrant groups are Kohn's (1959) *The Jewish Community in Utica, New York,* George Schiro's (1975) *Americans by Choice,* and Briggs's (1986) *Immigrants to Three American Cities.* Frasca's (1992) *The Rise and Fall of the Saturday Globe* and Ryan's (1981) *Cradle of the Middle Class* both discuss the rise of modern middle-class sensibilities in the Utica area with an emphasis on the national significance and exportation of such trends. Pula and Dziedzic's (1991) *United We Stand* details the textile mills in New York Mills with an emphasis on labor history. The best references on Utica's political machine are Witt's (1963) *The Democratic Party in Utica* and Bean's (1994) article *The Irish, the Italians, and Machine Politics.* Additional insight into Utica's history can be gleaned from Behren's (1997) *Pioneering Generations,* DeAmicis's (1997) "To Them That Has Brot Me Up," and several articles by Phillip Bean (1989, 1991, 1993).

Scholarly literature in published form is often difficult to find in rural communities, but luckily does exist in Cooperstown and Hartwick. Though old, Birdsall's (1925) *The Story of Cooperstown* remains the definitive history of the village and the surrounding area for the period through 1925. (The first edition especially is best as it is most complete.) Also helpful is a history by James Fenimore Cooper (1976), *History of Cooperstown*. Cooper's affinity for his father, William Cooper, does introduce some bias. Later authors have published updated histories and these are also quite helpful. The definitive book for the early history is Alan Taylor's Pulitzer Prize winning *William Cooper's Town* and should be read by anyone interested in the American frontier. William Cooper's own (1936 [1810]) book *A Guide to the Wilderness* is a good contemporary source. Butterfield's (1955) *In Old Otsego* gives short vignettes about Otsego County as a whole. Pearl Weeks's (1981) *History of Hartwick* is the most complete history of Hartwick, although a number of unpublished materials by Roy Butterfield at the Town of Hartwick Historical Society are also extremely useful. Early industry in the Cooperstown-Hartwick area is discussed in depth in Bohls's (1999) *Industrial Order in Leatherstocking Country*, Weeks's (1964) *Pioneer Industries*, and Gardner's (1974) *Reflections of an Early Mill Town*. Arndt's (1937) article *John Christopher Hartwick, German Pioneer of Central New York* and Gjernes's (1972) *Hartwick Seminary in Otsego County, New York* are helpful in understanding John Christopher Hartwick. The effect and ultimate end of geographical isolation in the area is best discussed by Grills's (1969) *Cooperstown and its Railroad* and Hanavan's (1989) *Radio and Rural Life*.

There are also a number of societies that are extremely helpful when looking for local history sources. In Utica, the Oneida County Historical Society is well staffed by very helpful volunteers. Located in a former Christian Science center, the spacious main floor features exhibits and the lower level consists of a library. The Town of Hartwick Historical Society has a small exhibit located in Kinney Memorial Library in Hartwick. There is also a large number of special collections including books, letters, newspaper scrapbooks, and other miscellaneous writings that are quite helpful. The staff of the library is particularly helpful. The New York State Historical Association contains a library and two museums (Fenimore House and the Farmer's Museum) on a beautifully landscaped campus in Cooperstown. The library has extensive collections of historical books and newspapers relevant to New York State and Cooperstown. Home to the State University of New York College at Oneonta's masters degree program in History Museum Studies, the library also contains numerous master's theses of interest to New York State history. Due to the program, the Cooperstown area may very well be the best studied of rural community in the United States and is a tremendous resource. The Village Library of Cooperstown also has some historical materials on Cooperstown. Of course, there are many other communities that need and deserve scholarly attention and they likely have similar organizations to concentrate on them.

Sources

Adler, P. A. and P. Adler. 1983. "Shifts and Oscillations in Deviant Careers: The Case of Upper Level Drug Dealers and Smugglers." *Social Problems,* 31: 195–207.

Albion, R. G. 1984. *The Rise of New York Port, 1815–1860.* Boston: Northeastern U. Press.

Allen, O. E. 1993. *The Tiger—The Rise and Fall of Tammany Hall.* New York: Addison-Wesley Publishing Company.

Allswang, John M. 1977. *Bosses, Machines, and Urban Voters.* New York: Kennikat Press.

Amato, P. R. and J. Zuo. 1992. "Rural Poverty, Urban Poverty, and Psychological Well-Being." *The Sociological Quarterly* 33: (2): 229–40.

Ames, L. J. and J. Ellsworth. 1997. *Women Reformed, Women Empowered: Poor Mothers and the Endangered Promise of Head Start.* Philadelphia: Temple U. Press.

Anechiarico, F. and J. B. Jacobs. 1996. *The Pursuit of Absolute Integrity: How Corruption Control Makes Government Ineffective.* Chicago: U. Chicago Press.

Aquila, R. 1977. *The Iroquois Restoration: A Study of Iroquois Power, Politics, and Relations with Indians and Whites.* Ph.D. Dissertation, Ohio State University.

Arkin, W. H. and R. Fieldhouse. 1985. *Nuclear Battlefields: Global links in the Arms Race.* New York: Harper Information.

Arndt, K. J. R. 1937. "John Christopher Hartwick, German Pioneer of Central New York." *New York History* 18: 293–303.

Aronoff, M. W. 1997. "Changing Rural Communities: Reconstructing the Local Economy of a Nonmetropolitan Community." In *Changing Rural Social Systems: Adaptation and Survival,* edited by Nan E. Johnson and Ching-li Wang. East Lansing, MI: Michigan State U. Press.

Ballard, P. L. and G. V. Fuguitt. 1984. *Changing Rural Village in America: Demographic and Economic Trends Since 1950.* New York: Harper Information.

———. 1985. "The Changing Small Town Settlement Structure in the United States, 1900–1980." *Rural Sociology* 50: 99–113.

Balzamo, W. and G. Carpozi. 1991. *Crime Incorporated or Under the Clock: The Inside Story of the Mafia's First Hundred Years.* New York: New Horizon Press.

Barlett, D. L. and J. B. Steele. 1994. *America: Who Really Pays the Taxes?* New York: Touchstone.

Barlett, P. F. 1993. *American Dreams, Rural Realities: Family Farms in Crisis.* Chapel Hill, NC: U. North Carolina Press.

Bassett Healthcare. 2001. *Web Site.* <<http://www. Bassetthealthcare.org>>; accessed 15 Nov. 2001.

Becker, H. S. 1963. *Outsiders; Studies in the Sociology of Deviance.* Glencoe, IL: Free Press.

Bean, P. A. 1989. "Fascism and Italian-American Identity, A Case Study: Utica, New York." *Journal of Ethnic Studies* 17 (2): 101–19.

———. 1991. "The Role of Community in the Unionization of Italian Immigrants: The Utica Strike of 1919." *Ethnic Forum* 12: 36–55.

———. 1993. "The Great War and Ethnic Nationalism in Utica, New York, 1914–1920." *New York History* 74 (4): 382–405.

————. 1994. "The Irish, the Italians, and Machine Politics." *Journal of Urban History* 20 (2): 205–39.

Behrens, J. 1997. *Pioneering Generations: The Utica College Story, 1946–1996.* Utica: Utica College.

Birdsall, R. 1925. *The Story of Cooperstown.* New York: Scribner's.

Bluestone, B. and B. Harrison. 1982. *The Deindustrialization of America.* New York: Basic Books.

Bohls, C. 1991. *Industrial Order in Leatherstocking Country: Textile Mills and Mill Workers in Otsego County, New York.* Master's Thesis. Cooperstown Graduate Program/State University of New York College at Oneonta.

Bourke, L. and A. E. Luloff. 1995. "Leaders' Perspectives on Rural Tourism: Case Studies in Pennsylvania." *Journal of the Community Development Society* 26 (2): 224–39.

Briggs, J. W. 1986. *An Italian Passage: Immigrants to Three American Cities, 1890–1930.* New Haven: Yale U. Press.

Brown, R. B., C. D. Hudspeth, and J. S. Odom. 1996. "Outshopping and the Viability of Rural Communities as Service/Trade Centers." *Journal of the Community Development Society* 27 (1): 90–112.

Burgess, E. W. 1925. "The Growth of the City." *Publications of the American Sociological Society* 18: 85–97.

Butterfield, R. L. 29 Apr. 1955. "An Otsego Pioneer." *The Otsego Farmer.*

————. 1969. "In Old Otsego." Cooperstown: Freeman's Journal.

CACI. 1987. *The Sourcebook of Zip Code Demographics.* Arlington, VA: CACI, Inc.

Castells, M. 1977. *The Urban Question: A Marxist Approach.* Cambridge: MIT Press.

Clarke, T. W. 1952. *Utica, for a Century and a Half.* Utica: Widtman Press.

Clavel, P. and N. Kleniewski. 1990. "Space for Progressive Local Policy: Examples from the United States and the United Kingdom." In *Beyond the City Limits,* edited by J. R. Logan and T. Swanstrom. Philadelphia: Temple U. Press.

Collins, R. 1975. *Conflict Sociology: Toward an Explanatory Science.* New York: Academic Press.

Comprehensive Advanced Planning Commission. 1993. *Report.* Cooperstown: Village of Cooperstown.

Cooper, J. F., S. M. Shaw, W. R. Littell, and H. H. Hollis. 1976. *History of Cooperstown.* Cooperstown: New York State Historical Association.

Cooper, W. 1936 [1810]. *A Guide in the Wilderness.* Cooperstown: Freeman's Journal.

Crisafulli, V. 1960. *An Economic Analysis of the Utica-Rome Area.* Utica: Utica College.

Daniels, T. 1999. *When City and Country Collide: Managing Growth in the Metropolitan Fringe.* Washington, DC: Island Press.

Davidson, O. G. 1996. *Broken Heartland: The Rise of America's Rural Ghetto.* Expanded Edition. Iowa City: U. Iowa Press.

DeAmicis, J. 1994. "The Search for Community." In *Ethnic Utica,* edited by J. S. Pula. Utica: Utica College.

————. 1997. " 'To Them That Has Brot Me Up:' Black Oneidans and their Families, 1850 to 1920." *Afro-Americans in New York Life and History* 21 (2): 19–38.

Deavers, K. 1992. "What is Rural?" *Policy Studies Journal* 20 (2): 184–89.

Department of Public Works. 1950. *Report on State Arterial Route Plans in the Utica Urban Area.* Utica: Author.

DHCR. See New York State Division of Housing and Community Renewal.

Dorian, E. 1962. *The Sex Cure.* New York: Beacon.

Duncan, C. M. (Ed.) 1992. *Rural Poverty in America.* New York: Auburn House.

Duncan, C. M. and S. Sweet. 1992. "Introduction: Rural Poverty in America." In *Rural Poverty in America.* New York: Auburn House.

Ehrenhalt, A. 1989. "The Rise and Fall of a Haughty Political Machine." *Governing* 2 (6): 32–38.

———. 1992. *The United States of Ambition.* New York: Times Books.

Ellis, D. M. 1979. *New York: State and City.* Ithaca: Cornell U. Press.

Ellis, D. M., J. A. Frost, H. C. Syrett, and H. J. Carman. 1957. *A Short History of New York State.* Ithaca: Cornell U. Press.

Ellis, D. M. and D. M. Preston. 1982. *The Upper Mohawk Country: An Illustrated History of Greater Utica.* Woodland Hills, CA: Windsor Publications.

Encyclopedia Brittanica. 1976. *Baseball.* Volume Two, 728–246.

FBI. See Federal Bureau of Investigation.

Federal Bureau of investigation. 2001. *Index of Crime by Metropolitan Statistical Area, 1999.* <http://www.fbi.gov/ucr/Cius_99/w99tbl06.xls

Fischer, J. R. 1997. *A Well-Executed Failure: The Sullivan Campaign against the Iroquois, July–September 1779.* Columbia, SC: U. South Carolina Press.

Fitchen, J. M. 1991. *Endangered Spaces, Enduring Places.* San Francisco, CA: Westview Press.

———. 1992. "On the Edge of Homelessness: Rural Poverty and Housing Insecurity." *Rural Sociology* 57: 173–93.

Francaviglia, R. V. 1996. *Main Street Revisited.* Iowa City: U. Iowa Press.

Frasca, R. 1992. *The Rise and Fall of the Saturday Globe.* Selinsgrove, PA: Susquehanna U. Press.

Frisbie, W. P. and D. L. Poston, Jr. 1975. "Components of Sustenance Organization and Nonmetropolitan Population Change: A Human Ecological Investigation." *American Sociological Review* 40: 773–84.

———. 1976. "The Structure of Sustenance Organization and Population Change in Nonmetropolitan America." *Rural Sociology* 41: 354–70.

———. 1978. Sustenance Differentiation and Population Redistribution. *Social Forces* 57: 42–56.

Frommer, H. 1988. *Primitive Baseball.* New York: Atheneum.

Fuguitt, G. V. 1985. "The Nonmetropolitan Population Turnaround." *Annual Review of Sociology* 11: 259–80.

Fuguitt, G. V. and J. D. Kasarda. 1981. "Community Structure in Response to Population Growth and Decline: A Study in Ecological Organization." *American Sociological Review* 46: 600–15.

Gans, H. J. 1962. *The Urban Villagers.* Glencoe, IL: Free Press.

Gardner, L. W. 1974. *Recollections of an Early Mill Town: Toddsville.* Publisher Not Listed.

Garreau, J. 1992. *Edge City: Life on the New Frontier.* New York: Doubleday.

Garrison, W. C. 1992. *The Southern New York Railway*. Master's Thesis. Cooperstown Graduate Program/State University of New York College at Oneonta.

Gibson, C. (United States Bureau of the Census) 1998. *Population of the 100 Largest Cities and other Urban Places in the United States: 1790 to 1990*. United States Census Bureau Population Division Working Paper No. 27. Washington, DC: United States Census Bureau.

Gjernes, M. 1972. *Hartwick Seminary in Otsego County, New York: 1812–1934*. Master's Thesis. Cooperstown Graduate Program/State University of New York College at Oneonta.

Goffman, E. 1959. *The Presentation of Self in Everyday Life*. New York: Doubleday.

Goode, E. and N. Ben-Yehuda. "Moral Panics: Culture, Politics, and Social Construction." *Annual Review of Sociology* 20: 149–71.

Gottdeiner, M. 1994. *The New Urban Sociology*. New York: McGraw Hill.

Gould, S. J. 1989. "The Creation Myths of Cooperstown." *Natural History* (November): 14–24.

Granovetter, M. 1985. "Economic Action and Social Structure: The Problem of Embeddedness." *American Journal of Sociology* 91: 481–510.

Graymont, B. 1990. *The Iroquois in the American Revolution*. Syracuse: Syracuse U. Press.

Greenhouse, C. 1986. *Praying for Justice: Faith, Order, and Community in an American Town*. Ithaca: Cornell U. Press.

Griffith, D. 1993. *Jone's Minimal: Low Wage Labor in the United States*. Albany: State U. of New York Press.

Grills, R. A. 1969. *Cooperstown and its Railroad: A History of the Cooperstown Railroad Company and its Effect on the Community of Cooperstown, 1865–1903*. Master's Thesis. Cooperstown Graduate Program/State University of New York College at Oneonta.

Gusfield, J. R. 1963. *Symbolic Crusade: Status Politics and the American Temperance Movement*. Urbana: U. Illinois Press.

Handler, R. and E. Gable. 1997. *The New History in an Old Museum: Creating the Past at Colonial Williamsburg*. Durham, NC: Duke U. Press.

Hanavan, J. 1989. *Radio and Rural Life: A Case Study of WGY and Otsego County*. Master's Thesis. Cooperstown Graduate Program/State University of New York College at Oneonta.

Harris, C. and E. Ullman. 1945. "The Nature of Cities." *The Annals of the American Academy of Political and Social Science* 252: 7–17.

Harrison, B. and B. Bluestone. 1988. *The Great U-Turn*. New York: Basic Books.

Hassett, E. (Ed.) 1992. *Not So Long Ago: 1940–1949 Utica and Environs*. Utica: North Country Books.

Heaton, T. B. and G. V. Fuguitt. 1980. "Dimensions of Population Redistribution in the United States Since 1950." *Social Science Quarterly* 61: 508–23.

Hoyt, H. 1933. *The Structure and Growth of Residential Neighborhoods in American Cities*. United States Federal Housing Administration. Washington, DC: Government Printing Office.

Humphrey, C. R. and K. P. Wilkinson. 1993. "Growth Promotion Activities in Rural Areas: Do They Make a Difference?" *Rural Sociology* 58 (2): 175–89.

Hurd, D. H. 1868. *History of Otsego County*. Philadelphia: Everts & Farris.

Huxley, A. 1992 [1932]. *Brave New World*. New York: HarperPerennial.

Inciardi, J. A. 1992. *The War on Drugs II*. Mountainview, CA: Mayfield.

Jacobs, J. 1992 [1961]. *The Death and Life of Great American Cities*. New York: Vintage Books.

Jacobs, J. B. 2001. *Gotham Unbound: How New York City Was Liberated from the Grip of Organized Crime*. New York: New York U. Press.

Jacobs, W. R. 1972. *Dispossessing the American Indian: Indians and Whites on the Colonial Frontier*. New York: Scribner's.

Jackson, K. T. 1985. *Crabgrass Frontier: The Suburbanization of the United States*. New York: Oxford U. Press.

Johansen, H. E. and G. V. Fuguitt. 1973. "Changing Retail Activity in Wisconsin Villages: 1939–1954–1970." *Rural Sociology* 38: 207–18.

———. 1979. "Population Growth and Retail Decline: Conflicting Effects of Urban Accessibility in American Villages." *Rural Sociology* 44: 24–38.

Johnson, K. M. 1982. "Organization Adjustment to Population Change in Nonmetropolitan America: A Longitudinal Analysis of Retail Trade." *Social Forces*, 60: 1123–39.

———. 1989. "Recent Population Redistribution Trends in Nonmetropolitan America." *Rural Sociology* 54: 301–26.

Judd, D. and S. Fainstein. 1999. *The Tourist City*. New Haven: Yale U. Press.

Kantor, P. and S. David. 1987. *The Dependent City: The Changing Political Economy of Urban America*. Glenview, IL: Scott, Foresman, & Co.

Kay, J. H. 1998. *Asphalt Nation: How the Automobile Took Over America and How We Can Take It Back*. Berkeley: U. California Press.

Kephart, W. M. 1987. *Extraordinary Groups*. Third Edition. New York: St. Martin's.

Kehoe, A. B. 1992. *North American Indians: A Comprehensive Account*. Second Edition. Englewood Cliffs, NJ: Prentice-Hall.

Kirshenblatt-Gimlet, B. 1998. *Destination Culture: Tourism, Museums, and Heritage*. Berkeley, CA: U. California Press.

Kobler, J. 1973. *Ardent Spirits: The Rise and Fall of Prohibition*. New York: Putnam.

Kohn, S. J. 1959. *The Jewish Community of Utica, New York, 1847–1948*. New York: American Jewish Historical Society.

———. 1994. *Kehillah, the Jewish Community*. In *Ethnic Utica*, edited by J. S. Pula. Utica: Utica College.

Kulik, G. 1989. "Designing the Past: History-Museum Exhibitions from Peale to the Present." In *History Museums in the United States: A Critical Assessment*, edited by W. Leon and R. Rosenzweig. Urbana: U. Illinois P.

Kunstler, J. H. 1994. *The Geography of Nowhere*. New York: Touchstone.

Lacey, R. 1991. *Little Man: Meyer Lansky and the Gangster Life*. Boston: Little, Brown & Co.

Lang, F. 1927. *Metropolis*. Madacy Entertainment.

Larkin, F. D. 1998. *New York State Canals: A Short History*. Fleischmanns, NY: Purple Mountain Press.

Le Corbusier. 1987 [1929]. *The City of To-Morrow and its Planning*. Mineola, NY: Dover Publications.

Lenig, D. 1965. "The Oak Hill Horizon and its Relation to the Development of Five Nations Iroquois Culture." *Researches and Transactions of the New York State Archaeological Association* 15: 1–114.

Levine, H. G. and C. Reinarman. 1992. "From Prohibition to Regulation: Lessons from Alcohol Policy for Drug Policy." *The Milbank Quarterly* 69 (3): 1–34.

Levine, P. 1985. *A. G. Spaulding and the Rise of Baseball.* New York: Oxford U. Press.

Lewis Mumford Center for Comparative Urban and Regional Research. 2001. *Metropolitan Racial and Ethnic Change—Census 2000.* Data Extracted 5 November 2001; <<http://www.albany.edu/mumford/census/>>

Lichter, D. T. and G. V. Fuguitt. 1980. "Demographic Response to Transportation Innovation: The Case of the Interstate Highway." *Social Forces* 59: 492–512.

Lockheed Martin Corporation. *Lockheed Martin Consolidation Plan to Yield $1.8 Billion in Annual CostSavings.* Press Release: <<http://lmms.external. lmco.com/newsbureau/pressreleases/1995/9572.html>>; Accessed 29 Nov. 2001.

Logan, J. R. and H. Molotch. 1987. *Urban Fortunes: The Political Economy of Place.* Berkeley: U. California Press.

Logan, J. R. and T. Swanstrom. (Eds.) 1990. *Beyond the City Limits: Urban Policy and Economic Restructuring in Comparative Perspective.* Philadelphia: Temple U. Press.

Look Magazine. 8 July 1958. Report from Utica. *Look* 22: 35–36.

Lyson, T. A. and W. W. Falk. (Eds.) 1993. *Forgotten Places: Uneven Development in Rural America.* Lawrence: U. Press Kansas.

———. 1989. *Two Sides of the Sunbelt: The Growing Divergence between the Rural and Urban South.* New York: Praeger.

MacCannell, D. 1999. *The Tourist: A New Theory of the Leisure Class.* Berkeley: U. California Press.

Markusen, A. 1987. *Regions: The Economics and Politics of Territory.* Totowa, NJ: Rowman & Littlefield.

Marx, K. 1985 (1848). *The Communist Manifesto.* New York: Penguin Books.

———. 1990 (1867). *Capital; Volume One.* New York: Penguin Books.

Matsuoka, J. K. and M. Benson. 1996. "Economic Change, Family Cohesion, and Mental Health in a Rural Hawaii Community." *Families in Society* 77 (2): 108–16.

Mattson, G. A. 1997. "Redefining the American Small Town: Community Governance." *Journal of Rural Studies* 13: 121–30.

McFarlane, S. K. 1960. *The Characteristics, Problems, and Potential of Manufacturing in the Utica Area.* Ph.D. Dissertation: Syracuse University.

Merton, R. K. 1968. *Social Theory and Social Structure.* Revised Edition. New York: Free Press.

Miller, N. J., S. Schofield-Tomschin, and S. Kim. 1998. "Consumer's Apparel and Home Furnishings Inshopping Behavior in Rural Communities." *Clothing and Textiles Research Journal* 16 (4): 157–66.

Mohawk Valley EDGE. 2001. *Web Site.* <<http://www.ocedge.org>>; accessed 20 Nov. 2001.

Moore, M. 1989. *Roger & Me*. Warner Brothers Entertainment.

Mulligan, R. E. Jr. 1972. *The Sullivan Expedition of 1779 and Some Problems of Supply*. Master's Thesis. Cooperstown Graduate Program/State University of New York College at Oneonta.

Musto, D. F. 1999. *The American Disease: Origins of Narcotic Control*. Third Edition. New York: Oxford U. Press.

Nash, J. C. 1989. *From Tank Town to High Tech: The Clash of Community and Industrial Cycles*. Albany: State U. of New York Press.

National Baseball Hall of Fame and Museum (NBHFM). 1997. *Attendance Statistics*. Cooperstown: NBHFM.

National Archives. 1998a. Fort Stanwix Boundary Line Treaty. *National Archives Microfilm Publication No. 668: Ratified Indian Treaties; 1722–1868, No. 7 frame Nos. m=0138–142, pg. M-5*. Washington, DC: National Archives & Records Administration.

———. 1998b. Treaty of Fort Stanwix. Fort Stanwix Boundary Line Treaty. *National Archives Microfilm Publication No. 668: Ratified Indian Treaties; 1722–1868, No. 9 frame Nos. m=0152–153, pg. m-5, P=0148–151, pg. m-4*. Washington, DC: National Archives & Records Administration.

Nelli, H. 1990. *The Business of Crime: Italians and Syndicate Crime in the United States*. Chicago: U. Chicago Press.

Neil, C. and M. Tykkylainen. 1998. *Local Economic Development: A Geographical Comparison of Rural Community Restructuring*. New York: United Nations University Press.

Newsweek. 24 Feb. 1958. *Wide-Open Town*.

Nestle, D. F. 1959. *The Leatherstocking Route: From the Mohawk to the Susquehanna by Interurban*. Publisher not listed.

New York State Division of Housing & The U. S. Housing & Home Finance Agency. 1954. *SPUR: Study Project Urban Renewal Report 1: 315: Utica Urbanized area*. New York: NYS Division of Housing.

New York State Division of Housing and Community Renewal (DHCR). 1961. *Special Community Survey: An Analysis of Moderate-Income Housing Needs with Special Emphasis on Housing for the Aging: Utica, New York*. Albany: Author.

New York State Division of Housing and Community Renewal (DHCR) and Urban Renewal Administration, United States Housing and Home Finance Agency. 1963. *Industrial Renewal: Determing the Potential and Accelerating the Economy of the Utica Urban Area*. Albany: Author.

New York State Historical Association (NYSHA). 1997. *The Farmer's Museum; Fenimore House Museum: Visitor's Guide*. Cooperstown: NYSHA.

———. 1998a. *Attendance Figures for The Farmer's Museum*. Cooperstown: NYSHA.

———. 1998b. *Attendance Figures for Fenimore House Museum*. Cooperstown: NYSHA.

Noble, A. G. 1999. *An Ethnic Geography of Early Utica, New York: Time, Space, and Community*. Lewiston, NY: Edwin Mellon Press.

OCPD. See Otsego County Planning Department

Oestreicher, R. 1988. "Urban Working-Class Political Behavior and Theories of American Electoral Politics, 1870–1940." *The Journal of American History* 74: 1257–86.

Olasky, M. 1995. *The Tragedy of American Compassion*. Washington, DC: Regnery Publishing.

Oneida Nation. 2000. *Oneida Nation Web Site*. <http://www.oneida-nation.net>; (3 December 2000).

Oneonta, City of. 17 March 2000. *Common Council Minutes*. Oneonta, NY: City of Oneonta.

Otsego County Planning Department. 1997. *1996 Building Report for Otsego County*. Cooperstown: OCPD.

Padilla, F. M. 1992. *The Gang as an American Enterprise*. New Brunswick, NJ: Rutgers U. Press.

Parce, M. Spring 1957. *Era Comes to an End*. Oneonta *Daily Star* Column on Display at Hartwick Historical Society, Hartwick, New York.

Pinkerton, J. R., E. W. Hassinger, and D. J. O'Brien. 1995. "Inshopping by Residents of Small Communities." *Rural Sociology* 60 (3): 467–80.

Plunkitt, G. W. 1995 [1905]. *Plunkitt of Tammany Hall*. New York: Penguin Putnam.

Preston, D. M. and E. P. Hassett. (Eds.) 1995. *Focus on the Fifties: Utica and Vicinity, 1950–1962*. Utica: North Country Books.

Przybycien, F. E. and P. A. Romanelli. 1976. *Utica, A City Worth Saving*. Utica: Dodge-Graphic Press.

Pula, J. S. (Ed.) 1994. *Ethnic Utica*. Utica: Utica College.

Pula, J. S. and E. E. Dziedzic. 1991. *United We Stand: The Role of Polish Workers in the New York Mills Textile Strikes, 1912 and 1916*. New York: Columbia U. Press.

Rabrenovic, G. 1996. *Community Builders*. Philadelphia: Temple U. Press.

RadioStation.com. 1997. Radio Station Database. Accessed by Alexander R. Thomas; <http://www.radiostation.com>; (8 Nov. 1997).

Reinarman, C. 1997. "The Social Construction of Drug Scares." In Adler, P. A. and P. A. Adler. *Constructions of Deviance* (Second edition). Albany: Wadsworth.

Reiss, S. 1989. *City Games: The Evolution of American Urban Society and the Rise of Sports*. Urbana: U. Illinois Press.

Reuter, P. 1985. *Disorganized Crime*. Cambridge: MIT Press.

Ringholz, R. C. and K. C. Muscolino. 1992. *Little Town Blues: Voices from the Changing American West*. Salt Lake City: Gibbs-Smith Books.

Ryan, M. P. 1981. *Cradle of the Middle Class*. New York: Cambridge U. Press.

Saint Elizabeth Medical Center. 2001. *Web Site*. <<http://www.stemc.org>>; accessed 16 Nov. 2001.

Sant'Elia, A. 1973 (1914). "Manifesto of Futurist Architecture." In Appolnio, U. *Futurist Manifestos*. London: Thames & Hudson.

Sassen, S. 1991. *The Global City*. Princeton: Princeton U. Press.

Schwarzlose, R. A. 1980. "The Nation's First Wire Service: Evidence Supporting a Footnote." *Journalism Quarterly* 57 (4): 555–62.

Schiro, G. J. 1975. *Americans by Choice: Italians in Utica, New York*. North Stratford, NH: Ayer Co. Publishers.

Sheehan, R. Dec. 1949. "Take Utica, For Instance." *Fortune*: 126–30.

Shupe, B., J. Steins, and J. Pandit. 1987. *New York State Population: 1790–1980*. New York: Neal-Schuman Publishers.

Smith, D. C. 1990. *The Mafia Mystique*. Lanham, MD: University P. of America.

Springwood, C. F. 1996. *From Cooperstown to Dyersville: A Geography of Baseball Nostalgia*. Boulder: Westview Press.

Storper, M. and R. Walker. 1989. *The Capitalist Imperative: Territory, Technology, and Industrial Growth*. New York: Basil Blackwell.

Strobel, P. A. (Ed.) 1867. *Memorial Volume of the Hartwick Synod of the Lutheran Church*. Philadelphia: Lutheran Publication Society.

Tauxe, C. S. 1993. *Farms, Mines, and Main Streets: Uneven Development in a Dakota County*. Philadelphia: Temple U. Press.

Taylor, A. 1995. *William Cooper's Town*. New York: Knopf.

Thomas, A. R. 1998. *Economic and Social Restructuring in a Rural Community*. Ph.D. Dissertation: Northeastern University.

———. 1999. Untowning Hartwick: Restructuring a Rural Town. *Electronic Journal of Sociology* 4 (1). *[iuicode: 100.4.1.4]*

Thomas, A. R. and L. Cardona. 2002. *Retail in Greater Cooperstown: 1997 and 2001*. Oneonta: SUNY Oneonta Center for Social Science Research.

Thomas, A. R., M. Mansky, D. Frimer, and C. J. Natale. 2002. *Hartwick Retail Practices Survey: General Report*. Oneonta: SUNY Oneonta Center for Social Science Research.

Tuck, J. A. 1977. "A Look at Laurentian." *New York State Archaeological Association Researches and Transactions* 17: 31–40.

Turkus, B. B. and S. Feder. 1992 [1951]. *Murder Inc.: The Story of the Syndicate*. New York: Da Capo Press.

UGEC. See Utica Gas & Electric Company.

United States Bureau of Labor Statistics. 2001. *National Employment, Hours, and Earnings*. <http://stats.bls. gov/ceshome.htm>; (accessed 3 January 2001).

———. 1984. *Employment, hours, and earnings, States and Areas, 1939–82*. Washington, DC: U. S. Government Printing Office.

United States Bureau of the Census. 1946. *U. S. Census of Agriculture: 1945*. Volume 1, Part 2. Washington, DC: U. S. Government Printing Office.

———. 1947. *County and City Data Book*. Washington, DC: U. S. Government Printing Office.

———. 1952. *County and City Data Book*. Washington, DC: U. S. Government Printing Office.

———. 1957. *County and City Data Book*. Washington, DC: U. S. Government Printing Office.

———. 1962. *County and City Data Book*. Washington, DC: U. S. Government Printing Office.

———. 1967. *County and City Data Book*. Washington, DC: U. S. Government Printing Office.

———. 1972. *County and City Data Book*. Washington, DC: U. S. Government Printing Office.

———. 1977a. *County and City Data Book*. Washington, DC: U. S. Government Printing Office.

———. 1977b. *1974 Census of Agriculture*. Volume 1, Part 32. Washington, DC: U. S. Government Printing Office.

———. 1979. *State and Metropolitan Area Data Book*. Washington, DC: U. S. Government Printing Office.

————. 1980. *1980 Census of Population and Housing*. Washington, DC: U. S. Government Printing Office.

————. 1982. *State and Metropolitan Area Data Book*. Washington, DC: U. S. Government Printing Office.

————. 1986. *State and Metropolitan Area Data Book*. Washington, DC: U. S. Government Printing Office.

————. 1989. *1987 Census of Agriculture*. Volume 1, Part 32. Washington, DC: U. S. Government Printing Office.

————. 1990a. *1990 Census of Population and Housing, Summary Tape File 3A*; generated by Alexander R. Thomas; using 1990 Census Lookup; <http://venus.census.gov/cdrom/lookup>; (19 October 1997).

————. 1990b. *1990 Census of Population and Housing, Summary Tape File 3C*; generated by Alexander R. Thomas; using 1990 Census Lookup; <http://venus.census.gov/cdrom/lookup>; (19 October 1997).

————. 1991. *State and Metropolitan Area Data Book*. Washington, DC: U. S. Government Printing Office.

————. 1994. *1992 Census of Agriculture*. Volume 1, Part 32. Washington, DC: U. S. Government Printing Office.

————. 1997a. *Census of Agriculture*. Washington, DC: U. S. Government Printing Office.

————. 1997b. *State and Metropolitan Area Databank*. Washington, DC: U. S. Government Printing Office.

————. 1997/1998. *State and Metropolitan Area Data Book*. Washington, DC: U. S. Government Printing Office.

————. 2000. *Metropolitan Area and Central City Population Estimates for July 1, 1999 and April 1, 1990 Population Estimates Base*. <http://www.census.gov/population>; (3 January 2001).

United States Library of Congress. 31 May 1779. George Washington Papers at the Library of Congress, 1741–1799: Series 4. General Correspondence. 1697–1799. *Letter from George Washington to John Sullivan, May 31, 1779*. <http://memory.loc.gov/ammem/gwhtml/gwhome.html>; (accessed 30 Jan. 2001).

Utica Gas & Electric Company. 1923. *The Upper Mohawk Valley: A Land of Industry*. Utica: Utica Gas & Electric Company.

Utica Urban Renewal Agency. 1970. *Report*. Utica: Author.

Vaughn, S. D. 1978. *Water-Powered Industry on Fly Creek: A Survey of Archaeological Sites*. Master's Thesis. Cooperstown Graduate Program/State University of New York College at Oneonta.

Vidich, A. J. and J. Bensman. 1968. *Small Town in Mass Society: Class, Power, and Religion in a Rural Community*. Revised Edition. Princeton: Princeton U. Press.

Vlasich, J. 1990. *A Legend for the Legendary: The Origin of the Baseball Hall of Fame*. Bowling Green, OH: Bowling Green U. Popular Press.

Wachs, M. and M. Crawford. (Eds.) 1992. *The Car and the City: The Automobile, the Built Environment, and Daily Urban Life*. Ann Arbor.: U. Michigan Press.

Wallerstein, I. 1979. *The Capitalist World Economy*. New York: Cambridge U. Press.

Walsh, J. J. 1982. *Vignettes of Old Utica.* Utica: Utica Public Library.

Warren, R. C. 1978. *The Community in America.* Third Edition. Chicago: Rand McNally Publishing.

Weber, M. 1992 [1930]. *The Protestant Ethic and the Spirit of Capitalism.* New York: Routledge.

Weeks, P. A. 1964. *Pioneer Industries.* Hartwick, NY: Hartwick Reporter.

———. 1981. *History of Hartwick (Village and Town).* Richfield Springs, NY: Heritage Press.

White, D. F. (Ed.) 1999. *Exploring 200 Years of Oneida County History.* Utica: Oneida County Historical Society.

Williams, P. B. 11 Nov. 1959. *Industrial Changes in Utica since 1940.* Utica: Utica Public Library.

Wirth, L. 1938. "Urbanism as a Way of Life." *American Journal of Sociology* 44: 1–24.

Witt, S. K. 1963. *The Democratic Party in Utica.* Master's Thesis: Syracuse University.

Wright, F. L. 1958. *The Living City.* New York: Horizon Press.

Wyld, L. D. 1962. *Low Bridge! Folklore and the Erie Canal.* Syracuse: Syracuse U. Press.

Young, F. W. 1999. *Small Towns in Multilevel Society.* New York: University Press of America.

Zogby International. 2001. *Web Site.* <<http://www.Zogby.com>>; accessed 21 Nov. 2001.

Index